Tru

True Mission

Socialists and the Labor Party Question in the U.S.

Eric Thomas Chester

Pluto Press

LONDON • STERLING, VIRGINIA

First published 2004 by
Pluto Press
345 Archway Road, London N6 5AA
and 22883 Quicksilver Drive, Sterling, VA 20166–2012, USA

www.plutobooks.com

British Library Cataloguing in Publication Data
A catalogue record for this book is available from the British Library

ISBN   0 7453 2215 8 hardback
ISBN   0 7453 2214 X paperback

Library of Congress Cataloging in Publication Data
Chester, Eric Thomas.
    True mission : socialists and the Labor Party question in the U.S. /
Eric Thomas Chester.
        p. cm.
    ISBN 0–7453–2215–8 — ISBN 0–7453–2214–X (PBK)
    1. Socialist parties—United States—History. 2. Elections—United
States—History. 3. Third parties (United States politics)—History. 4.
United States—Politics and government. I. Title.

    JK2265.C46 2004
    324.273'7—dc22

                                                            2003022872

10   9   8   7   6   5   4   3   2   1

Designed and produced for Pluto Press by
Chase Publishing Services, Fortescue, Sidmouth, EX10 9QG, England
Typeset from disk by Stanford DTP Services, Northampton, England
Printed and bound in the European Union by
Antony Rowe Ltd, Chippenham and Eastbourne, England

To Jeff and the Next Generation
of Democratic Socialists

Contents

Acknowledgements

Electoral politics has been the touchstone for left-wing politics in the United States. One of the recurring points of controversy has focused on the possible creation of a viable party that would not adopt an explicitly socialist program and yet would be independent of the Democratic Party. Frequently, this debate has been more narrowly focused on the potential for a political party based directly on the trade unions, a labor party. In researching this question, I have had the opportunity to look at several key moments in U.S. history from a distinctive perspective.

Wherever possible, I have relied on primary sources and archival documents. My recent projects had examined aspects of Cold War history, and I have found it refreshing to be able to explore the relevant archives without having to deal with the hassles and endless delays involved in the federal government's declassification process. Yet my experience proved useful. I found that even on the Left there is often more going on than appears on the surface. I have tried to probe beyond the official record to examine the ideological debates and the tactical maneuvering that was often occurring in closed caucuses and confidential letters.

I want to thank the librarians and archivists at Harvard University, the Tamiment Institute at New York University, the University of Vermont, the Wisconsin Historical Society, Columbia University and the Indiana Historical Society for their assistance and their patience. I wish to particularly thank the librarians at the Robert Frost library at Amherst College who quickly and politely responded to frequent questions from a wandering scholar.

The staff and editors at Pluto Press were diligent and persistent in bring this work to publication. My agent William Goodman gave me helpful feedback on the manuscript. Julia Wrigley and Anne D'Orazio reviewed the manuscript and aided in its publication. My partner Susan Dorazio gave me the emotional support I needed to complete this project.

Needless to say, any mistakes or errors in analysis that remain are my responsibility, and not that of any of those who gave me their advice and assistance.

Preface

The most contentious issues dividing the U.S. Left have always been those related to the Democratic Party. Successive generations of activists have been drawn into the web of mainstream liberalism, each time hoping to transform the Democrats and each time being rebuffed. In spite of this, a series of grass-roots movements, from industrial unionism to civil rights and the anti-war movement, have challenged the existing power structure by tapping into the pervasive popular discontent. Yet each time these movements begin to gain momentum they run up against the tight constraints imposed by the politics of the two party system.

Pressed into a search for an alternative, activists have sought out the potential for an independent politics, separate from and independent of the Democratic Party. At this point, radical activists confront a crucial question: is it possible to create a viable independent party that limits its program to the reform of the existing capitalist market economy, or does an independent party need to start with a rejection of the market economy and a commitment to the formation of a democratic socialist society? It is this question that stands at the center of my work.

I started writing this book in the aftermath of the presidential election of 2000. Ralph Nader's candidacy on the Green Party ticket had, once again, brought the potential for independent politics to the forefront of political debate. As a socialist and a historian, I began to reflect upon the implication of Nader's candidacy for socialist theory and practice. My own formative experiences took place during the 1960s, when I actively participated in the Human Rights Party of Michigan. The HRP cooperated with the Peace and Freedom Party of California in an effort to initiate a national network of independent parties that could present a credible alternative to anti-war militants who might otherwise be drawn into the unending effort to capture the Democratic Party. I have, therefore, sustained a continuing interest in issues related to independent political action.

My curiosity was further piqued by the success of several newly formed non-sectarian socialist parties in Western Europe. Throughout Europe, the demise of the Soviet Union has led to the collapse of Communist parties. At the same time, most of the social democratic parties of Western Europe have jettisoned their previous role as advocates of structural reform in their rush to occupy the corporate Center. These recent developments have led to a vacuum on the Left that new democratic socialist parties have sought to fill. Parties such as the Scottish Socialist Party and the Red–Green Alliance of Denmark have overcome the fragmentation of the radical Left by providing an organizational framework in which socialists coming from a variety of tendencies can feel at home and can participate fully in determining policies and strategy.

Thus, with the hope for a socialist electoral politics in the United States reinforced by developments in Western Europe, and with Nader's candidacy sparking renewed interest in third party politics, I began looking into past experiences in independent politics. As an active member of the Socialist Party USA, I was especially interested in studying how the Socialist Party responded to previous third party formations.

Closely related to the questions posed by a broadly based third party are the issues raised by a more narrowly focused party linked organically to the trade unions. I found the question of the labor party to be of particular interest. My father was close to the Independent Socialist League, an offshoot of Trotskyism that merged into the Socialist Party in 1958. I remember listening to discussions while still a teenager concerning the possible formation of a labor party as an essential step toward a mass-based socialist movement.

Marxists have traditionally started with the belief that the primary purpose of electoral politics is a deepening of class-consciousness within the working class. A critical link in this process would be the formation of a party that represents the working class, in opposition to the mainstream parties, which merely represent differing wings of the capitalist ruling class. This has usually been framed in terms of the creation of an explicitly socialist party. Still, there have also been tendencies within the socialist movement that have looked toward the creation of a political party directly connected to the trade unions as a necessary transitional stage. Such a labor party would not be a socialist party, but rather a party of reform, and yet it would have a clear class basis, and, so it has been argued, its formation would represent an important step forward for the working class.

These are the concerns and the historical and personal context that provided the basis for my research. My book examines several critical moments in U.S. history when the potential for a definitive break with the two party system seemed tantalizingly immediate. I also examine the Nader campaign of 2000 within the historical framework set by earlier precedents in third party politics.

In the past, much of my research has dealt with aspects of the Cold War. I have therefore come to assume that a search for the truth requires probing well beneath the surface of events. The U.S. government consistently lies and distorts the truth for its own strategic needs. I found that those on the Left are more open, but, even so, much of what occurs is shaped by events that are undertaken in secret, in closed caucuses or confidential letters. I have therefore utilized a wide array of sources from books and journal articles to contemporaneous newspapers and personal correspondence from archival papers.

A project such as this is bound to be an interactive experience. I began as a skeptic of third party politics and I remain unconvinced. Personality-driven campaigns based on an anti-corporate populism resonate within the U.S. political context. Nader's candidacy was one of several that fit this same pattern. Yet in spite of an initial burst of popular enthusiasm, these ventures into third party politics tend to be short-lived. Starting with a political program that is remarkably like that of the liberal wing of the Democratic Party, and with a similar social base rooted in the professional middle class, third parties are unable to develop the ideological foundation that is needed to maintain a politics that remains consistently independent of the two party system. As a result, these parties tend to remain at the edge of the Democratic Party, and are soon coopted back into it. As I write in the summer of 2003, it would seem that the Green Party has traveled a substantial distance with considerable rapidity along this very trajectory.

In distinction to my views on third party politics, I began this project with a generally favorable attitude toward the concept of a labor party. I felt that at some time in the future socialists would act as the loyal left-wing of a trade union based political party. However, I found as I probed the history of this question that the labor party was an artificial construct within the U.S. context.

Throughout most of U.S. history, trade unions have represented a small minority of the total workforce. Furthermore, the great majority of trade union officials have remained committed advocates of one of the two mainstream parties, usually the Democratic Party. In those few cases where a significant segment of the union officialdom has considered independent politics, labor based political formations have quickly shifted to become a component of a more broadly based cross-class third party. This deliberate effort to blur the class basis of an independent electoral formation reflects both the weakness of the trade union movement and the opportunistic pragmatism that characterizes officials trained in the short-run calculus of business unionism.

The entire idea of a labor party should be abandoned as an ideological myth within the context of the United States. At the same time, the anti-corporate populism of third party politics, as epitomized by the Nader campaign, is incapable of establishing the organizational or ideological grounding for a definitive break with the two party system. This takes us back to the fundamental choice confronting radical activists. Only an explicitly democratic socialist party that is open to a range of tendencies can provide the organizational framework for a genuinely independent politics. We should look to the new wave of socialist parties in Western Europe for useful guidelines, but we also need to look back to the Socialist Party prior to World War I. The SP's left-wing explicitly rejected the labor party perspective and, instead, sought to solidify its links to militant workers at the grass-roots level. These are lessons worthy of our attention.

My book should be relevant to the democratic socialists of today who are trying to work out a principled and effective electoral strategy. Yet even those who start from a very different political perspective will find that my research adds to a keener understanding of decisive moments in U.S. history. My work is therefore offered as a contribution to both socialist theory and strategy, and to the social and political history of the United States.

1
Introduction

The Democratic and Republican parties have dominated the U.S. political scene since the Civil War. The development of a viable alternative to these two corporate parties through the formation of a political party that could effectively represent the interests of working people has been a priority objective of the Left for more than a century. By the turn of the twentieth century, mass-based socialist parties rooted in the working class were flourishing in virtually every country in Western Europe. Yet Britain and the United States stood apart from this insurgency, as working people remained content with the nebulous promises of liberal reformism, and with the limited options presented by the politics of the lesser evil.

In frustration, one strand of thought within the socialist movement began advancing the idea of an intermediate stage, a nominally independent party that would not advance a socialist vision, but which would instead seek to gain incremental social reforms. Such a party, of necessity, could only constitute a pallid substitute for a mass-based socialist party. Socialist proponents of this perspective argued for the creation of a labor party, a party based directly on the affiliation of trade unions, in distinction to a third party founded on individual memberships and established on a program designed to appeal to middle-class reformers.

The labor party question has divided the U.S. Left for a century and more, and yet labor parties have been few in number, and transitory in nature. Third parties have occurred more frequently and have achieved greater success. Still, none of these middle-class reform parties have succeeded in becoming genuinely independent parties. In the end, third parties have either dissolved or been absorbed back into the two party system.

I have focused on several critical moments in the history of this debate. In addition, I have brought the issue up to the present by analysing Ralph Nader's presidential campaign of 2000. I have closely examined each of the electoral formations involved, while observing the reaction within the socialist movement to these formations. My work begins with a study of Henry George's campaign for mayor of

New York City in 1886, followed by a look at the controversies within the Socialist Party at its zenith, from 1909 to 1912. It proceeds to an analysis of the Conference for Progressive Political Action and Senator Robert La Follette's presidential campaign of 1924, and, then, to an examination of the debates within the Socialist Party in relation to Fiorello La Guardia's 1937 campaign for mayor of New York City as a candidate of the American Labor Party. In the final chapter, I set the Nader campaign within this historical context.

HENRY GEORGE AND FRIEDRICH ENGELS

In 1886, Henry George stood at the head of an independent municipal ticket initiated by the New York City Central Labor Union. George was well known as a social reformer and as the author of the single-tax theory of taxation, which sought to levy a property tax on land and landed property as the primary source of public revenues. Trade union officials sought out George as a candidate for mayor, convinced that only a celebrity could defeat the entrenched Democratic Party machine of Tammany Hall. His candidacy generated enthusiastic popular support. Indeed, it is possible that Henry George would have been elected mayor of New York City had there been an accurate tallying of the votes, but Democratic Party regulars made sure of their continuing stranglehold over City Hall through the use of fraud and coercion.

For Friedrich Engels, Henry George's campaign promised to become a crucial turning point for the U.S. working class. Engels was optimistic that the success of the New York campaign would spark the formation of a nationwide labor party, and he urged socialists to work for George's election. In his view, such a nationwide labor party would quickly be transformed into a genuinely socialist party, since, once in motion, the U.S. working class would soon catch up to its European comrades.

Engels was mistaken at every level. The United Labor Party emerged out of the George campaign, but it soon disintegrated, with its leaders, including Henry George, scurrying back into the two party system. Furthermore, even before this collapse, socialists had been expelled from the ULP for challenging George's ideological control over the new party.

The first chapter traces the Henry George campaign from the 1886 election through the demise of the United Labor Party, counterposing the actual events in New York to the assessment of those events by Engels in London.

THE SOCIALIST PARTY AND THE LABOR PARTY

Socialists in the United States were so disillusioned by the Henry George campaign that they resolved to remain aloof from any future third party formation. In 1901, only 15 years after George's campaign for mayor, the Socialist Party was formed from the merger of two smaller organizations. Over the next decade, the SP grew into a mass party. By 1912, the Party had more than 120,000 members, a press that was read by several hundred thousand sympathizers, and a presidential candidate, Eugene Victor Debs, who had become a respected, even revered, national figure.

The Socialist Party ultimately failed to establish itself as a credible alternative to the two mainstream parties, but not because its members were lured back into the fold. It was undermined in part by two bitter splits in which the moderate leadership pushed more radical elements out of the Party, but, more important, it was crushed by government repression for its opposition to World War I.

From its founding, the Socialist Party was deeply divided between radicals and moderates, with the labor party one of the issues in dispute. Moderates in the Socialist Party leadership looked to the rapid electoral success of the British Labour Party as a model. In Britain, a small social democratic party, the Independent Labour Party, had acted as the catalyst to the creation of a mass-based political party linked directly to the trade unions.

Influential moderates within the Socialist Party sought to emulate the British experience. Yet the rank and file of Party activists, whatever their political orientation, were committed to building a distinctly socialist party. Since calls for the formation of a labor party were met with a crescendo of hostility, labor party advocates within the SP opted to work through clandestine networks.

The second chapter examines the Socialist Party in its heyday, focusing on the efforts of a substantial segment of the SP's leadership to convince progressive union officials to initiate a public call for a labor party. It also examines the volatile debates that ensued within the Socialist Party as news of these secretive maneuvers leaked out to the general membership.

THE LA FOLLETTE CAMPAIGN

The next two chapters focus on the turbulent years following World War I, culminating in 1924 in Senator Robert La Follette's independent presidential campaign. The majority of those in the left-wing of the Socialist Party had left in 1919, certain that the Russian Communist Party would set the strategic guidelines for revolutionaries around the world. Most of those who remained in the SP looked to the British Labour Party as an attractive alternative. Hopes for a labor party in the U.S. were rekindled when the myriad craft unions within the railroad industry, representing 1.5 million workers, became interested in forging a broadly based coalition of progressive forces.

The railway system had been nationalized during World War I, and then returned to private ownership in 1920. Trade union membership mushroomed under William McAdoo, the government's director general of railroads and the Secretary of the Treasury. With privatization came a devastating assault on wages and working conditions, as the railroad corporations sought to reverse the gains achieved during the war. Even narrowly focused craft union leaders came to see the virtues of returning the railroads to social control under a quasi-public authority.

Only a mass movement held the potential for reversing the privatization of the railroads. Railroad union leaders looked to progressive farmers, and even to the Socialist Party, for support. In February 1922, the first meeting of the Conference for Progressive Political Action was convened in Chicago. The Socialist Party eagerly attended, its leaders convinced that the CPPA would serve as the basis for an independent labor party. Yet most of the railroad union leaders never gave the slightest indication that they were prepared to break with the two party system. Only in the summer of 1924, when the Tea Pot Dome oil reserve scandal had eliminated McAdoo as a tenable presidential candidate, did railroad union officials rally behind the idea of an independent presidential campaign.

Not only did La Follette gain the organizational backing of the CPPA and the railroad unions, he even succeeded in gaining the endorsement of Samuel Gompers and the American Federation of Labor. The 1924 election remains, to this day, the only time that the AFL supported an independent candidate for president. When Gompers insisted that the AFL set the direction for the campaign at the Congressional level, La Follette and the CPPA agreed. La Follette then proceeded to wield his influence to block socialist candidates whose candidacies might have caused the defeat of those moderate Democrats supported by the AFL. Unwilling to jeopardize their links to the CPPA, the leaders of the Socialist Party pressured locals to withdraw Congressional candidates in closely contested elections.

Only a small left-wing grouping openly challenged the underlying assumptions of the labor party perspective, while criticizing the Party's willingness to subordinate its politics within La Follette's progressive coalition.

When the votes were counted, La Follette's received 16 percent of the total tally, while carrying his home state, Wisconsin. For the railroad union leaders, the campaign had been a dismal failure. The CPPA was quickly dissolved and the AFL, and the railroad unions, resumed their roles as loyal supporters of the Democratic Party. La Follette died a few months after the campaign, and the progressives were swept up into the New Deal a few years later. For the Socialist Party, the La Follette campaign had been a disaster, undercutting its ideological cohesion and undermining its organizational underpinnings. Nevertheless, the moderate majority remained committed to the labor party perspective. Debs was one of the few to hail the collapse of the CPPA, for it had left the Party free to pursue a truly socialist politics.

TROTSKY, THOMAS AND LA GUARDIA

During the period from 1936 to 1938 the Socialist Party, as well as the U.S. Left, was again divided by the labor party question. The New Deal policies of President Franklin Roosevelt commanded overwhelming support within the working class. Thus, any challenge to the two party system was bound to remain small and marginalized. Yet the 1930s were also the years of the Great Depression, a time when many young people were radicalized well beyond the bounds set by New Deal reforms. Furthermore, the militant organizing drives led by the Congress of Industrial Organizations (CIO) in the mass production industries brought millions of workers into a more politicized milieu, where the idea of an independent labor party was up for debate.

These conflicting currents were difficult to decipher, and to analyse. The Socialist Party remained an influential force on the Left, although it was overshadowed by the Communist Party, which became increasingly enmeshed within the Democratic Party through its acceptance of the Popular Front. SP activists scoffed at the New Deal, but they still sought to retain their influence within the newly formed CIO unions, and within the broad social movements of that era. This tangled situation was made even more complex by the shifting positions of Leon Trotsky and his supporters. The Trotskyists, after entering the SP in the late spring of 1936, actively participated in the Party's internal disputes until their expulsion in the fall of 1937.

Underlying differences within the SP were crystallized by the La Guardia campaign of 1937. La Guardia had been elected mayor of New York City in 1933, standing as an honest reformer battling the corrupt Democratic Party machine. In July 1936, top union officials in the garment industry, many of them former members of the Socialist Party, launched the American Labor Party as an electoral vehicle to lure socialist voters into voting for New Deal Democrats. After helping Roosevelt to win a second term in 1936, the ALP turned to the municipal election of 1937, and the reelection of Fiorello La Guardia.

In the spring of 1937, the issues raised by the La Guardia campaign ignited a bitter controversy within the Socialist Party, when Norman Thomas withdrew as the socialist candidate for mayor. The Clarity Caucus, the left-wing of the SP, condemned Thomas for undermining the Party's commitment to independent political action. With the SP evenly divided, the Trotskyists could have allied with Clarity, with the very real possibility of defeating Thomas and his supporters. Instead, Trotsky ordered his adherents to provoke an immediate split, convinced that any further effort to build links to social democrats would be pointless, and that Trotskyists had to build their own distinct organizations.

Over the summer of 1937, the Socialist Party went through a wrenching and demoralizing rift. The Trotskyists hammered away at the question of the labor party, insisting that socialists had no role in the formation of a labor party, but should rather concentrate their energies on building the socialist movement.

In October 1937, as the Socialist Party finalized the expulsion of the Trotskyist cadre in its midst, Trotsky determined upon yet another drastic shift in perspective. He concluded that his supporters should become vocal proponents of a labor party. This represented a direct reversal of previous policy, one not justified by developments in the United States. Stalin was ruthlessly purging the Old Bolsheviks who remained in the Soviet leadership, and sending them to concentration camps. At the same time, Trotskyist leaders in Europe were being hunted down and assassinated by the Soviet secret police.

Trotsky came to see the defeat of Stalinism as the central task for revolutionary socialists in the West. In the United States, the Communist Party had entered the American Labor Party, where it soon became an influential force. Trotsky was convinced that the

ALP, and other similar third parties, could provide an important arena in which to confront the CP and its call for a Popular Front.

Thus, a year after the contentious disputes around the La Guardia campaign, all of the participants could be found working together within the American Labor Party. Norman Thomas facilitated the entry of individual SP members into the ALP, while the leaders of the Clarity Caucus, disoriented by the split with the Trotskyists, abandoned their opposition to that policy. Finally, the newly formed Trotskyist organization, the Socialist Workers Party, urged its members to enter the ALP, where they cooperated with Socialist Party activists in countering Communist influence.

Throughout these many twists and turns, the American Labor Party remained what it had always been, a trade union pressure group bargaining with the Democratic Party bosses while blocking any effort to initiate a genuine break with the two party system. The collapse of Clarity and the Trotskyists as principled opponents of the ALP represented a pivotal defeat for those interested in pursuing a truly independent politics.

THE NADER CAMPAIGN

The experience of the Socialist Party from 1936 to 1938 represents the last of the historical moments that constitute the subject of this work. My final chapter looks at the most recent experiment in third party politics, the 2000 presidential campaign of Ralph Nader, with the aim of placing this campaign into the historical context set by the preceding case studies.

The unrelenting globalization of capital has significantly altered the logic of the two party system. In the past, the Democratic Party sought to coopt dissident movements with limited reforms. Over the last years, the Democrats have moved to capture the corporate Center. Progressives have been isolated and rendered ineffectual, as the Democratic leadership actively pursues the profit oriented interests of a substantial segment of big business. More fundamentally, the range of social reforms that can be achieved within the capitalist system has been drastically narrowed, as corporations shift vast investments overnight, and at the slightest provocation.

Not surprisingly, the rise of the transnational corporation has spurred a renewed interest in independent politics. The Green Party seemed to present a new alternative, one that was environmentally sensitive and grass-roots oriented. Still, the Greens stumbled, deeply divided and without a clear program, until they turned to Ralph Nader as their celebrity spokesperson. Nader had successfully fostered a national reputation as a consumer advocate, starting with his exposure of unsafe cars in the 1960s. His network of non-profit organizations has continued to function as a consumer watchdog exposing corporate abuses.

During the 2000 presidential campaign, Nader raised millions of dollars and vocally challenged both of the mainstream presidential candidates. In the end, he received 3 million votes, nearly 3 percent of the total, becoming the swing factor in a tightly contested election. It was evident from the start that a Nader campaign would be personality driven. Nader formulated his own program, while making it clear that he was not bound by the platform of either wing of the Greens. Furthermore, Nader's campaign apparatus dwarfed that of the Greens, who were in no position to retain any significant control over their own candidate. Indeed, while Nader attacked the two mainstream candidates for their traditional, hierarchical style of politics, his own campaign was marked by the same style, top-down and personality focused.

The Nader campaign is hardly the first case of a personality-driven third party campaign. Indeed, the track of the Nader campaign in 2000 follows closely that of the La Follette campaign in 1924. In both of these cases, the Left looked to a well-known personality in order to achieve an instant credibility as an electoral alternative. Nevertheless, the coalition that had been organized around the La Follette campaign disintegrated shortly after the election. Progressive presidential campaigns based on celebrities have never provided the basis for a viable, ongoing third party.[1]

Of course, history never provides us with carbon copies, but the similarities are striking. Although the Greens have certainly gone further than previous progressive movements in creating a distinct organizational structure, the political perspective that they represent has consistently failed to provide the groundwork for a genuinely independent party.

TOWARD THE FUTURE

The United States has had more than a century of experience with the question of a labor party. In focusing on several key moments in this history, certain conclusions appear evident. To start, the two party system has proven to be surprisingly resilient. In spite of dramatic changes in the economic and social setting, the Democratic and Republican parties continue to dominate the political scene, as most Americans remain trapped within the logic of the lesser evil.

On the other hand, U.S. history has been marked by a series of social movements that have contested the boundaries of the two party system. Each successive social movement has challenged the existing order, and thus, of necessity, has collided with the corporate controlled parties. As activists seek to transcend the limited range of reforms doled out by the political structure, whether controlled by Democrats or Republicans, calls for a new third party inevitably come to the surface.

For socialists, for whom class conflict is central, an independent party based directly on organized labor has frequently acted as an intriguing chimera. Yet throughout the history of the American Federation of Labor, and that goes back to 1886, the great majority of union officials have sought to cultivate close ties to the Democratic Party. As a result, labor parties have been infrequent, and transient. Furthermore, these momentary formations have usually remained within the orbit of the Democratic Party. Finally, the leaders of these parties, pragmatic union officials accustomed to working toward the immediate gain, have frequently looked to noted middle-class reformers for candidates. Thus, the inherent logic of the labor party, within the context of the United States, has led away from a class based party and toward a progressive third party based on a platform that can cut across class lines.

Third parties have arisen more frequently and proven to be more successful than labor parties, and yet none of them have succeeded in developing a nationwide base of popular support over an extended period of time. Furthermore, these electoral formations have been unwilling to cut their ties to the two mainstream parties. Ultimately, third parties have either dissolved or been absorbed back into the two party system.

An electoral strategy based on remaining at the edge of the Democratic Party is bound to fail. The pressures to conformity are too great, and the potential perquisites that come with cooptation are too attractive, to make any other outcome a realistic possibility. Only a party that severs all of its ties to the two party system, one that views itself as an iconoclastic alternative to the entire range of political perspectives coexisting within the mainstream parties, can establish the ideological grounding needed to sustain a viable, credible, independent electoral alternative.

There has been only one political party in the history of the United States that has succeeded in this task, the Socialist Party of the early twentieth century. The SP fiercely guarded its organizational identity, while creating its own distinct culture of resistance. By presenting a distinctive worldview, the SP provided its militants with the motivation to retain their radical vision, and to reject the blandishments offered by the proponents of liberal reforms. I would suggest that this experience remains a salient one a century later. The true mission of socialists is to build a socialist movement, and not to be waylaid into the illusory temptations of a non-socialist formation of progressives, whether it be a labor party or a third party.

2
Engels and the Henry George Campaign of 1886: "Historic" Development or Blind Alley

Henry George was one of the most celebrated social reformers of the nineteenth century. In 1886, he was a candidate for mayor of New York City on an independent ticket nominated by a labor-based coalition initiated by a federation of local trade unions. His campaign attracted the enthusiastic support of tens of thousands of workers, drawn into an insurgency that threatened the hold of a powerful and corrupt political machine.

To Friedrich Engels, Karl Marx's friend and colleague, Henry George's campaign seemed an historic breakthrough, a striking signal that the United States working class was ready to abandon its illusory hopes in the lesser evil, and to rally around an independent party of the working class. Engels believed that not only could such a party speedily gain a mass base, but that it would also be quickly won to a socialist perspective. He was convinced that the strong showing of independent candidates in the municipal elections of November 1886 marked "the entry of the Americans into the movement," an event that would be hailed as "of world historic importance."[1]

Certainly there were reasons for Engels to be pleased, and yet the entire effort would prove to be evanescent, leaving the U.S. working class just where it had been before, and where it remains to the present day, within the grip of the two party system of patronage politics. Henry George lost the election, although he was credited with 30 percent of the total vote. The party that emerged from this campaign, the United Labor Party, soon purged socialist activists from its ranks, and, shortly thereafter, it disintegrated. In taking a close look at the 1886 campaign, it is instructive to contrast the actual course of events with Engels' assessment of these events and his hopes for the future. The point is not to refute Engels, but to use this case study as a starting point to more clearly understand these critical questions.

UNION MILITANTS JAILED

The first half of the nineteenth century had seen several efforts to create local third parties rooted in organized labor. These efforts had been transitory and localized,[2] with politics on the national level dominated by the unresolved and interconnected issues of slavery and the westward expansion. By 1886, two decades after the Civil War, rapid industrialization and the closing of the Western frontier had created the prerequisites for a sustained working-class movement. Yet the Civil War had engendered a configuration of party loyalties that remained ingrained in the popular consciousness. Indeed, only the Great Depression, and the New Deal, would bring a significant shift in these sectional and class allegiances.

In New York City, working men had been voting Democratic for decades prior to the Civil War. (Women would only win the right to vote in federal elections in 1920, and in New York state elections in 1918.) Tammany Hall had constructed a well-oiled machine, based on the distribution of government jobs to loyal supporters and the solicitation of bribes from local businesses. The Democratic bosses also cultivated their ties to the Catholic Church, a force of particular significance within the Irish working class. Disgusted with the venal politics of Tammany Hall, middle-class reformers sought to end this corrupt system of patronage politics by bringing "good government" to the thriving metropolis.

Only the organized working class could provide the basis for a radically new pattern of politics on the municipal level. In 1882, the Central Labor Union was formed, linking skilled workers organized into local craft unions with unskilled workers enrolled into branches of the Knights of Labor. The Central Labor Union of New York City was hardly typical of the local labor federations that were beginning to be formed around the country. Several of its constituent unions were composed of German-speaking workers, and, within these unions, activists from the Socialist Labor Party soon came to the forefront. Calls for a labor party had been a staple of SLP propaganda for some years prior to 1886.[3]

Irish nationalists were also active in the new union federation, honing a weapon forged during the Irish land wars, the economic boycott. When George Theiss, the owner of the Alhambra saloon, a popular beer garden and concert hall, refused to negotiate with unions representing the waiters, bartenders and musicians he employed, a 15-day boycott, organized by the Central Labor Union, convinced him to sign an agreement resolving the dispute. One provision of the agreement provided for a $1,000 payment by Theiss to the unions as compensation for the costs of the boycott. Theiss paid the full amount, and then went to the district attorney claiming extortion.[4]

When the issue was presented to a grand jury, five German-American socialists who had been members of the boycott organizing committee were indicted on felony charges. The five union militants were immediately tried, and convicted, before Judge George C. Barrett, a prominent member of the New York judiciary, and a Democratic Party mainstay. On July 2, 1886, Judge Barrett sentenced the five union advocates to prison terms ranging from 18 to 45 months, to be served doing hard labor at Sing Sing maximum security prison in upstate New York.[5]

In justifying the sentences, Barrett made it very clear that the charges of extortion were a pretext. The distribution of leaflets in front of the saloon had constituted "an unrestrained exercise of the dangerous power of combination." Beyond the desire to deter boycotts, Barrett was incensed at the spread of socialist ideas throughout the German-American community. The five activists were charged with "Socialistic crimes." Furthermore, the severity of their actions was "heightened by the fact" that the five were "not American citizens."[6]

INITIATING AN INDEPENDENT CAMPAIGN

Thus, the harsh prison terms meted out by Judge Barrett were a blatant attempt to quash the spread of radical ideas in the immigrant community. Union activists were infuriated by Barrett's draconian sentences. Under intense pressure from an incensed rank and file, the Central Labor Union initiated a discussion of independent politics. On July 11, 1886, the CLU established a Committee on Political Action to further the goal of an independent slate. The committee returned with a report calling for a ticket pledged to the goal of achieving a "redemption of our city government from the hands of plunderers whose acts of spoilation have brought disgrace upon our city, and through whom the administration of justice has become a farce." The Central Labor Union then issued a call for a conference of sympathetic "trade and labor organizations" based on one delegate per 100 members. The vindictive jail terms given the five union activists had sparked the creation of a municipal labor party.[7]

When the convention met on August 5, 402 delegates from 165 unions and organizations represented 40,000 members. Most of the organizations at the conference were craft union locals and Knights of Labor assemblies, but the Socialist Labor Party and the Greenback Party were directly represented as well. Most of the delegates were disgusted with Tammany Hall, convinced that it was time for working people to vote for an independent slate of union members, since there were "men in our ranks who were just as shrewd as any other." By an overwhelming vote of 362 to 40, the delegates approved a motion to nominate an independent slate for the municipal elections, and then adjourned.[8]

The conference reassembled on August 19, and selected a seven-person committee to investigate the potential for an independent slate. Although several members of the committee were committed socialists, the chair, James P. Archibald, was an official of the paperhangers' union and a Democratic Party stalwart. The conference also chose John McMackin, an official of the painters union, as the chair of its executive committee. An Irish immigrant, McMackin had worked as a painter before becoming a leading official in the local Painters' Union and an influential member of the Central Labor Union. Within the CLU, McMackin was seen as a moderate, ideologically hostile to the tenets of socialist thought.[9]

Over the next few weeks, the conference of delegates met at regular intervals to organize the basis for an independent slate of candidates for municipal office. Delegates approved a platform that included a series of reforms of special interest to working people, including an eight-hour day, a graduated income tax, and the abolition of child labor.[10]

HENRY GEORGE

On August 20, the candidate selection committee conferred with Henry George. George had already established a solid reputation as a social reformer. His 1879 book, *Progress and Poverty*, had become a huge popular success. George believed that the government should rely on a single tax, one that would fall on the increasing value of land. Over time, this tax would be steadily increased until all of the revenues generated by pure rents would go to the government, and property owners holding undeveloped land would be forced to sell.[11]

George understood that the increasing value of land did not just reflect the monopoly holding of a scarce resource, but that it also stemmed from capital improvements constructed on the land, whether in the form of office buildings, residential homes or irrigation ditches.

As a believer in the capitalist market economy, George had no desire to inhibit private sector investment, so his single tax would have excluded property improvements from taxation.

Henry George had moved to California as a youth, where he had started his career as a printer and journalist, rising to become the part owner and editor of one of San Francisco's leading daily newspapers.[12] Railroads dominated the economy and the politics of California. Railroad lines were given huge subsidies to lay tracks through the fertile inland valleys of California. Land grants provided to the railroad corporations by the state as an incentive to building new lines soared in value as previously isolated areas became newly accessible. As a result, railroad magnates reaped vast fortunes, and the railroads became land holding companies. Thus, George's proposed land tax made a certain sense in nineteenth-century California, but it had far less relevance to a densely settled metropolis such as New York City.

Progress and Poverty was widely read even in Europe. Marx did not publicly comment on its thesis, but he did critique it in a letter to a friend and comrade in the United States, Friedrich Sorge. The single-tax plan, if implemented, would still "leave *wage labor*, and hence *capitalist production*, in existence." According to Marx, George had not articulated a radical critique of monopoly rule, but rather his single-tax plan represented "simply an attempt, trimmed with socialism, to save capitalist rule."[13]

The Central Labor Union had initiated the slate of independent candidates for the 1886 election, but in seeking out Henry George union leaders had substantially diluted the slate as a genuine expression of working-class politics. Instead, the campaign had moved significantly toward becoming yet another venture in middle-class reform politics. Although George had once worked as a printer and a journalist, and had retained his membership in the typographers' union, he had long ceased to be either a working printer or journalist.[14] As an editor and publisher, he had become an entrepreneur, and his politics reflected his rise to affluence.

HENRY GEORGE AS CANDIDATE

George agreed to run for mayor, but only if 30,000 signatures were collected on nomination petitions. In a letter to Archibald and the selection committee setting out his terms, George declared his support for an independent "working-man's party," committed to fighting "industrial slavery," as exemplified by child labor and poverty. Yet he also admonished that such a campaign "ought not to be lightly entered into." In addition to union members, there were "thousands and thousands heartily sick of the corruption of machine politics." These supporters of civic reform would back an independent ticket, but only if it "gave fair promise of success." Thus, any third party activity "must manifest strength at the outset" if it were "to prove formidable at the polls."[15]

George's contingent acceptance was met with avid enthusiasm. The organizers of the effort believed that George's candidacy would lend legitimacy to the ticket, and, perhaps, even give it a reasonable chance of winning. A campaign structure was placed in motion, funded by an assessment of 25 cents for each member claimed by one of the endorsing organizations. With local unions solidly behind the campaign, eager activists quickly collected 39,000 signatures. A convention of delegates was then set for September 23, 1886, to make official George's nomination for mayor of New York City.[16]

In 1886, New York City was confined to the lower half of Manhattan. Within this densely populated area, with a population of 1.2 million, lay the financial, commercial and communications center of the United States. As the campaign gained momentum, newspaper coverage blossomed. In London, Engels received reports directly from comrades who had relocated to the United States, and indirectly through journals and newspapers. With Marx's death in March 1883, Engels had become the focal point for Marxists around the world. Although he had not previously devoted much thought to the situation in the United States, his attention was drawn to the apparent willingness of American trade unions to break with the two party system. In a letter to August Bebel, one of the leaders of the German Social Democratic Party, Engels hailed the independent ticket in New York City, as well as similar ones in Chicago and Milwaukee. In spite of "colossal blunders," presumably the selection of Henry George as the standard bearer, the U.S. working class was finally in motion, and once under way "things will go faster there than anywhere else."[17]

On September 23, the nominating convention of the independent municipal slate convened, with 409 delegates representing 40,000 members in attendance. The delegates registered a decisive vote of 360 to 38 to formally offer the nomination for mayor to Henry George. A new platform written by George was then adopted, a platform based on single-tax theory. In levying property taxes, vacant land should be assessed at the value of comparable land that had already been developed. This would force the owners "to build on it themselves, or give up the land to those who will." The property tax rate would also be increased so that "the enormous value" of land arising from the pressing density of people in New York City would be tapped for the public good, with the increase in revenues being allocated for public education and mass transit. Another key plank decried the pervasive corruption in New York's politics, and called for "honest government" and a reform of the patronage system.[18]

Although the campaign had been initiated by the Central Labor Union, the revised platform omitted any mention of working-class issues such as the eight-hour day, child labor, or the rights of trade unions to organize and strike. In rewriting the platform, Henry George had shifted the direction of the campaign from that of working-class reformism to one that could appeal to middle-class progressives.[19]

From the start of the campaign, George defended this shift toward the middle class as a strategic priority. A day after the nominating convention, the candidate informed the *New York Times* that he "would simply give the people an honest government" while working for social reform. Furthermore, George was convinced that "his support outside of the labor organizations would be much stronger than anticipated."[20]

As the campaign gained momentum, Engels received a series of reports on the U.S. scene from a close personal source. Eleanor Marx, one of Karl Marx's three daughters, and an outstanding activist in her own right, arrived in New York City on September 10, 1886. She and her partner Edward Aveling had been invited by the Socialist Labor Party to tour the United States, and the two would travel to 40 cities during the next three months, returning to Europe on December 25, 1886.[21]

On September 29, the Avelings met with Henry George for a brief, confidential conversation. George made it clear that he rejected the socialist analysis of capitalist society, and indeed that he did not view the market economy "as the basis" of "the ills" of society. Nevertheless, the Avelings were generally pleased with their reception, and during their stay in New York they urged SLP clubs in the area to actively participate in the George campaign.[22]

At a raucous rally of thousands on October 5, George formally accepted the nomination, and the campaign moved into high gear. For five weeks, the city was crowded with political rallies, as Tammany Hall vied with trade union militants for working-class support. Union leaders around the country viewed the Henry George campaign as a matter of critical importance. The Knights of Labor had attracted hundreds of thousands of new members through their participation in a wave of mass demonstrations for an eight-hour day that had swept through the country in the spring of 1886. Terence Powderly, the Grand Master Workman of the Knights, came to New York to speak at an election eve rally for George, and then toured the city with the candidate on election day.[23]

SAMUEL GOMPERS AND HENRY GEORGE

This would prove the heyday of the Knights of Labor, as the organization spiraled downward to dissolution, unable to consolidate a durable organizational structure. Although the Knights attempted to organize workers by industry rather than craft, craft unions of skilled workers were being formed as a rival force within the union movement. The Federation of Trades and Labor Unions of American and Canada brought many of these craft unions into a loose confederation. (In December 1886, the Federation of Trades would merge with dissident elements from the Knights of Labor to form the American Federation of Labor (AFL).) On a state and local level, these lines blurred. The New York City Central Labor Union enrolled both craft unions and Knights of Labor assemblies as affiliates. At the state level, the Workingmen's Assembly, which acted as labor's lobby to the state legislature, drew from Knights of Labor assemblies and Federated Trades affiliates.[24]

Samuel Gompers stood at the nexus of this emerging network of unions. A cigar maker by trade, Gompers was vice-president of the Cigar Makers Union, one of the largest unions in New York City. In addition, he was also the president of the Workingmen's Assembly, president of the Federation of Trades legislative committee, and the prospective president of the American Federation of Labor. At 36, Gompers was already a confirmed and cautious pragmatist. In his view, unions existed for the primary purpose of extracting immediate concessions in wages and working conditions for their members. Gompers had worked with socialist activists within the Central Labor Union, and he would, on occasion, voice a tenuous sympathy for the goal of an alternative society. Nevertheless, he consistently subordinated the struggle for fundamental change to the exigencies of the immediate tactical advantage.[25]

Gompers was wary of independent politics, but he was also infuriated by Judge Barrett's decision to jail the Theiss boycott committee. As Henry George's campaign for mayor gained momentum, Gompers threw himself into the effort. He chaired the citywide organization of Henry George Clubs, while also coordinating the speakers bureau. At the rally at Coopers Union that formally initiated the campaign, Gompers urged the workers of New York City to vote for George to demonstrate to those who have "imprisoned our brothers, indicted our fellows and held the menace of the penitentiary over our heads" that "we cannot be clubbed into submission."[26]

At a citywide meeting of cigar makers, Gompers further clarified his position. He "had always opposed independent political action, but he thought the time had come when workingmen should select, as well as vote" for, and elect their own candidates. This was particularly true for the campaign for mayor, where Henry George stood an excellent chance of being elected.[27]

Ever the pragmatist, Gompers' energetic participation in the Henry George campaign did not signify a severing of ties to the political parties of the corporate establishment. On October 31, two days before the election, Gompers joined with eight other members of the Workingmen's Assembly executive committee in an official list of endorsements. While urging "every member of organized labor" to "work for the election of Henry George" as mayor of New York City, the union officials also opted to "recommend the election" of nine candidates to the state legislature. Seven of the nine were Tammany Hall Democrats.[28]

SOCIALISTS AND THE GEORGE CAMPAIGN

As the Central Labor Union mobilized its forces for the fall election, the Socialist Labor Party gave its enthusiastic support to the campaign. None of the socialist delegates to the CLU delegate conferences challenged the choice of Henry George as the candidate for mayor. Furthermore, no objection was raised to the adoption of a platform based on levying a single tax on land. Instead, socialist speakers were sent around the city to agitate for the Henry George and the trade union slate. The *Volkszeitung*, a German-language weekly, with direct ties to the SLP, gave extensive coverage to George's campaign. Along side the *Leader*, a daily which had been created specifically to publicize the independent ticket, and which was largely supported by trade union affiliates of the Central Labor Union, the *Volkszeitung* was one of the very few newspapers in New York City to endorse the independent ticket, and Henry George.[29]

The socialist presence in the campaign became even more visible when Governor David Hill decided to commute the sentences of the five union boycott leaders to 100 days served. Upon their release, the five German-American socialists returned to New York City and immediately appeared at a protest rally. One of them, Paul Wilzig, addressed the crowd, denouncing Hill, a Democrat, as a "demagogue," who had acted purely out of self-interest. He warned the workers of New York to not be deceived into voting for Hill, or any other Democrat, and, instead, to hold firm for independent political action and Henry George.[30]

With the Central Labor Union, and the Socialist Labor Party, gearing up for the election, George attempted to expand his base of support in organized labor, hoping to attract a broader constituency. In doing so, he sought to distance himself from the recent upsurge in working-class militancy. When George spoke to the waiters union, the same union that had provided the spark for his campaign by organizing an effective boycott of Theiss' saloon, he warned his supporters that it would be his "sworn duty" as mayor to enforce the law. This would be "absolutely necessary" since, "as a class, working men have nothing to gain from disorder." After all, "if the laws do not suit them, let them change the laws." Henry George was convinced that control of the state was "within their reach," and, thus, "no appeal to force" was warranted.[31]

These comments constituted a pure, undiluted statement of liberal reformism, with its blind faith in the efficacy of legal and constitutional procedures. Of course, George had also been emphasizing the pervasive corruption of Tammany Hall, which had repeatedly demonstrated its flagrant disregard for the democratic rights of its opponents. Indeed, Henry George himself would soon get a very thorough and personal lesson in the intricacies of election fraud as practiced by the Democratic Party machine of New York City.

THE CATHOLIC CHURCH AND THE GEORGE CAMPAIGN

George also sought to counteract the hostility of the Catholic Church through his public association with one of the most prominent priests in New York. Father Edward McGlynn had served as the principal priest of St. Stephen's for 25 years. A maverick and a progressive,

McGlynn had publicly defended the single-tax theory in 1882, and had then established a continuing relationship with its author. McGlynn's superior, Archbishop Michael Corrigan, was his antithesis, and his nemesis.[32]

On August 23, Corrigan privately warned McGlynn to abstain from any comments concerning the municipal election. In defiance of this order, McGlynn addressed a crowded rally of 2,300 Henry George supporters on October 2, a rally that had been organized for the specific purpose of bringing the campaign to a more upscale, middle-class audience. Corrigan was furious, ordering McGlynn to refrain from any public statement in support of Henry George or the single-tax theory. McGlynn refrained from further public appearances during the campaign, but he proceeded to test the limits of the archbishop's warning, joining George and Terence Powderly on a tour of polling stations on election day. McGlynn's continuing support for George provided a significant boost for the campaign within the Irish working-class community.[33]

As election day approached, the independent slate seemed to be gaining momentum. George addressed three or four street rallies a night, with each rally attracting hundreds of enthusiastic supporters.[34] All of those disaffected by the corruption of the patronage system were being drawn to the George campaign. In a last ditch effort to hold the working-class vote, Tammany Hall induced the Catholic Church hierarchy to directly enter into the fray.

Tammany boss Richard Croker persuaded Joseph John O'Donohue, a leading figure in the Irish community, to publicly query the Church as to its position on the single tax. O'Donohue, a prosperous merchant and a long-time Democratic Party leader, had hoped to be slated as the party's candidate for mayor, only to see Abram Hewitt chosen instead. (Hewitt was the wealthy owner of an iron works and an influential member of the city's business establishment.) Disappointed, O'Donohue met privately with the head of the slate, hoping to convince Hewitt to accept his selection as the Democratic nominee for president of the board of aldermen. Hewitt rejected the idea, insisting that "we mustn't load down the ticket with Irishmen." Dismayed, O'Donohue complained to friends that Hewitt was "a narrow-minded bigot."[35]

Still, the Henry George campaign threatened the Democratic Party's hold over the working-class vote. Overcoming his distaste for Hewitt, O'Donohue agreed to write Monsignor Thomas Scott Preston, vicar general of the archdiocese, asking the hierarchy to clarify its attitude toward Henry George and the single tax. In an open letter dated October 25, Preston informed O'Donohue that "the great majority of the Catholic clergy in this city are opposed to the candidacy of Mr. George." Indeed, "his principles" were "unsound and unsafe, and contrary to the teachings of the Church." Should such a program be put into practice, the consequences "would prove the ruin of the working-men." Preston's letter was circulated as a leaflet to parishioners leaving Mass on the following Sunday, the last Sunday before the election.[36]

ELECTION DAY

November 2, election day, saw a large turnout at polling places around the city. Voting at the time was by open ballot, so votes could be directly bought, and Tammany Hall did just that. At certain polling places, gangs of toughs, with the complicity of the police, made sure that only Democratic voters could cast their ballots. Ringers were brought in from the surrounding areas, some of them voting at more than one precinct. Ballot boxes were stuffed with spurious ballots, while other containers holding votes for Henry George were cast into the East River.[37]

From the vantage point of a century later, it is difficult to be certain who actually won the election, but it is clear that fraud was widespread and egregious. The final tally showed the Democratic candidate ahead, with George credited with 68,000 votes, or 31 percent of the total votes officially counted. Henry George generally sidestepped charges of election fraud, opting instead to emphasize the potential for future campaigns. On election night, he told a reporter that he was pleased with the initial tallies, which indicated that he had made "a very good showing." He went on to promise that the role of working people in independent politics had "only just begun."[38]

Engels received reports of the 1886 election results with considerable enthusiasm, certain that "the political action of the working class as an independent party" was "henceforth established" in the United States. In a letter to another one of Karl Marx's daughters, Laura Lafargue, Engels conceded that the platform of the new party, with its emphasis on the single tax, was problematic. Although Henry George had "a nostrum of his own, and not a very excellent one," still Marxists could not "expect even [the] American masses to arrive at theoretical perfection in six or eight months."[39]

Engels was being disingenuous. The platform of the independent slate had not been revised because the working class of New York City had been enraptured by the tenets of single-tax theory, a scheme for social reform that had little relevance to an industrial and commercial metropolis. Indeed, the thrust of the initial platform developed by the Central Labor Union, with its call for a graduated income tax and an eight-hour day, demonstrated that. The problem arose when leaders of the Central Labor Union determined that a credible, even victorious, campaign required a celebrity candidate, one with broad popular appeal that could reach the wider community of middle-class reformers. This would become a recurring theme of labor party politics in the United States, the search for a personality who would appeal to a broad spectrum of voters, most particularly middle-class progressives.

THE UNITED LABOR PARTY

Within a week of the election, November 6, a packed meeting of 4,000 assembled at Cooper Union to launch a new party, the United Labor Party. George promised that "the ball had been set rolling." The mobilization of forces in support of his candidacy, along with the sizable vote he had garnered, had been a lesson to the machine politicians of the two establishment parties, guaranteeing that "they would never again sneer at political labor movements." Gompers addressed the gathering, reiterating his support for Henry George, while underlining his belief that "workingmen had the perfect right to boycott any one they pleased."[40]

Feelings of good will were deepened several days later when Henry George spoke to a Cooper Union rally organized by the Socialist Labor Party as a celebration of the municipal campaign. George thanked the socialists for their "warm and steady support," noting that they had muted "all of their differences for a common cause."[41]

Nevertheless, in spite of the profuse expressions of unity, the coalition that had been constructed during the campaign was beginning to unravel. Those who attended the rally on November 6 that launched the United Labor Party were greeted with a single large banner. It read: "Abolish All Taxes But One on Land." Thus, the two wings of the Central Labor Union, both the socialists and the proponents of business unionism, were given clear warning that the ULP would be a party narrowly founded on the single tax.[42]

At the same meeting, a resolution was passed establishing a three-person executive committee, charged with the responsibility for drawing up a constitution and bylaws. Since the party would be organized on a statewide basis, a founding convention was scheduled for the following summer in Syracuse. All three members of the executive committee, McGlynn, McMackin, and James Redpath, were close allies of Henry George.[43]

The three-person executive committee proceeded to adopt a tentative constitution for the United Labor Party on December 1. This created a county convention for New York City with representation by state assembly districts. Primaries would be held for ULP members based on one delegate per 200 votes received by Henry George in that district. The statewide convention was constituted on a similar basis, with districts outside of New York City being allotted a share of the total delegates.[44] By shifting from a system of direct representation by unions to one based on geographical districts, what had begun as an independent municipal slate initiated by a local union federation had been transformed into a third party of progressive reformers dominated by Henry George and his supporters. The United Labor Party, despite its name, was not a true labor party, and, indeed, union leaders began distancing themselves from it.

Gompers, who had always been wary of independent political action, cited these developments as sufficient reason to spur his withdrawal from the new party. In a later interview with the *Volkszeitung*, Gompers argued that the potential for a viable independent party had ended in the fall of 1886 "when a self-appointed executive committee had the impudence to take the leadership of the movement out of the hands of the Central Labor Union." After that, Gompers had "wanted nothing more to do with it."[45]

For the militants of the Socialist Labor Party, who had been buoyed by the hope that the success of the New York City campaign could lead to the formation of a labor party on a nationwide basis, a break with Henry George was far more difficult. An editorial in the *Volkszeitung* declared that socialists had supported George "not on account of his single-tax theory, but in spite of it." After all, "the burning issue" was "not a land tax, but the abolition of all private property in [the] instruments of production." Still, the SLP continued to praise George as the candidate and leader of the ULP.[46]

ENGELS AND THE UNITED LABOR PARTY

From his vantage point in London, Engels remained convinced that the United Labor Party could become a focal point for a broadly based independent working-class party. In November 1886, he wrote Sorge that for "a country that has newly entered the movement, the first really crucial step is the formation by the workers of an independent political party, no matter how, so long as it is distinguishable as a labor party." Working people in the United States were confused in their views, but they would be "impelled onwards by their own mistakes, and [would] learn by bitter experience," but first they had to "have a movement of their own."[47]

The German-Americans of the Socialist Labor Party were "doctrinaire and dogmatic." They needed to become fluent in English so that they could fully enter the movement, where they could use their knowledge of Marxist theory as a guideline to action. As socialists and revolutionaries they could help their U.S. comrades "see that any movement which does not constantly bear in mind that the ultimate goal is the destruction of the wage system must necessarily go astray and come to nothing."[48]

In a letter written during the closing days of 1886 to Florence Kelley, who was translating Engels into English, Engels again emphasized that the "great thing is to get the working class to move *as a class*," since, once in motion, it would "soon find the right direction." With this in mind, socialists in the United States should work within the coalescing third party movement. Indeed, a "million or two of working-men's votes next November for a bona-fide working-men's party is worth infinitely more at present than a hundred thousand votes for a doctrinally perfect platform."[49]

Thus, Engels continued to urge socialists in the United States to actively participate within a broad working-class party. At the same time, he stressed the necessity of socialists acting as a distinct tendency within the broader party. In late January 1887, Engels sent an updated preface prepared for the U.S. edition of his *Condition of the English Working Class*. Along with the preface, Engels sent a personal letter to Kelley once again praising the United Labor Party, and urging socialists to work within it. Engels concluded that "all of our practice" had shown that it was "possible to work along with the general movement of the working class at every one of its stages without giving up or hiding our own distinct position, and even organization."

Should the "German-Americans choose a different line," they would "commit a great mistake."[50]

Still, Engels did not believe that socialists should submerge their own distinct position while acting as a left-wing minority within a mass-based working-class party committed to social reform. On the contrary, he was convinced that socialists should be outspoken in articulating their own perspective and differentiating it from the views held by the majority of the party. Engels then proceeded to act in accordance with these guidelines.

The U.S. preface to the *Condition of the English Working Class* provided Engels with his only public opportunity to comment on the 1886 election. He began by noting that a wave of strikes had preceded the election, and that this had led to "the next step," the "formation of a political workingmen's party, with a platform of its own." Still, this represented "but a beginning," since "in the long run" the working class through its political party needed to "proclaim as the ultimate end" the "direct appropriation of all means of production" to "be worked in common by all for the account and benefit of all."[51]

Engels was especially interested in the potential for a new electoral formation that would bring together several reform groups and trade unions into one broadly based independent party. With the onset of the 1886 election campaigns, labor activists and social reformers around the country began to conceive of a single nationwide third party that could contest the presidential election of 1888. In September 1886, a conference initiated by the Greenback Party, with support of dissident elements within the Knights of Labor, met in Indianapolis and agreed to issue a call for a national convention of all third party forces to be held in Cincinnati the following February. (Greenbackers had gained significant support in farm districts with calls for a sizable expansion of the money supply.) With the striking success of the Henry George campaign, organizers of the Cincinnati convention looked to the United Labor Party as an important component of this wider coalition.[52]

Engels criticized the Socialist Labor Party for becoming an isolated clique. Although he remained hopeful that it could "play a very important part in the movement," to do so its members would "have to become out and out Americans." In light of this, he urged the SLP to work within this new electoral formation, "no matter how inadequate a provisional platform" it might adopt. Nevertheless, "there cannot be any doubt that the ultimate platform of the American working class must, and will be, essentially the same as that now adopted by the whole militant working class of Europe."[53]

Having articulated his perspective on the U.S. political scene, Engels proceeded to directly attack Henry George and his single-tax theory. This theory, as adapted by the United Labor Party, was "too narrow to form the basis for anything but a local movement." In any case, socialists "demand the resumption, by society, of the land, and not only of the land, but of all other means of production likewise." Although Henry George proposed that pure rents derived from the ownership of land be taxed for the public good, his plan would leave land privately owned and controlled. In contrast, "what Socialists demand implies a total revolution of the whole system of social production," while the single tax "leaves the present mode of production untouched."[54]

THE CATHOLIC CHURCH ATTACKS

The publication of the preface could only have reinforced the disquiet felt by Henry George toward the socialist contingent in the United Labor Party. Still, during the winter and spring of 1887 the leadership of the ULP was preoccupied by continuing attacks from the Catholic Church. On November 21, 1886, Archbishop Corrigan issued a pastoral letter, read in every parish in the New York City region, attacking socialism and defending property rights. Corrigan did not specifically mention Henry George, but he referred to the public debate on "the right of property or ownership in land," and he warned parishioners to spurn "theories however specious," or be subject to "the risk of embracing falsehood for truth."[55]

In rejecting and condemning socialism and the single tax, Corrigan had to concede that a capitalist market economy engenders intolerable inequalities in income and wealth. Yet the Church's solution to these crucial issues came to nothing more than pious platitudes. The archbishop ended his pastoral statement with citations from an 1878 encyclical by Pope Leo XIII in which the Pope had admonished "the rich [to] give of their superabundance to the poor," or be punished by "divine judgment" to the "eternal punishment" of hell. The poor who waited with patience and obedience would "be blessed," and would reap "the reward of eternal happiness."[56]

Corrigan's attack on the single tax badly hurt the ULP in the Catholic communities of New York. Father McGlynn tried to deflect this ideological assault in a newspaper interview given within days of the pastoral letter. In the interview, McGlynn reaffirmed his belief in Henry George and the single-tax theory. For Corrigan and the Catholic hierarchy, this open challenge to their authority had to be crushed. Having been already temporarily suspended as parish priest, McGlynn was temporarily removed from his post as principal priest at St. Stephen's. Soon after, on December 4, 1886, he was ordered to go to Rome for a further review of his case. When he refused, he was permanently suspended from all duties as parish priest. In July 1887, Corrigan went even further, banning McGlynn from the priesthood.[57]

As these events unfolded, George was establishing his own weekly newspaper, the *Standard*. The paper was created as George's own personal forum, and it was subsidized by the Land and Liberty League, an educational organization established to promote single-tax theories. George responded to the Catholic Church's attacks on McGlynn and himself with a series of editorials in the first issues of the *Standard*, but his effort met with little success.[58]

THE UNITED LABOR PARTY SPLITS

In the midst of this acrimonious dispute, divisions within the United Labor Party receded in importance, at least through the winter of 1887. Nevertheless, there were increasing signs of tension between socialist sympathizers and single-tax supporters. One issue arose as a consequence of the launching of the *Standard* in January 1887. Louis F. Post, the managing editor of the new publication, and a prominent supporter of George and the single tax, had previously served as the editor of the *Leader*, the newspaper founded in the summer of 1886 as a vehicle for the Henry George campaign. Serge Schewitsch, an exiled member of the Russian nobility and a staunch member of the Socialist Labor Party, took over from Post. George was not pleased to see an avowed socialist selected as the editor of the *Leader*, but the two newspapers avoided sniping at each other through the first months of 1887.[59]

Nevertheless, links between Henry George and the German-American socialists of the Socialist Labor Party grew increasingly strained, particularly when the SLP issued a thorough critique of single-tax theory, written by its most renowned author, Laurence Grönlund.[60] Born in Denmark, Grönlund had studied law at the University of Copenhagen, but left before graduating. In 1867, at the age of 21, he immigrated to the United States, where he moved to Chicago and practiced law. After being attracted to social reform movements, Grönlund became further radicalized and joined the Socialist Labor Party.

In 1884, Grönlund published one of the first books to develop a socialist vision of a future society. *The Cooperative Commonwealth* sold well, establishing Grönlund as a public figure. Elected to the SLP's executive committee in 1886, he was the logical choice to refute the arguments of Henry George. In the spring of 1887, his tract *The Insufficiency of Henry George's Theory* articulated a crude but effective analysis of the single-tax theory from a Marxist perspective.[61]

Grönlund pointed out that in a capitalist society land and capital "together constitute [the] means of labor, [the] means of production." Thus it was essential to demand "that both land and capital be placed under collective control." Since the single-tax theory focused exclusively on the proceeds of owning land, socialists had to call for a more comprehensive analysis. Grönlund was confident that ULP members were "far more advanced than Henry George," and would insist on creating a party "whose aim is the abolition of the wage-system."[62]

Yet despite this ideological critique of the single-tax theory, Grönlund still sought to mollify its adherents and avoid a split within the United Labor Party. Indeed, the pamphlet emphasized that socialists continued to "highly esteem the noble qualities" of Henry George, "his head and heart." The Socialist Labor Party continued to view George as "the forerunner of Socialism in these United States, and the entering wedge for [its] ideas into American minds."[63]

Relations between George and the SLP became even more contentious as the date for the February convention in Cincinnati approached. George opposed the Greenback Party's plan for a significant expansion of the supply of money. In addition, it was becoming increasingly clear that he would only support a third party that focused its platform on the imposition of a single tax on property. As a result, the United Labor Party declined its invitation to the Cincinnati convention, acting in accordance with George's desires.[64]

Throughout the spring of 1887, Engels continued to diligently follow political developments in the United States. Although he remained optimistic, he was becoming increasingly skeptical, especially after he learned of George's decision to bypass the Cincinnati convention of third party movements. In an April letter to Sorge, Engels noted the deepening tensions, remarking that George was becoming "more and more set on his land fad," thus leading him to "suppress all that is socialist." Another letter to Sorge, from June

1887, found Engels "fed up with Father McGlynn" and with George who "has turned into a real founder of a sect."[65]

Cooperation between single-tax supporters and socialists fell apart as the United Labor Party prepared for its first statewide convention, to be held in Syracuse, New York, in August 1887. In part, the division stemmed from the considerable differences in political perspective between the two groups, as well as Henry George's insistence on maintaining total control of ULP policy. Yet the split also reflected a tactical shift in focus. In the fall of 1886, during his campaign for mayor of New York City, Henry George had viewed the socialist presence as an asset, both because of the number of committed activists the SLP could mobilize for the campaign, and because the socialist vision had a considerable appeal to significant segments of the city's working class. As the United Labor Party directed its energies to statewide elections, George viewed a visible socialist presence as an electoral liability.

The first open skirmish erupted in May, as Henry George and his supporters opted to create a greater ideological distance between themselves and the radical Left. On May 5, the general convention for the New York City area met to adopt a proposed platform to be presented at the Syracuse convention. Socialist delegates advanced a resolution recognizing the inherent conflict between workers and corporations, and supporting the militant actions of the organized working class. This would seem a rather tepid resolution for a supposed labor party, and yet the motion failed. Instead, the convention adopted a proposal declaring that "there was no enmity between labor and capital," and urging both sides to join in harmony and cooperation for the greater good.[66]

Dismayed, the Socialist Labor Party convened a meeting on May 21 of all of its sections in the New York metropolitan area. Although several of those in attendance held that the SLP should immediately leave the United Labor Party, the majority, led by Serge Schewitsch, insisted on remaining. The majority decided to present a distinct slate of candidates for delegates to the Syracuse convention, one pledged to present a class conflict plank for incorporation into the party's platform.[67]

These incidents brought the two sides to the brink of an open rupture. Still, the ULP leadership indicated its willingness to tolerate a socialist presence, but only on a clearly subordinate basis. John McMackin told the *New York Times* in late June that the party would be fielding a complete slate of candidates in the upcoming state elections. He felt certain that the SLP would continue to support the ULP ticket, since they could "not lead, and the next best thing" would be "to follow in the wake."[68]

The Socialist Labor Party scrambled to remain in the United Labor Party, but on terms that would not totally dilute its socialist perspective. A review in the *Leader* of June 28, 1887 lauded Grönlund's pamphlet and its critical analysis of the single-tax theory, while still praising Henry George as the standard bearer of independent politics. Although the *Standard* did not respond, George was becoming increasingly distrustful of his erstwhile socialist allies.[69]

After months of escalating tension, the final break came during the weeks leading up to the Syracuse convention. When SLP members pledged to a class conflict perspective did well in the delegate selection process, Henry George moved quickly to defeat this challenge to his dominant position within the ULP. In an article appearing in the July 30 issue of the *Standard*, he held that the public sector should be limited to those cases "where competition fails to rescue liberty of action and freedom of development." The Socialist Labor Party, with its "childish notions of making all capital the property of the state," represented a threat to the United Labor Party. At about the same time as this diatribe appeared in print, George was privately warning a supporter that a showdown with the socialist grouping within the ULP was "inevitable, sooner or later."[70]

On August 4, John McMackin ruled as chair of the ULP county convention for the New York City area that SLP members were ineligible for election as delegates to the statewide convention. His ruling was upheld by the entire convention. Although the Central Labor Union, which had initiated the ULP, accepted the SLP as one of its affiliates, and although SLP members had been welcomed as activists throughout the entire campaign for mayor, McMackin ruled that a provision in the United Labor Party rules that required members to have "severed all connections with all other political parties" prohibited joint membership in the SLP. McMackin defended this ruling by arguing that the ULP could not "afford to tolerate Greenback, Irish, German or Socialist factions."[71]

The Socialist Labor Party, which had been muting its own political perspective in a futile effort to avoid conflict with Henry George and his coterie of supporters within the ULP, now found itself excluded from further participation in the party. Several SLP members proceeded to travel to the Syracuse convention, hoping to be seated in spite of the county convention ruling. As the state convention came to order on August 17, 1887, it became clear that the majority of delegates sided with Henry George. In an informal discussion, George advised Schewitsch that socialists would, of necessity, be excluded from the United Labor Party because they were "dreaded by the farmers of the state." The next day, eight delegates, including Schewitsch and Grönlund, were barred from further participation by a substantial majority of the convention. The SLP then created a new party, the Progressive Labor Party, which vitriolically condemned the ULP during the 1887 election, drew off 5,000 votes from the latter, and then dissolved.[72]

The Socialist Labor Party had pursued a policy similar to that proposed by Engels, with the result that it had helped to build a party from which it was soon excluded. In a letter to Sorge in early August, written during the Syracuse convention, Engels took a philosophical view of this debacle. U.S. workers would "astonish us all by the vastness of their movement, but also by the gigantic nature of the mistakes" they would make, and through which they would "finally work out their way to clarity."[73] Yet Engels had to concede, at least implicitly, that the Henry George campaign had not marked a significant step toward an independent politics. Thus, the "course of the movement" would "by no means follow the classic straight line, but travel in tremendous zigzags and seem to be moving backwards at times," but that was "of much less importance there [in the United States] than with us."[74]

A month later, Engels wrote Sorge that Henry George's "repudiation of the socialists" had provided "the greatest good fortune that could happen to us." His nomination was an "unavoidable mistake for which we had to pay." Still, "the masses" could "be set in motion only along the road that fits each country and the prevailing circumstances," which was "usually a roundabout road."[75]

While recognizing that the George campaign had not had the desired results, Engels evaded the implications of this failure for the strategic perspective he had urged upon socialists in the United States. The Socialist Labor Party had wielded considerable influence within the Central Labor Union, and yet they had made no effort to counter George's nomination for mayor. Indeed, the SLP had enthusiastically and uncritically endorsed the George campaign. Only after the election had it tentatively raised a socialist critique of single-tax dogma, only to find its members excluded from the United Labor Party.

THE UNITED LABOR PARTY DISINTEGRATES

The final stages in the dissolution of the United Labor Party can be quickly described. After refusing to seat any delegate who was a SLP member, the Syracuse convention of the ULP nominated Henry George for the top post on its statewide ticket. Since the position of governor was not up for election in 1887, George was nominated as secretary of state. The campaign was modestly successful, with George receiving 68,000 votes, or 7 percent of the total. Yet George was a practical politician, eager to make an immediate impact on mainstream America. His near victory as mayor of New York City had left him with unrealistic expectations, even the hope of a credible campaign for president in 1888. The election results of 1887 demonstrated that the ULP was a marginal third party, with slim hopes of quick electoral victories at either the state or national levels.[76]

During his lengthy stay in California, Henry George had been allied with liberal reformers within the Democratic Party. Indeed, he had even served as a delegate to the 1872 Democratic Party convention. At that point, George had hoped for a fusion effort of Democrats and Republicans in support of free trade through a general and substantial reduction in tariffs.[77] With his disappointing showing in the election of 1887, George sought an expedient path back to the safe waters of the two party system. He soon found one.

Groping for a popular issue to improve his re-election chances, President Grover Cleveland opted to focus his annual message to Congress on the high protective tariff. His speech of December 6, 1887, emphasized that tariffs on the "necessaries of life" were excessively steep, and should be significantly reduced. For Henry George, the proposed tariff reduction represented "not merely an economic reform, but a great moral and political reform." George hailed Cleveland's speech as an effective "means of bringing the whole subject of taxation" into "the fullest discussion." The paramount objective of the single-tax theory, according to its founder, Henry George, had been to shift the structure of taxes away from those that fell on working people, and the tariff was one of the most egregious examples of such indirect taxes.[78]

Within days of Cleveland's message to Congress, George began signaling his readiness to abandon his tentative support for an independent politics. An editorial in the *Standard* of December 17, 1887 suggested that "independent political action" should be considered "as only one of various means." George went on to suggest that single-tax supporters should be prepared to shift their support to Cleveland if the Democratic platform held firm to the need for tariff reduction. Henry George had returned to the politics of the lesser evil, and, to add insult to injury, he had done so on the basis of an issue of peripheral concern to working people.[79]

With George moving toward the Democratic Party, the ULP quickly disintegrated. McGlynn, as its president, insisted that the party would continue to field its own slate in the fall of 1888, and that its candidates would not focus on the tariff issue. In February, with McGlynn still adamant, George endorsed President Cleveland's re-election bid, and then resigned from the United Labor Party. Undeterred, the ULP went forward with its own presidential slate, which received 3,000 votes in New York, after which the party dissolved.[80]

All of the major figures in the Henry George campaign soon returned to the political mainstream. Ironically, Edward McGlynn wound up supporting the Republican presidential candidate, Benjamin Harrison, who went on to defeat Cleveland. McGlynn then dropped out of politics, and, in 1892, was reinstated as a parish priest, and assigned to a small town outside of New York City.[81]

The trade union officials most associated with the George campaign quickly withdrew from any further participation in third party politics. John McMackin became a Republican stalwart, and was rewarded with a series of patronage jobs, culminating in his appointment as New York State Commissioner of Labor from 1901 to 1905. For Gompers, the Henry George campaign marked a turning point, confirming his belief in the futility of independent political action. As president of the American Federation of Labor, Gompers generally discouraged affiliate unions from active participation in the electoral arena. Then, in 1906, he abandoned this perspective and adopted the policy of "rewarding labor's friends." From then on, Gompers actively promoted progressive candidates, usually Democrats, who campaigned within the framework of the two party system.[82]

Henry George remained a committed proponent of the single-tax theory, but he spurned any further commitment to independent politics, endorsing the Democratic presidential candidates in 1892 and 1896. In 1894, when a group of Chicago labor activists, Populists, and single-tax sympathizers came together to form an independent third party, George discouraged this effort, and urged the dissidents to remain within the Democratic Party.[83]

Thus, every one of the leading personalities of the Henry George campaign had re-entered one of the two mainstream parties within two years of the 1886 election. The ULP rapidly collapsed, and, indeed, popular support for a labor party would remain dormant for more than two decades. Contrary to Engels' enthusiastic predictions, the Henry George campaign proved to be a transitory happenstance leading nowhere, rather than a stepping stone to a vibrant, radical third party. Yet even in February 1888, as the ULP was disintegrating, Engels was certain that the "two great Anglo-Saxon nations" were "sure to set up [a] competition in Socialism," after which there would "be a race with ever-accelerated velocity."[84]

ENGELS AND THE LABOR PARTY

Obviously, Engels totally missed the mark in this prediction. It would be too easy to dismiss this error as merely another instance of revolutionary optimism, the inclination of socialists to exaggerate the potential for rapid social change from within capitalist society. The problem runs far deeper. Engels' position was untenable at every level, from the tactical to the strategic and theoretical.

Before moving to an assessment of the flaws in Engels' perspective, it is important to understand where he actually stood. Advocates of a labor party have cited carefully chosen sections of Engels' letters to his U.S. correspondents to argue that he was committed to a pragmatic posture in which socialists would submerge their politics within a broad working-class party. Yet the preface to the *Condition of the English Working Class*, which was written several months before the split in the United Labor Party, includes an incisive critique on Henry George from the perspective of revolutionary socialism. Engels believed that socialists should participate within a broadly based labor party, but he also insisted that they should articulate their own, distinct position, even if this led to confrontations with the reformist majority.

Nevertheless, Engels proposed a strategic perspective that was certain to fail. Those organizing a labor party always view the electoral arena as a means of making an immediate impact on U.S. public policy. To do this, the party's platform has to be limited to demands that can quickly attract a large number of voters, thus validating the labor party as a credible electoral force within the American mainstream. In the United States, socialism has always represented a minority viewpoint within the working class. Those who advocate a labor party are bound, therefore, to view an organized socialist tendency as a threat to their underlying strategic vision. Henry George was quite willing to have socialist activists working in his campaign for mayor, particularly since they had a base of support within the working class of New York City, but only if they followed his lead on the party's program, and kept silent about their own. Once the scope of the campaign moved beyond New York City, George was unwilling to tolerate any socialist presence at all.

When Henry George moved to oust socialists from the ULP, Engels realized that his policy suggestions had proven to be a failure. Unfortunately, his analysis did not move beyond a dismissal of George as a sectarian ideologue. Yet George had not sought the nomination as a candidate for mayor of New York City. Quite the contrary, the union leaders of the Central Labor Union had pleaded with him to accept the nomination. This desire to place a celebrity at the head of the ticket is a consistent strand in the history of U.S. third parties. In search of a rapid rise to electoral success, the pragmatic leaders of these parties look to prominent personalities, hoping to capitalize on their celebrity to win votes. The celebrity then campaigns on his own, without roots in the social movement that has generated the independent party. Often, the famous candidate has little or no commitment to independent political action, leaving the party adrift when the celebrity returns to the fold of the two party system. (The Progressive Party campaign of 1948 of Henry Wallace is a textbook example of this phenomenon.)

Labor parties have not been immune to this cycle of failure. Union officials are schooled in the pragmatic logic of the tactical maneuver. From this perspective, nominating a well-known personality seems a logical course of action. Furthermore, union officials have sought to enhance the credibility of an independent slate by widening its appeal to include middle-class social reformers. As an electoral tactic, this has made sense, but it has also diluted the class basis of the campaign. Thus, the decision to nominate Henry George was bound to undermine the United Labor Party as a truly independent working-class party. Socialists should have opposed his nomination, and they certainly should have resisted the revisions George made to the initial platform. Instead, the Socialist Labor Party kept quiet during the mayoralty campaign, a move Engels supported in his overly enthusiastic response to its initial success.

The errors in Engels' analysis extended far beyond the willingness to passively acquiesce to George's nomination. Engels realized that the U.S. working class was very different than the working class of most European countries, and yet, while recognizing these differences, he failed to come to terms with the consequences in strategy and tactics. In a society where class lines were less rigidly defined, and where social mobility remained a tantalizing prospect, U.S. workers generally accepted the individualistic ethic of a capitalist market economy. The resulting lack of class consciousness found its electoral expression in an acceptance of lesser-evil politics, and a loyalty to the two party system.

Engels stood with other socialists in the firm conviction that it was essential for working people to definitively break with the Democratic and Republican parties. There can be no doubt that this question has been the touchstone of left-wing politics in the United States. With this as the strategic goal, Engels proposed a stage theory of development. First, workers would create their own independent party on a platform of concrete reforms. Then, this party would sharpen its politics, and formulate a socialist critique of capitalist society, while articulating a program of fundamental structural change. Finally, the party would accept a Marxist analysis of society and move toward a revolutionary confrontation with the state. Although Engels recognized that these stages would not be reached in a smooth, steady process, and that setbacks were likely along the way, he held on to this fundamentally flawed approach to U.S. politics until his death in 1895.

Engels believed that socialists should always act as an integral element of the existing working-class movement, the left-wing of a mass party. In the United States, where the working class has never demonstrated the class consciousness seen in Western and central Europe, this meant becoming the radical opposition within a broad political party of social reform. Implicitly, Engels was formulating a recurring theme on the American Left, the proposition that a socialist strategy must necessarily be tailored to the unique circumstances of this country. Yet Engels saw this as a temporary adaptation, one that would be rapidly transcended as the U.S. working class approached, and even surpassed, its European comrades. Thus, while arguing for a strategic perspective specifically adapted to the United States, he refused to accept the wide gap in class consciousness between the working class of the United States and Western Europe as more than a brief, transitory discrepancy.

Engels has proven to be wrong on both counts. The majority of the U.S. working class has consistently remained within the constraints of the two party system, accepting the pragmatic appeal of the lesser evil. During several volatile moments of crisis, a substantial segment of the U.S. working class has been attracted by the potential of a third party. Yet without the anchor of a radical, democratic socialist program, electoral formations such as the Henry George campaign soon falter, collapsing back into the folds of the electoral mainstream. A definitive break with the Democratic Party can only come as part of a sharp ideological rejection of liberal reformism. Third parties based on a program of progressive reforms are quickly integrated into the system. As the Henry George campaign of 1886 all too clearly demonstrates, political formations based on the official trade union structure are far from immune from this cycle of cooptation.

Furthermore, it is essential that an independent party truly and totally break with the capitalist parties. All too often, third parties have remained on the edge of the Democratic Party, attempting to act as a progressive pressure group on that party's leaders. Although the United Labor Party only existed for a brief period, and therefore did not establish any organizational ties to the two corporate parties, it is clear that its leaders, from George to McMackin to Gompers, viewed the election of 1886 as a single, unique, event, with limited implications for the future. Indeed, in the final days of the campaign, Gompers could exhort union members to vote for Henry George for mayor of New York City, while simultaneously endorsing Tammany Hall Democrats for the state legislature.

Engels' analysis was therefore fatally flawed. The fundamental strategic imperative for socialists in the United States is no different from that in any other advanced capitalist country. In the U.S., as elsewhere, socialists should focus their energies on building a dynamic democratic socialist party as an integral component of a militant working-class movement. Furthermore, rather than hoping to discover a quick and easy path through participation in a broad third party, U.S. socialists should accept their position, for now, as the radical gadflies of a society permeated by the individualistic search for wealth and power.

3
The Political Party of the Working Class: The Socialist Party and the Labor Party Question

By 1912 the Socialist Party of America had become an influential force in U.S. politics. A scant eleven years after its formation in 1901, it had grown from 10,000 to more than 120,000 members, while electing mayors, state representatives, and even one Congressperson. Hundreds of thousands of working people throughout the United States avidly read newspapers and magazines that were closely linked to the Party. In both the Industrial Workers of the World (IWW) and the American Federation of Labor, a significant section of union activists and labor leaders looked toward the Socialist Party as an influential ally.

This experience stands in direct contradiction to the perceived wisdom, according to which third parties are destined for failure in the United States. In spite of an electoral system rigged against dissident voices, and a culture steeped in a pragmatic rejection of ideologies, the Socialist Party blossomed and flourished. It remains to this day the sole example of an independent nationwide political party that succeeded in building a solid and consistent base of popular support.

Nevertheless, in spite of the Party's impressive growth, many of its leaders had become disenchanted. They were eager to become a pressure group within a looser, less ideologically defined party linked directly to the AFL and its affiliated trade unions. Prominent moderates were convinced that such a labor party would quickly become a major party, and that socialists would serve as important advisors within it. Yet before a sizable section of the AFL leadership would even consider such a plan, the Socialist Party would first need to be transformed, its radical left-wing marginalized and isolated.

The moderate leaders of the SP could not openly advance such a labor party perspective, since the overwhelming majority of the rank and file remained fiercely committed to the Party, and were totally uninterested in submerging it within a wider, and less radical, formation. The result was a bitter irony. As the Socialist Party grew in size and influence, its leaders became increasingly committed to the clandestine pursuit of a different strategic vision, in the futile hope that their actions would clear the way to the formation of a new labor party that could rapidly attract a majority of the working class.

THE EMERGENCE OF THE SOCIALIST PARTY

The decision of the British Trades Union Council to establish the Labour Representation Committee had an enormous impact on the Left in the United States. Initially formed to support labor candidates in the 1900 elections to Parliament, the effort gained momentum in 1906 with the election of 29 labor candidates. At this point, the Labour Representation Committee was transformed into the British Labour Party. For many socialists in the United States, this rapid rise to electoral success appeared to show the way forward.

The Socialist Party of America had been formed a year later, in 1901. A loosely organized, decentralized organization, the SP included a wide range of political tendencies and factions, held together by a basic belief in the need for an independent electoral party committed to a democratic socialist perspective. The Socialist Party was deeply divided, with a third of the membership aligned with the radical Left. Radical dissidents were committed to building a political party that could not just win elections, but that could also challenge the conservative leadership of the American Federation of Labor at the workplace. Party moderates rejected this approach, insisting that the Party had no business intervening in the internal affairs of trade unions, and should instead focus on gaining their support for the socialist ticket. Moderates also stressed the importance of electoral victories in gaining the step-by-step reforms that would eventually lead to a socialist transformation of society.

In spite of these divisions, the SP was united in the proposition that a mass-based democratic socialist party could be built in the United States, following the course already set in most Western European countries. Eugene Victor Debs was the popular symbol of the democratic socialist movement in the United States. An ally of the radical Left within the Party, he adamantly opposed any alliance with a third party of progressives. To Debs, the "overthrow of capitalism" constituted "the object of the Socialist Party." The SP would therefore "not fuse with any other party and it would die rather than compromise."[1]

During the initial years of the Labour Representation Committee, Debs rejected the idea of a labor party, and instead insisted that only an explicitly socialist party could truly represent the interests of the working class. According to Debs, trade unions were not and could "not become a political machine," nor could unions "be used for political purposes." Those who argued for "working class political action not only" had "no intention to convert the trade unions into a political party but they would oppose any such attempt on the part of others."[2]

Although Debs held firmly to these views, many of the moderate leaders of the Party came to reject these shared assumptions, although they did so covertly and by implication, rather than by way of a direct challenge. By 1909, the Socialist Party had grown to 40,000 members. It had become a small mass-based party, and yet socialism remained very much a minority viewpoint within the working-class movement. Most workers, as well as most trade union officials, remained bound to the two party system. Increasingly frustrated, leading members of the Socialist Party came to believe in a labor party as an alternative to an explicitly socialist party. They visualized a two-step process, beginning with the transformation of the Socialist Party into a more monolithic organization, holding a clearly reformist perspective. Calls for a socialist future would be downplayed, and the Party would emphasize even more strongly its support for a program of social reforms that could appeal to the craft unions of the American Federation of Labor. Once this happened, a new, more moderate Socialist Party could play a key role in the formation of a labor party backed by a substantial segment of the established unions. This strategic perspective took the Independent Labour Party of Britain as its model. The ILP, an organization of moderate socialists, had acted as the catalyst for the Labour Party, and had then continued as an integral component of the Labour Party coalition. The SP moderates envisioned that once the AFL, or at least a substantial number of its larger affiliates, agreed to create a labor party, the Socialist Party would cease nominating its own candidates, and would act as a left-wing tendency within the wider party.

THE MILWAUKEE AND NEW YORK LOCALS

The Socialist Party had a truly national presence, with strength in virtually every region of the country except the South. Nevertheless, there were only two locals that by their size and their ability to elect officials up to the Congressional level exerted a dominant influence within the Party. Both of these locals, New York City and Milwaukee, were aligned with the moderate wing of the Party.

Relations between the leadership of both of these locals were close and generally harmonious. Nevertheless, there were distinct differences in their objective situations, and in their political perspectives. In Milwaukee, the Party grew out of the large German-American working-class community. Milwaukee socialists looked to the German Social Democrats as a model, and, indeed, the German party exerted a dominant influence within the Second International, the international network of social democratic parties.

In Germany, the party had preceded the trade unions. Although the links between the union bureaucracy and the party apparatus were extensive, the party officially declared it would not interfere in trade union affairs, and vice versa. This became the official position of the Socialist Party of America, and its implementation worked well in Milwaukee. Local unions, most especially the Brewery Workers, were led by German-American socialists, who endorsed and sponsored the Socialist ticket. In turn, the Milwaukee local cooperated with AFL union leaders and praised their policies. With this as its base of support, the Milwaukee local elected Emil Seidel mayor in April 1910, and sent Victor Berger to Congress that November.[3]

Berger was the most prominent member of the Milwaukee local, and the most vocal advocate for the Socialist Party's right-wing. Born and raised in the German-speaking Jewish community residing in the Rumanian region of the Austro-Hungarian empire, he immigrated to the United States with his family in 1878. Berger soon settled in Milwaukee, blending into the large German community while teaching high school. In 1898, Berger joined with Gene Debs in founding the Social Democratic Party, which merged with a splinter group from the Socialist Labor Party three years later to form the Socialist Party of America.[4]

Berger reigned as the undisputed boss of the Milwaukee local, ruthless, egotistical and driven. An ineffectual speaker, and a ponderous writer, Berger was nonetheless a skillful editor and a political leader with a clear strategic vision. Berger made no pretensions to being a revolutionary socialist. Instead, he focused on winning elections and legislating an extensive program of social reforms. Berger became the chief nemesis of the radical Left, the leading exponent of "sewer socialism." Yet on a national level he never commanded the influence of his New York rival and colleague, Morris Hillquit.[5]

New York City provided a very different setting than Milwaukee. By 1910, New York City had incorporated Brooklyn and the other outer boroughs, encompassing a population of nearly five million. Furthermore, unlike Milwaukee, it had grown into an ethnically diverse metropolis. The Socialist Party had developed a solid core of support in the Jewish community of the Lower East Side, a crowded, noisy neighborhood of tenement slums and garment sweatshops. Socialist activists had been instrumental in the formation of the International Ladies Garment Workers Union (ILGWU), which only succeeded in organizing a significant sector of that industry after winning two tumultuous strikes in 1909 and 1910.[6]

Yet New York was also the financial, commercial and communications center of the United States. It featured a large working class, Irish and Italian as well as Jewish, but it also supported a growing and influential middle class. Although the Socialist Party could win elections within the Lower East Side, indeed it would send Meyer London to Congress in 1914 and 1916, it remained a marginal force in city politics. New York City municipal politics were defined by the ongoing battle between Tammany Hall and a loose coalition of "good-government" progressives.

Morris Hillquit, the outstanding leader of the New York socialist scene, emerged from the hothouse milieu of the Lower East Side. A Russian-Jewish immigrant, as a teenager he worked in a shirt factory. At the age of 18, he joined the Socialist Labor Party, a committed Marxist. When the SLP tried to organize shops on the Lower East Side, Hillquit became an organizer for the United Hebrew Trades. From there, he attended law school and soon became a successful lawyer. In July 1899, Hillquit spearheaded a split from the SLP, forming a short-lived group nicknamed the Kangaroos. He then led this group into the Socialist Party of America.[7]

Hillquit would act as a powerful influence within the Socialist Party from its formation in 1901 to his death in October 1933. A competent writer, he was also an excellent tactician and a skillful negotiator. While Berger starkly articulated his belief in reform and moderation, Hillquit wrapped himself in the supposed Marxist orthodoxy of the Second International. Yet underneath the ponderous rhetoric, Hillquit was cautious and pragmatic. In 1910, he served as a "legal representative" to the International Ladies Garment Workers Union during a mass strike of cloakmakers. The strike came to an end with the

Protocol of Peace, a negotiated settlement that mandated compulsory arbitration of disputed issues in the New York garment industry.[8] Given his political perspective, it is hardly surprising that Hillquit perceived the virtues of a labor party. Nevertheless, he moved quietly and discreetly, avoiding any public statements that would commit him to this position.

THE CIRCLE OF SOCIAL WORKERS REFORMERS

In its desire to broaden the appeal of the Socialist Party, the New York local began looking toward a loose circle of middle-class reformers. Hillquit undertook a concerted effort to recruit prominent progressives to the Socialist Party, where several of them then rose to influential positions. In particular, the SP succeeded in attracting a stratum of social workers. Starting in the 1890s, settlement houses were established in the slums of the larger cities of the Northeast and the Midwest. Indeed, by 1910 more than 400 had been established. Settlement houses were inspired by the progressive ethic of social reform. A new profession, the social worker, was created to staff these institutions, drawing on college educated young people fired with the desire to help the poor.[9] Not surprisingly, most of those recruited from this background gravitated to the moderate Center of the party.

The success of the British Labour Party had a special appeal to Hillquit and the New York leadership. A political party directly tied to the official union structure seemed to provide a solution to the Socialist Party's continued isolation. A labor party would command the resources and the loyal base of support that could not only win elections in New York City, but could possibly even gain victories at the state and national level. Yet the impetus for the creation of a labor party came initially from a tight, interlocking social network of middle-class reformers, several of whom had been drawn from social work into the socialist movement.

Five prominent individuals were at the center of this informal network. All five knew each other well, and were interlinked by close friendships and marriage. Three of them had worked together as resident staff members of the same Lower East Side settlement house, while all five had experience as social workers in the urban slums of the Chicago and New York metropolitan areas. Four of the five would be elected to the Socialist Party's National Executive Committee, the leadership body that set policy between conventions. Finally, all five would leave the Socialist Party as ardent supporters of the U.S. war effort during World War I.

Robert Hunter was a central figure in the drive toward a labor party. The son of a prosperous carriage manufacturer, Hunter was dismayed by the poverty and unemployment that gripped the country in the aftermath of the 1893 crash. After opting to become a social worker, he moved to Chicago in 1896, where he worked for three years with Jane Addams and her Hull House. Disillusioned with liberal reformism, Hunter was recruited to the socialist movement by Algie Simons, a social worker himself, who would join with Hunter in promoting the formation of a labor party. In 1902, Hunter moved to New York, where he headed the staff at the University Settlement House on the Lower East Side. The following year he left social work to write one of the first sociological studies of life in the slums. His book, *Poverty*, brought Hunter widespread public recognition.[10]

The heir to a considerable fortune, Hunter also married into one of the richest families in New York City. His father-in-law, Anson Phelps Stokes, was a wealthy merchant and investment banker, with extensive holdings in the railroads and mines of the West. With his marriage to Caroline Phelps Stokes in May 1903, Hunter entered into the select circle of the city's social elite. Hunter looked the part, always "the well-groomed, impeccably dressed gentleman," whose "entire demeanor" succeeded in "conveying wealth and good breeding."[11]

Hunter traveled widely in Europe, where he met with prominent members of the British and European Left. Upon joining in 1905, he quickly assumed a prominent position within the Socialist Party, campaigning for the New York state assembly in 1908, and governor of Connecticut in 1910. From 1909 to 1912, Hunter served on the seven-member National Executive Committee of the Socialist Party, setting policy guidelines for the Party.[12] Inspired by the British Labour Party's dramatic gains in the parliamentary elections of 1906, Hunter would take the lead in the effort to transform the Socialist Party into the catalytic force for an American labor party.

Although Hunter had been impressed with the British model during his visits to Europe, one of his friends and comrades had actually participated in the formative stages of the Labour Party. John Spargo was born in Cornwall, England, and began working as a stone cutter while still a teenager. Soon afterward, Spargo became a member of the Social Democratic Federation, a small organization of socialist militants. After moving to Wales in 1895, he quickly attained a position of influence within the local trade union movement. In

1900, Spargo campaigned for Keir Hardie in his successful effort to gain a seat in parliament as a candidate of the Labour Representation Committee.[13]

Having immigrated to the United States in February 1901, Spargo promptly joined the New York local of the Socialist Party, aligning himself with its moderate leadership. Although Spargo had casually met Robert Hunter in Britain, the two only became close friends in 1904, when they worked together on a committee organized to pressure the state of New York into a more vigorous enforcement of its child labor laws. Later that year, Spargo moved to Yonkers, a suburb of New York City, where he helped found a settlement house, and then served for a brief time on its staff.[14]

With Hunter's support, Spargo authored a sequel to *Poverty*, *Bitter Cry*, which focused on the impact of poverty on children. The book established Spargo as a national figure. Elected to the National Executive Committee in 1909, he remained an influential figure in the Socialist Party until his resignation in the spring of 1917. Spargo responded enthusiastically to the call for an American labor party.[15]

Hunter reached out to others in his personal network of social workers. Algie Simons was a prominent leader in the Chicago local. Raised on a family farm in Wisconsin, he attended the University of Wisconsin in Madison, where he took classes from well-known progressive professors. Shortly after graduating, Simons moved to Chicago to work as a social worker in the slum district adjoining that city's stockyards. Horrified by the pervasive misery of the slums, Simons joined the Socialist Labor Party in 1897.[16]

Two years later, Simons left social work to become a journalist and editor in the socialist press. He joined Hillquit in the Kangaroo faction that broke with the Socialist Labor Party, and then merged with a group led by Eugene Debs to form the Socialist Party. Starting on the Left of the party, Simons drifted rightward. From 1900 to 1908, he edited the *International Socialist Review*, seeking to establish it as the foremost journal of socialist theory in the United States. He also served on the SP's National Executive Committee from 1907 to 1910. Simons had also been impressed by the success of the British Labour Party, and was eager to further a similar formation in the United States. Indeed, Simons and his wife May "shared a love for England developed through several visits there and nourished by warm relationships with English friends."[17]

Hunter, Spargo and Simons would work closely with Hillquit in promoting the idea of a labor party. Other personalities who had been recruited into the Socialist Party from the same closely-knit circle would prove to be more skeptical of the labor party perspective. When Hunter, Spargo and Simons sought to enlist their friends as allies, they precipitated an acrimonious debate within the Socialist Party. The political differences that emerged were embittered by the strains placed on close and long-standing personal relationships.

Independently wealthy, William English Walling was nevertheless drawn to social work, serving on the staff of Chicago's Hull House from 1896 to 1899. There he developed a close relationship with Algie Simons, and with Robert Hunter. In April 1902, Hunter wrote Walling asking him to join the staff at the University Settlement House. (A year later, Walling served as an usher at Hunter's marriage ceremony.) In New York, Walling combined journalism and social work. Then, inspired by the 1905 revolution that swept Russia and nearly toppled the Czar, Walling traveled throughout Russia, meeting with a range of revolutionary figures, including Lenin and Trotsky. Upon his return, he wrote steadily for the socialist press, although he did not officially join the SP until 1910. Never elected to national office, Walling was still a figure of considerable renown and credibility among the rank and file members of the Socialist Party.[18]

James Graham Phelps Stokes, the fifth member of this informal network, graduated from Columbia University medical school a committed social reformer. His wealthy family fostered a tradition of public service. As the son of Anson Phelps Stokes, J.G. Phelps Stokes reversed the family's priorities, serving on the board of directors of mineral and railroad interests in Nevada, while devoting most of his time and energy to progressive causes.[19]

Stokes also served on Hunter's staff of social workers at the University Settlement, where he and Walling worked together and became close friends. The connections within this social circle grew even tighter when Hunter married one of Stokes' sisters. Stokes joined the Socialist Party in 1906, and was elected to the National Executive Committee for a one-year term of office in 1908.[20]

The scion of one of the wealthiest families in America, Stokes opted to marry Rose Pastor, a Jewish working-class immigrant. Born in the Jewish Pale of Czarist Russia, Pastor's family immigrated to London, and then on to Cleveland. At 13, Pastor started working in a cigar factory. Her life seemed destined to be marked by hard work at minimal pay until she began writing a series of letters to the *Jewish Daily News* detailing her experiences at work and in the community. Her letters proved so popular that in early 1903 she was hired as a staff reporter, and moved to New York City. When rumors of dissension within the University Settlement House came to the attention of the editors of the *Daily News*, Pastor was assigned to interview Phelps Stokes. Soon after, the two started dating, and in July 1905 they were married, to the delight of the tabloids. The two traveled around the country, speaking to large crowds eager to see the millionaire and his immigrant wife. Although the marriage was a happy one at first, the couple later diverged, both politically and personally.[21]

KEIR HARDIE AND THE LABOR PARTY

It was this circle of social worker reformers that would spark the drive to create a labor party in the United States. Although moderate socialists looked to the formation and success of the British Labour Party as a model of a successful working-class party, the AFL leadership had already drawn a very different set of conclusions from the British experience. A narrow craft unionist to his core, AFL president Samuel Gompers distrusted politicians, convinced that skilled workers had to rely on their own strength, and skills, to extract decent wages and working conditions from their employers. After participating in the Henry George campaign of 1886, Gompers worked within the two party system, but he also discouraged AFL affiliate unions from becoming too deeply enmeshed in electoral politics.[22]

All of this changed in January 1906, with the election of 29 candidates of the Labour Representation Committee to the British parliament. In both Britain and the United States, trade unions were under attack by a hostile judiciary. When Welsh workers on the Taff Vale Railway went out on strike, and set up a peaceful picket line, the company responded by suing the union for damages. In July 1901, a five-member panel of the House of Lords unanimously affirmed a lower court ruling finding the union liable for damages. Ultimately, the union had to pay more than $100,000 in fines.[23]

In the United States, courts were moving along similar lines, issuing sweeping injunctions to block mass picketing, and even prohibiting the boycotting of goods made by strikebreakers. When workers at the Buck's Stove Company went on strike in August 1907, the AFL added the firm to its consumer boycott list. A district judge granted Bucks an injunction, and, in December 1908, Gompers was sentenced to a year in jail for contempt of court. Six years later, the Supreme Court finally reversed the lower court's ruling on a technicality.[24]

Thus, in both countries the union movement sought legislative remedies to counteract damaging court rulings. The newly elected Labour Party bloc in the House of Commons insisted that the repeal of Taff Vale become a legislative priority. By December 1906, both houses of parliament had passed a bill reversing the Taff Vale judgment, thereby legalizing peaceful picketing during strikes.[25] The AFL leadership came under tremendous rank and file pressure to ensure a similar victory in the United States.[26]

Gompers moved quickly to channel the impact of the British elections into a safe outlet. In February 1906, only weeks after the British election, he advised the AFL executive committee that it was essential to meet directly with President Theodore Roosevelt, and with Congressional leaders, so as to insist on the implementation of a series of legislative demands. In line with this strategy, "a petition or statement" had to "be drafted." Six weeks later, the executive committee adopted a "Bill of Grievances," a modest list of social reforms, among them a strictly enforced eight hour day for government workers and relief from judicial injunctions during strikes. Four months later, with little having been accomplished, the AFL executive committee informed its affiliates that those in Congress who acted as a "true friend to the rights of labor" should "be supported." Although the AFL threatened to promote "a straight labor candidate" should "both parties ignore labor's legislative demands," the executive committee urged its affiliates to vigorously support those candidates of the two mainstream parties who "stand for the enactment to law of labor and progressive measures." In defending this new interest in electoral politics, the AFL executive committee pointed to the recent British elections, without mentioning the Labour Party, where the election of 54 trade unionists had "had a wholesome effect upon the government."[27]

Gompers would insist that this new policy was "non-partisan politically," but in fact he worked closely with the Democratic Party leadership in targeting key Republicans for defeat in the 1906 Congressional elections. Two years later, Gompers placed the AFL apparatus solidly behind William Jennings Bryan, the Democratic presidential nominee. Gompers viciously attacked Gene Debs, alleging that there was a "strong suspicion" that his whistle-stop travels aboard his own chartered train, the Red Special, were being lavishly funded by Republican corporate moguls who were eager to supply "the money for any branch of the campaign where it" could be "expected to do the most harm to the unions and their friends."[28] In fact, the American

Federation of Labor had become a subordinate element within the Democratic Party coalition, and so it has remained.

Gompers would not publicly concede that the new AFL policy directive constituted a direct response to the 1906 British election, but it was widely understood that this was the case. At the November 1906 AFL convention, held in Minneapolis, Victor Berger spoke for independent political action, and a rejection of the two party system. In taunting the AFL leadership for its sudden interest in electoral politics, Berger pointed out that the sole "reason for this change in the policy of the Executive Council was because they had success in the political movement in England."[29]

In responding to Berger, Gompers limited his remarks to a reiteration of the lesser evil argument as a basis for electoral politics. His close ally, Andrew Furuseth, the president of the Sailors Union of the Pacific, defended the AFL policy by countering that a working-class party in the United States could not hope to attain the electoral breakthrough that the British Labour Party had already achieved. Given the class composition of most Congressional districts, an "independent political party" would "not get a corporal's guard in Congress."[30]

Thus, by the fall of 1908, Gompers and the AFL leadership were solidly entrenched within the two party system. It was at this historical moment that Keir Hardie visited the United States, where he promoted the virtues of a labor party to Socialist Party activists. Hardie was born into a poor working-class family, and raised in the slums of Glasgow and the coalfields of western Scotland. Starting at the age of ten, he continued to work as a miner for the next 13 years. The coalminers' union was tightly aligned with the Liberal Party, and Hardie entered politics as a dedicated Liberal.[31]

By his early twenties, Hardie had emerged as a militant union leader, having coordinated a series of bitter strikes in the coalfields. Blacklisted as a miner, Hardie worked for two years as a journalist, before returning as a regional secretary of the miners' union. As the Liberal government continued to provide police protection for strike-breakers, Hardie grew increasingly disillusioned. He responded by moving toward a social democratic perspective, questioning the narrow limits of liberal reformism. After an unsuccessful effort to gain a seat in parliament as an independent in 1888, Hardie again ran as an independent in 1892, and won when the Liberals tacitly supported him. Shortly afterward, he helped to found the Independent Labour Party, which criticized the Liberals from the perspective of a moderate, reformist socialism.[32]

In 1895, the ILP decided to stand several candidates in swing districts. The Liberals then withdrew their support from Hardie, thus frustrating his bid for re-election. From this point on, Hardie concentrated on promoting the creation of a labor party. Finally, in February 1900, the Labour Representation Committee was formed as a loose coalition of the ILP and affiliated trade unions. The LRC sponsored a list of candidates on a platform of modest reforms, without a hint of a socialist vision. Hardie was one of two LRC candidates to be returned to parliament in the elections of October 1900.[33]

By this time, it was clear that the LRC could not become a major electoral force in direct opposition to the Liberals. On the other hand, the Liberals, who had lost the 1900 elections, came to view a tacit alliance with the labor insurgents as a tactical necessity. In February 1903, Ramsey MacDonald, as secretary of the Labour Representation Committee, met secretly with Jesse Herbert, the deputy chief whip for the Liberals. MacDonald reassured Herbert that LRC candidates were "in almost every case earnest Liberals."

Herbert then conferred secretly with Hardie, who confirmed his support for a tacit alliance. A month later, MacDonald and Herbert Gladstone, the chief whip of the Liberals, signed a pact. Under its terms, Gladstone pledged to use his influence to make sure that local Liberal associations would refrain from nominating candidates in 30 specified parliamentary districts. In return, the LRC would leave the field clear for the Liberals in every other district. The clandestine pact worked as the Liberals swept to victory, while the LRC succeeded in electing 29 candidates. In each of these 29 districts, the Liberals had refrained from nominating their own candidate.[34]

The results of the 1906 election turned Hardie into a noted celebrity and the foremost exponent of the labor party perspective. As such, he began traveling widely and frequently, spreading the message of social democratic reformism. Yet Hardie knew of, and approved of, the secret agreement with the Liberals. From July 1907 to April 1908, Hardie undertook a world tour, beginning with an extended stay in Canada. While there, he was distressed to see the impact of U.S. radicals on the Canadian Left. Nevertheless, he was hopeful that a new infusion of moderates would "make it too hot for the IWW type." The goal was to isolate the "impossibilist element which for the moment dominates the movement, and which has had to be downed everywhere – including the United States of America – as a preliminary to Socialism becoming a living, vitalizing power."[35]

Thus, even before coming to the United States, Hardie was convinced of the need to exclude the IWW, and the rest of the radical Left, from positions of influence within the Socialist Party. Of course, the right-wing of the SP had been trying to isolate the Left since its formation in 1901, but Hardie set this struggle within a broader strategic framework. In September 1908, Hardie undertook another lengthy tour, this time to the United States to observe the political scene in the midst of a presidential campaign. He arrived in New York, traveled extensively through the Midwest, and then returned to New York before returning to England.[36]

While in the New York City area, Hardie resided at Robert Hunter's country estate in an affluent Connecticut suburb. Although they came from diametrically different social backgrounds, their political views had virtually converged. Hunter had visited London in 1899, but had been disaffected by the fragmentation of the English Left. He had then proceeded to Scotland, where he had spent several days engrossed in friendly discussions with Hardie, this at a time when the Labour Representation Committee was in the process of being formed.[37]

Hardie had been very clear in his political orientation, laying out a strategy that he would meticulously follow for the next decade and more. In his view, "the most important work to be done was to take all unions" and move them "out of the Liberal and Tory parties, and to have them form an independent political body." Hardie had been certain that "in the beginning this organization could hardly be socialist." Yet since "socialism expressed the hopes and aspirations of the working class," a labor party "must, in the end, become socialist."[38] U.S. advocates of a labor party would act in exact accordance with this strategy.

During his visit to New York, Hardie visited with progressive trade union officials, as well as leading members of the Socialist Party, hoping to bring the two groups into a close working relationship. Hardie was convinced that the British experience could be repeated in the United States, but only if two conditions could be met. AFL officials had to be persuaded to loosen their ties to the Democratic Party, just as British union officials had slowly withdrawn from active participation in the Liberal Party. At the same time, the Socialist Party had to demonstrate its commitment to a strategic vision rooted in electoral reformism, thus laying the groundwork for it to become the loyal left-wing of a broad, non-socialist political party based directly on the trade unions.

In assessing his New York stay in the fall of 1908, Hardie concluded that the "most hopeful sign in America" was the increasing "number of Trades Union officials who" were "openly taking sides with Socialism." Indeed, the "imperative need of the hour" remained "an understanding between" the SP and the AFL to bring about a "united party."[39]

Hardie then toured the United States, before returning to New York City in January 1909. There he delivered a public speech on the necessity of establishing a broadly based labor party that would, nevertheless, draw "inspiration from the Socialist ideal." On the eve of Hardie's return voyage, Hunter hosted a large gathering of friends and sympathizers. Local union officials lauded Hardie, while indicating their interest in the British Labour Party's success in the 1906 election. Still, the officials were cautious, one of them chastising socialists "to show a better spirit than heretofore," and urging them "to learn that they cannot convert men by vilifying them."[40]

Hardie then addressed the gathering, expressing his fervent belief that "trade unionists must unite with the Socialists." Although U.S. corporations were "more unscrupulous" than those in Britain, still with "unity and a genuine working class movement," the barriers to fundamental social change could be overcome. A labor party could attract 3–5 million votes in the 1912 presidential election, thereby bringing "a real political division between the labor and the capitalistic class."[41]

LABOR PARTY SUPPORTERS BEGIN ORGANIZING

Hardie's visit galvanized the moderate leadership of the Socialist Party, most particularly local leaders in New York and Milwaukee. The Party's local in Los Angeles had already swung its support to a locally based labor party. In northern California, a local labor-based party, the Union Labor Party, had been formed in 1901 to contest San Francisco's municipal elections. The deployment of police to break a bitter strike of teamsters had inspired the city's unions to create an electoral alternative. From 1901 to 1907, the ULP controlled city hall, and yet its administration accomplished virtually nothing in the way of progressive legislation. The mayor, and his colleagues on the city council, did succeed in lining their pockets with bribes from corporations seeking municipal franchises and waivers from the city's regulatory agencies. After a series of scandals culminating in trials and convictions, the ULP lost the municipal elections of 1907, was returned to office in 1909, and then had the good grace to fade away.[42]

In spite of its name, the Union Labor Party was not a true labor party in that local unions did not directly affiliate to the party. Instead, the party's internal structure rested on neighborhood-based clubs sending delegates to citywide conventions. Nevertheless, the ULP had been initiated by local unions, and the mayor and many of its elected city council members were union officials. A significant factor in the municipal politics of San Francisco, it never emerged as a truly independent party. Indeed, its most popular official, Mayor Eugene Schmitz, hoped to win the Republican nomination for governor, while most of the union officials that backed it were active in the Democratic Party.[43]

It is difficult to understand how the ULP could have been viewed as an attractive model, but it was. Los Angeles trade union officials eagerly sought to emulate its success in their community. In 1902, they initiated their own Union Labor Party to field an independent slate of candidates for the 1902 municipal elections. The Los Angeles Socialist Party then withdrew its own candidates and endorsed the ULP slate. When the ULP candidate for mayor received only 20 percent of the vote, AFL unions lost interest in further independent campaigns. Within the SP, the LA local's decision to endorse the candidates of another party met with harsh criticism, so Los Angeles withdrew its support for a labor party. The Socialist Party then resolved at its 1904 national convention that "no state or local organization shall under any circumstances fuse, combine or compromise with any political party or organization." The resolution passed overwhelmingly.[44]

Undaunted, Job Harriman, a well-known attorney, a prominent member of the Los Angeles local and a close personal friend of Hillquit, continued to act as a fervent proponent of a labor party. In November 1908, soon after Hardie's initial stay in New York, Harriman wrote to Hillquit, prodding him into taking immediate action. Harriman's letter is instructive, since it lays out so clearly the strategic vision that would guide the actions of the moderate leadership of the Socialist Party for the next three decades and more. Harriman reminded Hillquit that he had been certain for several years "that the greatest service" that "Socialists could do to the Labor and Socialist movement would be to amalgamate with the Labor movement, and, at the same time, continue" as a "propaganda organization."[45]

The immediate task required the calling of "a political convention of both organizations, the Socialists and the American Federation of Labor, within the coming year." This convention would adopt a common platform, one that "would fall somewhat short of the Socialist platform," but that would focus on planks such as an eight-hour day, an anti-injunction plank to stop judicial strikebreaking, and the "public ownership of all monopolized industries." This stretched the outer limits of the program set by progressive reformers.[46]

Harriman reassured Hillquit that "Socialists do not compromise anything when they unite with the working class, for the interests of the working class are fundamentally revolutionary." Still, he was quick to reject an alliance with "any reform party," such as the Progressives, since these formations did "not exist in the primary interests of the working class."[47]

Harriman was not only an articulate advocate of labor party politics, but he was also convinced that the AFL leadership was ready to break with the two party system. This assessment not only reflected the over-optimism of an enthusiast, it constituted a fundamental flaw in the argument. Harriman held that Gompers' policy had "failed," but socialists within the AFL should not "endeavor to crush him," but rather should "show leniency toward him."[48]

Hillquit had been persuaded by Hardie and Hunter, so he already agreed with Harriman's underlying argument. Nevertheless, Hillquit was far more cautious in his tactics. He did not publicly advocate the formation of a labor party, and, indeed, he denied that he held such a view. At the same time, he quietly supported efforts to call a convention along the lines proposed by Harriman, while also working to transform the SP so that it would project a more moderate image, and thus would appear a more attractive ally to progressives within the AFL leadership.

Hillquit and Harriman joined with other influential moderates in a broad, informal, and secretive network that would continue to remain in contact through World War I. Its members sought to "revolutionize" the Party, drastically altering its purpose and direction to make it more acceptable to sympathetic trade union officials and liberal middle-class reformers.[49]

THE FIRST PUBLIC DEBATE

From the start, Robert Hunter was at the focal point of the effort to initiate a labor party, hoping to persuade his circle of social worker reformers to provide their support. Yet one member of this group of friends and colleagues, William English Walling, spurned Hunter's efforts, and went public with his disagreements.

In an article for the *International Socialist Review*, Walling severely reprimanded the British Labour Party. He argued that "the program and tactics of the British party" were "as far as possible from social democracy," and that its goals were "wholly removed from genuine Socialism." Walling then turned to the issue of whether socialists should support the formation of a labor party in the United States. A "labor party in America would be far more disastrous" than it had been in Britain. Although the Socialist Party had succeeded in attracting members from among the unskilled blue-collar workforce, the American Federation of Labor had targeted its organizing at the small elite of highly skilled workers. Thus, unlike the Socialist Party, a labor party based on the AFL would necessarily represent the interests of "a small proportion of the community," those in the "ranks of organized and skilled labor," while tending to the "exclusion or subordination" of the great mass of unskilled workers.[50]

Hunter responded to Walling's critique in the following issue of the *Review*. He did so by focusing exclusively on a defense of the British Labour Party, while totally ignoring Walling's remarks on the United States. This reflected a general pattern. Moderates within the SP leadership were anxious to extol the virtues of the British Labour Party, but they were unwilling to publicly cite its accomplishments as a guide to socialist tactics in the United States.

From Hunter's perspective, the Labour Party constituted "the only prospect for Socialism in England." Indeed, it was "a magnificent body" that brought together those who refused "to remain the lackeys of [the] Liberals." In defending Labour, Hunter stressed its origin as a coalition of organizations. The Labour Party was "not a party," but rather "a federation of several distinct organizations, all of which" kept "their own identity," and carried "on their separate work with precisely the same freedom inside and outside the federation as before the organization of the party." As an electoral formation, it represented "an alliance between a political party – the Socialist – and a body of Trade Unionists." Ironically, this is exactly the argument Lenin would make a decade later in advising the newly formed British Communist Party to enter the Labour Party at the same time that left-wing currents throughout Europe were leaving social democratic parties to form separate, and antagonistic, Communist parties.[51]

Hunter's argument was specious. The British Labour Party constituted a political party, with a coherent, albeit moderate, political perspective, and its slate of candidates reflected this perspective. It differed from the orthodox social democratic parties of Western

Europe in that it was tightly controlled from the top by a few union officials, who voted by bloc at annual policy-making conventions. Furthermore, the Labour Party consistently focused on a program of immediate social reforms, while minimizing any consideration of the urgent need for a fundamental transformation of capitalist society.

Hunter stressed the influence of moderate socialists such as Keir Hardie within the Labour Party. Indeed, a majority of those in Labour's parliamentary delegation were members of socialist organizations, either the Independent Labour Party or the Fabian Society. Yet the ILP leadership had joined with the trade union contingent in defeating every effort to insist that "a belief in Socialism" should constitute "a basis of entrance into the new party." Passage of such a constitutional provision "would smash the Labour party," since it "would immediately destroy" the underlying alliance that had led to its formation. Thus, by breaking the link between socialists and trade union officials, "the whole purpose and object of the alliance would be defeated." Socialists within the Labour Party were "satisfied to be patient," certain "that the time" was "near when" the "entire labor movement" would "of its own volition, and without a word of urging, come out for the entire Socialist program."[52]

THE HIDDEN MANIFESTO

By the summer of 1909, the network of Socialist Party leaders committed to the formation of a labor party was already in place. Hillquit and Hunter, two key members of this secretive grouping, visited with J.G. Phelps Stokes at his family's estate in Connecticut, hoping to convince him of the necessity of a new strategic vision. Hunter argued that the party had to be changed, transformed into a grouping similar to the Independent Labour Party of Britain, while Hillquit "expressed no dissent, but, on the contrary, vigorously supported his [Hunter's] arguments."[53]

These preliminary discussions quickly proceeded to a concerted plan of action. Hillquit and Spargo drafted a manifesto addressed to the Socialist Party membership to be publicly issued under the signatures of "friendly AFL men," viewing it as an important step in launching a broadly based labor party. Prominent moderates, including Berger, Hunter and Simons, knew of the manifesto, and approved of its contents.[54]

The manifesto was set in type, although it was never openly circulated. It forcefully presented the moderate critique of the radical

Left, attacking those who were intent on "making the Socialist Party a sect." Yet the manifesto went further, delineating the underlying assumptions of the proponents of a labor party. It indicted the SP for having "failed to make satisfactory progress toward the attainment of the only aim which can justify the existence of a Socialist party in this or any other country." By this logic, the Socialist Party had foundered because it had not succeeded in enlisting the support of the majority of the working class. Although the SP had grown rapidly since its formation, it had "failed to enlist" in its "ranks the militant working class of the country."[55]

The manifesto did not expressly call for the submersion of the Socialist Party into a broader coalition, but it did cite the "growing demand for the formation of a labor party in this country." This demand reflected the inability of the SP to "successfully and courageously" fulfill "its true mission," to "unite the workers on the political field." To do this, the Party would have to gain the cooperation of the AFL leadership, and yet this could not possibly happen until the irresponsible radicals were excluded from its midst. Given the overriding necessity of creating a credible working-class party, the SP had to reach a definitive decision, for "we have come to the parting of the ways."[56]

THE SIMONS LETTER

The manifesto was never made public, overtaken by a furious debate that erupted within the Socialist Party. In the fall of 1909, the American Federation of Labor held its convention in Toronto, Canada. A high level delegation of SP leaders, including Algie Simons, decided to attend this gathering, hoping to discuss the possibility of a labor party with sympathetic union officials, both those within and outside of the Party. Those delegates who were SP members were shown the manifesto, and were asked to sign it as a first step toward a labor party.[57]

An enthusiastic advocate of the labor party, Simons found the convention rough going. Many of the progressives within the AFL leadership were former members of the Socialist Party, and they viewed it as a haven for radical extremists. Needless to say, this only reinforced Simons' belief in the need for a fundamental transformation of the Party. Shortly after returning from the convention, Simons wrote a long letter to his close friend William English Walling, hoping to convince him of the critical need for drastic action. In spite of their friendship, Simons knew that Walling was wary of the labor party, so Simons was not entirely candid in laying out his own perspective. Indeed, Spargo would later concede that Simons had written "more or less frankly" to Walling. Nevertheless, the letter would trigger an incendiary debate.[58]

Simons reported to Walling that he had met with the AFL delegates and encountered an "intense hatred against the Socialist Party, combined with a perfect willingness to accept the philosophy of Socialism." Although hostile to the SP, the progressive union officials, "nearly three-fourths" of them, were "ready and anxious for a working class party." To Simons, this further demonstrated the urgent need to immediately "reform the Socialist party [so] that it will fill the function for which it was intended." The SP had become "a hissing" within the working class, "a party of two extremes." On the one hand, stood "a bunch of intellectuals" such as Hillquit and Hunter, and, on the other hand, "a bunch of 'never-works', demagogues and would-be intellectuals, a veritable 'lumpen-proletariat.'"[59]

Simons stressed to Walling the importance of instituting "a reorganization of the SP." In this regard, he pointed to "the English policy," which was "doing something." The British Labour Party was "vitalizing the class struggle," even "rousing the antagonism of the capitalists." Simons had "full faith" that "out of such a fight" would "come clarity and revolutionary action." While the British were surging forward, "here we are dead," since "neither politically nor intellectually" were "we feared by the capitalists."

To move ahead, socialists in the United States had to absorb the lessons of the British experience. The American Federation of Labor came "much nearer [to] representing the working class than the SP." Thus, "unless we are able to so shape our policy and our organization as to meet the demands and incarnate the position of the workers, we will have failed of our mission." One essential aspect of this reshaping required a purge of the Party's membership, for "we must drive from our own ranks the demogogical politicians" who were "seeking to raise rebellion" against the Party's leaders. The current National Executive Committee was "more than willing to surrender their position if real workingmen" were "to take their places," but they would not readily cede power "to those who have never worked save with their jaws."

Simons' letter infuriated Walling. Deeply skeptical of its political direction, he was incensed by the implicit threat to engage in a collusive effort to retain control over the Party's leadership, no matter what the cost. Walling approached his close friends, J.G. Phelps Stokes and his wife, Rose Pastor Stokes. The two were as dismayed with Simons' letter as Walling had been.

Rose Pastor Stokes proceeded to caution Stephen Reynolds, a Terre Haute lawyer and a personal friend of Gene Debs. In her view, Simons' letter provided clear proof that the Party's leaders were "eager to combine with the conservative reactionary AF of L." The impetus for a labor party reflected "a desire to get into office and 'do something' right away," instead of "carrying forward the work of the S.P."[60]

In their desire to initiate a labor party, the members of the current National Executive Committee had determined "to perpetuate themselves, if they can, in their present office, unless such men are placed in office [who] will approve of the Compromise" they were planning. Stokes was "sick at heart" by the maneuvers of the Party leadership. The Left, "those who would not sacrifice principle for *votes*," needed to come together, "to stand in opposition" to the moderate majority.[61]

While Rose Pastor Stokes sent warnings to her circle of friends, Walling decided to circulate an open letter to a wide range of Socialist Party contacts, advising them of the secretive intrigues being undertaken by the Party's moderate leaders. Walling's letter hammered at the undemocratic implications of the moderates' position, as formulated by Simons, while attacking the underlying premises of the labor party perspective. The majority of the current National Executive Committee sought "to perpetuate itself, if possible, without regard to what actions the party takes." Indeed, the moderate majority believed that "they have a sacred mission to convert the present Socialist party into a labor party."[62]

Walling correctly understood that the SP moderates were inspired by the success of the British Labour Party. Yet, countered Walling, this was a party that dodged "the name of Socialist," renounced the class struggle and entered into "a working agreement with the Liberal Party in nearly every district in England." In their desire to catalyze a similar formation in the United States, the current executive committee pursued policies that were "sane, safe and conservative, guaranteed not to offend the reactionaries of the present Federation of Labor." Walling rejected this shift toward the opportune, convinced that "any further step towards the AFL must necessarily mean a complete and final abandonment of our Socialist principles and tactics."

The circular effectively warned SP activists of a covert scheme by some of its most influential members to fundamentally alter the Party's essential purpose. Yet Walling did not seem to fully comprehend the implications of the plan then being implemented by the SP leadership. Walling feared that if the moderates were "defeated in the coming election" to the National Executive Committee, they would leave the party to initiate "the organization of an 'Independent Labor'" Party. This missed the crucial point. The moderates had no intention of leaving the SP. They were confident of their ability to retain control over the Party apparatus, and they intended to use that power to transform the Socialist Party itself into the U.S. version of the British ILP. Thus transformed, having shed its left-wing dissidents, the party would be ready to cooperate with progressives within the AFL leadership in the formation of a broadly based labor party.

Walling's vehement rejection of a labor party perspective carried greater weight because he was not aligned with the Socialist Party's radical left-wing, having little sympathy with either the IWW or direct action. Indeed, Walling was convinced that the SP had been pursuing the correct policies since its formation eight years previously, and he lauded its rapid growth. With "the membership of the party," and the party press, "growing in a wonderful way," the push for the formation of a labor party could only obstruct and divert the SP from continued success.

Walling's circular letter set in motion a major upheaval within the Socialist Party. For Simons, it represented a "treacherous betrayal of confidence." Simons was not only discredited as an influential party leader, he was also personally hurt, for he had "valued" Walling's "friendship above [that] of any man" he had "known in the movement."[63]

The other members of the moderate majority on the National Executive Committee were embarrassed and dismayed by the controversy sparked by Simons' letter to Walling. In spite of their intention to act in secrecy, they now found themselves in the spotlight, and on the defensive. Spargo and Walling had been close friends, part of the same social circle that included Hunter and Phelps Stokes. Thus, Spargo's anger at Walling was both political and personal. Always a cautious strategist, Spargo addressed a confidential letter to Simons warning him "to be careful as to whom" he wrote "even intimating" their "plans."[64]

Spargo also sought to blunt the impact of the incident by diverting the attention of his critics to a secondary issue. Accordingly, he wrote a scathing letter to J.G. Phelps Stokes, condemning Walling as "mentally unbalanced [and] erratic," citing Walling's charge that

Spargo had joined with other influential party members "into a foul conspiracy to steal the election." Spargo insisted that Phelps Stokes reject this "infamous slander" or Spargo would refuse "under any circumstances" to "further association" with him.[65]

This coordinated effort to discredit Walling on personal grounds was further advanced at a public forum. When Victor Berger came to New York to deliver a speech at Cooper Union on the labor party, he vilified Walling as "a millionaire Socialist, or maybe an anarchist." Berger proceeded to deny Walling's claim of collusive behavior. He insisted that neither Berger nor the majority on the National Executive Committee were engaged in a "conspiracy to form a labor party." Indeed, this charge, said Berger, was nothing but "a lie." In fact, it was Berger and his allies who were lying.[66]

During the informal discussion that followed Berger's talk, Spargo reinforced his position. He insisted that he saw no "signs of a labor party today except in the Socialist party." Thus, the "Socialist party must take its stand as a labor party."[67] Spargo's disavowal was in direct contradiction to the thrust of the unpublished manifesto that he had recently helped to author, but then the manifesto had been withdrawn prior to being printed for public circulation in the wake of the furor ignited by the Simons–Walling interchange.

Berger's speech at Cooper Union left Walling exposed and vulnerable. After all, Berger was a powerful figure, the political boss of Milwaukee who would soon be elected to Congress in the November 1910 elections. Under this withering assault, Walling retreated, at least in public. In a letter to the *New York Call*, Walling denied that he had ever "stated in public or private a belief that there existed any conspiracy to form a Labor party."[68]

HARDIE AND KAUTSKY INTERVENE

The coordinated attack on Walling escalated with a personal intervention by Keir Hardie. Having returned to his parliamentary duties, Hardie kept abreast of the controversy raging within the Socialist Party. In a letter to the *New York Call*, he emphatically denied Walling's accusation of an implicit deal between the Liberals and the British Labour Party for the 1906 election. Hardie insisted that this was "not true, never was true, nor was there ever the slightest foundation for it." Labour had opted to limit the number of its parliamentary candidates solely because of the high costs of campaigning, and not because it sought to avoid dividing the left-of-center vote against the Conservatives. Hardie's claim was a conscious and deliberate falsification. He knew of the secret arrangement between the Liberals and Labour, and, indeed, he had expressly approved it.[69]

Hardie then clearly formulated the cornerstone beliefs of the proponents of the labor party. For socialism "to become a great political power in the United States, it must find ways and means whereby it can enlist the active support of the only class-conscious working class movement that exists, namely the trade unions." The Socialist Party could accept the position of "doctrinaire sectarians" such as Walling, in which case it would "remain for all time a neurotic, impotent, contemptible sect," or it could decide to join with progressive officials within the AFL and "become the great molding power" within the framework of a broad, non-socialist labor party.[70]

Hardie's letter set out a perspective that influential SP leaders, including Hillquit, would closely follow over the next three decades. Implicit in Hardie's position was a total dismissal of the Socialist Party as a meaningful political force. From this perspective, the sole purpose of the SP was to crystallize the formation of another, significantly more moderate organization. This at a time when the Party was rapidly growing, and when it had already enrolled 40,000 members.

In fact, the overwhelming majority of the Party's rank and file rejected the fundamental assumptions underpinning the labor party perspective. The rank and file believed in the Socialist Party, and they were convinced that it would continue to grow as an influential political force. Thus, no one, from Hunter to Hillquit, was prepared to openly call for the formation of a labor party in the United States. From his vantage point in Britain, Hardie had to publicly formulate what a substantial segment of the Party leadership believed, but would not publicly admit.

Hardie's intervention into the debate was critical, but it was followed by the publication of a commentary from an even higher authority. The German Social Democratic Party was viewed by socialists throughout the world as the embodiment of Marxist theory. Its size, and the close ties that had bound its leadership to Marx and Engels, guaranteed its standing. Furthermore, the German party's pre-eminent theoretician, Karl Kautsky, commanded overwhelming authority, even with those on the left-wing of the socialist movement.

When the British Labour Party applied to the International Socialist Bureau for direct affiliation to the Second International in October 1908, Kautsky presented a resolution accepting the Labour Party as an affiliate, while gently chastising it for "not expressly accepting the proletarian class struggle" as the underlying basis for its electoral campaigns. Still, Kautsky remained convinced that the Labour Party was implicitly committed to the class struggle in that it was "organized independently of the bourgeois parties." The resolution passed by a large majority, although it was sharply criticized by several of the more radical delegates to the Bureau.[71]

Since this issue had sparked a heated debate, Kautsky wrote a lengthy defense of his position in *Neue Zeit,* the foremost theoretical journal of the socialist movement. This article was then translated for publication in the *Call* in the wake of the Simons–Walling imbroglio. In defending the Second International's decision to accept the Labour Party as a full member, Kautsky also addressed the question of a labor party formation in the United States.

Kautsky recognized the ideological deficiencies of the British Labour Party. Indeed, he conceded that "the parliamentary and trade union leaders of the Labour Party" were "by no means independent." With "their ideas" still "saturated with bourgeois conceptions," the Labour Party had not broken with "the deeply rooted traditions of cooperation with the Liberals." Nevertheless, the creation of Labour as a nominally independent party represented a "step" toward the "ideal organization." Given "the peculiarity of England," it was necessary to create a new party based on the trade unions. Once formed, it was critical that socialists should join it, so that they could act as "the compass and the rudder" of an otherwise directionless organization. With socialists as a left-wing presence, the Labour Party would prove to be "a transitional stage which will sooner or later develop into a class conscious" party "with a definite Socialist program."[72]

With this rosy view of British politics in mind, Kautsky turned to the United States, where he saw the potential for a similar formation. Here too "the long wished for mass party of the proletariat may be formed into an independent political party in the very near future," through the medium of the American Federation of Labor. To Kautsky, the pattern followed the rule that "as in England, so in the United States." Once established, such a labor party would provide an electoral presence for the working class. The Socialist Party would then work within it while remaining a distinct organization with "theoretical and propagandist[ic] tasks."

In spite of the rhetorical differences, Kautsky had adopted the fundamental assumptions of Hardie's perspective, for both Britain and the United States. Unlike Hardie, Kautsky was willing to concede the shortcomings of the British Labour Party as delineated by its socialist critics. Yet ultimately none of this really mattered. Kautsky was certain that the weakness of the Left made it impossible to form an effective electoral presence on the basis of an explicitly socialist politics in either Britain or the United States. This made it essential for socialists to participate in the formation of a labor party, and then to function as a left-wing presence within it. In making this argument, Kautsky ignored the fact that the Socialist Party, USA, unlike organizations such as the Social Democratic Federation in Britain, had developed genuine roots within the working class. Implicitly, Kautsky was advancing a more sweeping argument. In most of Western Europe, social democratic parties were "mass parties" in that they constituted "the political representation of the whole proletariat engaged in its class struggle." Since the Socialist Party fell short of this standard, it had to be submerged into a broader formation.

DEBS GOES PUBLIC

With the advocates of a labor party attracting the support of influential European socialists, Walling turned to the most popular personality in the Socialist Party, Eugene Victor Debs. Enclosed with a cover letter from Walling, Debs received the initial letter from Simons. Debs notified Walling that he had "been watching the situation closely," and that he was convinced that the "Socialist Party has already catered far too much to the A.F. of L." The issue was one of vital importance, since the "revolutionary character of our party and our movement must be preserved in all its integrity, at all costs, for if that be compromised, it had better cease to exist."[73]

When Walling responded by urging a public statement of these views, Debs agreed that the "cowardly and compromising tendencies so much in evidence recently have got to be checked." As a result of this interchange, Debs' first letter to Walling was printed in the *International Socialist Review*, a monthly magazine controlled by those on the radical Left. To Robert Hunter and those in the moderate majority, the letter represented a genuine "blow," one that would soon lead to a concerted effort to block Debs' role as the Party's presidential candidate.[74]

In a private response to Hunter, Debs attacked Gompers, who was "kept where he" was "by the capitalists." His re-election as AFL president had been unanimous, with convention delegates who were SP members "slobbering over Gompers, and being puked on in return by him." There could be no conciliation across this divide for Gompers was "the deadly enemy of my class" and Debs was his. "Between us there can be nothing but war."

Debs also lambasted the actions of Hunter and his moderate allies while attending the 1909 AFL convention. "For alleged revolutionary Leaders [to] honey around and mix-up with such arch-traitors as run the A.F. of L. convention" was "absolutely inexcusable." It could only "muddle the situation," and thus make possible "the launching of a union labor party." Debs was adamantly opposed to the creation of a labor party. Instead, he stood forthrightly for an explicitly democratic socialist party, that is for "clear-cut action and uncompromising tactics."

HUNTER SEEKS TO CREATE A LABOR PARTY

Simons' letter had catalyzed the deep-seated differences within the Party. The widening divisions within the Party were reflected in the political maneuvers during the 1910 election to the National Executive Committee. Seven were to be selected from a list of 27 candidates through a system of preferential voting for a two-year term in office. In his circular letter response to Simons, Walling had urged those opposed to the formation of a labor party to join together to elect those who were "more uncompromising." He seems to have gotten little in the way of a positive response.[75]

Among the moderate party leaders, the necessity for cooperation was apparent. Berger and Hillquit formulated a common "list," which included the two of them, as well as Hunter and Spargo. Apparently, Simons was dropped from inclusion after having become a lightning rod for the anger felt by many rank and file members toward a leadership that was all too willing to tailor its politics to pragmatic expediency.[76]

With radicals and revolutionaries divided and disorganized, the moderates swept the January 1910 elections to the National Executive Committee. Even James F. Carey, a Massachusetts moderate whom Berger had placed "at the tail end" of the common list, succeeded in being elected. Walling was appalled by these results, which were "as bad as they could possibly be." He attributed the results to the organization of the moderates, who had created "a 'ticket', whereas our vote was scattered." In a letter to Debs, Walling warned that the "best people in the party are with you," but that this would be of little value as long as the Left remained diffuse and disorganized.[77]

For the proponents of a labor party, the 1910 elections to the National Executive Committee provided a striking confirmation of their hold over the party's apparatus. The intense debate triggered by Simons' letter had convinced them of the need for quiet discretion. Moderate leaders of the Socialist Party proceeded to put into operation a plan that they hoped would quickly lead to the formation of a broadly based labor party, but they did so in secret. The plan failed to move past the first phase of planning, but its existence demonstrates the hold that this goal had on prominent members of the Socialist Party.

Once again, Hunter took the initiative. Recognizing that a labor party could only succeed if a considerable section of the AFL leadership broke with the two party system, Hunter turned to Adolph Germer, a leader of the United Mine Workers in Illinois, and a veteran member of the Socialist Party. In March 1910, Hunter wrote to Germer proposing "a national conference to discuss political action." It was essential that the initiative for such a conference be taken by the progressive element within the AFL leadership. Of course, the Socialist Party would attend such a conference. Socialists would seek to provide overall leadership for the new formation, and, indeed, it "could be dominated at the start by Socialist elements." This was a concrete plan of action. Hunter urged Germer to discuss his proposal with other SP trade union officials, with the intent of bringing together an informal "conference as early as possible of our friends, so that we could plan some concerted action."[78]

Germer was impressed by Hunter's plan, and he began discussing it with his colleagues in the Illinois miners' federation. He also approached union leaders in several other unions, including the Western Federation of Miners. The response was positive, but tentative. Germer replied to Hunter that he was "much interested" in the proposed conference, but that he would need to gain the approval of a wide array of influential union officials.[79]

Hunter convinced Germer to attend a meeting of the Socialist Party's National Executive Committee scheduled for the spring of 1910 in Chicago. Although Germer met with Hunter, he remained wary. In a letter written shortly afterward, Germer advised Hunter that "a great deal depends upon what [Max] Hayes is willing to do." Hayes was an official of the Ohio typographers' union, and the leading spokesperson for the Socialist Party within the AFL.[80]

The conference was never convened. It would seem that the progressives within the AFL leadership were unwilling to break with the two party system, thus precipitating an open battle with Gompers, so the plan languished. Given the lack of support, Hayes withheld his support for the goal of a labor party. In a column appearing in the *International Socialist Review* in October 1910, Hayes warned his readers that a resolution favoring a labor party might be presented to the upcoming AFL convention. He was certain that socialists would "not take very kindly to the Labor party scheme," since such a formation "would tend to retard rather than aid" the socialist cause.[81]

The AFL remained tied to the two party system, targeting key Republican conservatives during the 1910 elections. This effort proved successful, as Democrats succeeded in gaining control of the House of Representatives. At the same time, the Socialist Party continued to gain in strength, with Victor Berger becoming the first socialist to be elected to the U.S. House of Representatives.

At the 1910 AFL convention, held in St. Louis soon after that year's Congressional elections, the sizable socialist contingent opted to avoid any challenge to the federation's leadership, and to remain silent. Hayes defended this decision, rationalizing that any resolutions criticizing Gompers "would have been defeated."[82] Thus, the drive to initiate a labor party seemed stymied, with AFL progressives reluctant to proceed with even the initial steps toward independent political action.

FRANK BOHN AND THE *INTERNATIONAL SOCIALIST REVIEW*

Nevertheless, while the SP moderates were forced to delay their immediate plans for a broadly based labor party, they continued to implement a strategy aimed at moving toward this goal. As a first step, they continued to pursue measures that would curb the influence of the radical Left within the Socialist Party, with the aim of making the Party a more appealing coalition partner to the AFL. Big Bill Haywood embodied the militant spirit that the moderates viewed as a direct threat to their plans to win over the AFL leadership. He was also closely linked to the *International Socialist Review*, a monthly magazine published by Charles Kerr that served as the leading forum for opponents of the labor party perspective.

Throughout the first years of its publication, the *ISR*, with Algie Simons as its editor, reflected a perspective firmly in the party's center, with many of its articles translated from *Neue Zeit*, the theoretical journal of the German Social Democratic Party. After January 1908, when Charles Kerr removed Simons as editor, its orientation shifted rapidly leftward, as it provided an organizational focus for the radical wing of the Socialist Party.[83]

The ideological development of the *ISR* reflected the evolution of its editorial staff, and most especially Frank Bohn, its associate editor. Bohn made an enormous impact on socialist politics during the heyday of the Socialist Party, and yet he is rarely mentioned in its history. A graduate of the University of Michigan, with a doctorate in economics, he joined the Socialist Labor Party in 1900, only to quit four years later, thoroughly disgusted with the authoritarian rule of Daniel DeLeon. Bohn was a founding member of the Industrial Workers of the World in 1905, and he worked as an IWW organizer in several organizing drives in the West. Bohn and Haywood met through the Wobblies, and became close friends. In 1910, the two cooperated in writing *Industrial Socialism*, a popular introduction to socialist theory. Their work sought to meld anarcho-syndicalism and revolutionary socialism into one coherent theory.[84]

Bohn began writing for the *International Socialist Review* in 1908, but he grew increasingly disillusioned with the IWW, and its syndicalist majority. In October 1911, he joined the *ISR* as a contributing editor, writing articles, touring the country promoting socialism and soliciting new subscriptions. Yet once Bohn joined the staff of the *ISR*, he became more deeply committed to the Socialist Party, entering into the heated debates within it. In cooperation with the other editors of the journal, Bohn formulated a revolutionary socialist perspective that viewed both the SP and the IWW as significant and integral components of a broader movement for revolutionary change. It was this group of editors and activists that would become the nucleus of the left-wing opposition within the SP.[85]

Bohn repeatedly attacked the effort to initiate a labor party. In an article appearing in the June 1911 issue of the *ISR*, he used the example of the Union Labor Party of San Francisco to condemn the entire perspective. A broad, non-socialist labor party would only provide a further obstacle to class-consciousness, since the Socialist Party was already "the political party of the working class." The millions of workers who remained aloof from the socialist movement needed to "be reached through Socialist agitation and Socialist education, not through the surrender of Socialist principles in order to be agreeable."[86]

Bohn then counterposed a potential labor party to the Socialist Party as it should be. A labor party would demand "bread and get crumbs," while the SP, which stood for "freedom for the workers," would soon have "a fight on its hands." In conclusion, Bohn insisted that the SP and a labor party were "not and never can be friends," for they were, "and must remain, irreconcilable enemies."[87]

Thus, the *ISR* continued to batter away at the labor party perspective. As the next elections to the National Executive Committee drew near, the underlying tensions within the Party grew sharper. Bohn and his colleagues at the *ISR*, Charles Kerr, Mary Marcy and Leslie Marcy, decided to bring together a slate of radicals to contest the election. Haywood was an obvious choice, although he was reluctant to accept, but Bohn and the *ISR* editors did their "utmost to persuade him," and they succeeded.[88]

Yet Bohn realized that the slate would have to reach beyond the revolutionary Left to have any chance of success. He was therefore willing to work for the election of prominent SP members who were not committed revolutionaries, but who were seen as sympathetic to industrial unionism, and who were hostile to the formation of a labor party.[89]

In an attempt to enlist Gene Debs in developing such a broad left-wing slate, Bohn wrote to Theodore Debs, Gene's brother, personal secretary and confidant. Seeking to explore Gene's position, Bohn advised Theodore that whatever he and the *ISR* editors decided to do, they hoped to "cooperate with both of you." Although Gene Debs was sympathetic to Bohn's efforts, he was not prepared to directly align himself in the Party's factional disputes.[90]

It is hard to judge why Debs was so reluctant to actively participate in the internal politics of the Socialist Party. Certainly, as the Party's perennial presidential candidate, and its most celebrated member, he sought to remain above the fray. Yet Debs was willing to publicly declare his adamant opposition to the plan for a labor party, even at the cost of acutely antagonizing the moderate leadership. Still, Debs was very concerned with the need to maintain a unified socialist party, and he may have felt that an open and direct confrontation with the moderates on this issue would trigger a split in the Party, which, in fact, it might well have done.

In any case, the *ISR* proceeded to present a radical alternative to the SP voters. Having opted to stand for the National Executive Committee, Bohn and Haywood issued open letters of acceptance. Haywood's statement focused on the importance of organizing the working class into unions that crossed craft lines. Rather than adhering to a neutral position, the Socialist Party should seek to "carry to the working class the message of industrial unionism."[91]

Bohn's acceptance statement explored a wider set of issues, holding that the Party's "present mission" was "one chiefly of propaganda and education," with an emphasis on "the revolutionary principles of solidarity, class action and the abolition of the private property system." While it maintained its commitment to a revolutionary political perspective, the SP had to safeguard against "the efforts, which we constantly see repeated, of allying the Socialist Party with cliques of trade union politicians." It was essential for the Party to uphold "its independent position," and reject "a spurious [electoral] victory obtained through an alliance with another organization of any kind whatever."[92]

THE MODERATES COUNTERATTACK

For the moderate leadership of the SP, the *ISR* initiated effort to create a cohesive left-wing slate for the National Executive Committee represented a threat that required an immediate response. Accordingly, the moderates launched a coordinated attack on the left-wing of the Party, beginning with the *International Socialist Review*. In November 1911, in the midst of the election campaign for the National Executive Committee, Robert Hunter attacked the *ISR* and its publisher, Charles Kerr. Hunter circulated a written proposal to the NEC urging it to initiate an investigation of the Kerr operation, insisting that his move to audit the books was not a ruse "to suppress the *Review*," but only an effort to make "one of our most boss-ridden institutions democratic." In fact, the *ISR* was edited by a collective, and seems to have functioned in general accord with democratic procedures. Needless to say, Hunter was not actually concerned with the internal workings of the *ISR*, or the distribution of its nonexistent profits, but rather with the intransigently radical politics expressed in its articles and editorials.[93]

Hunter's motion was endorsed by John Spargo, who made no effort to obscure the political purpose underlying the proposed investigation. The *ISR* was "wholly given up to the advocacy of policies which have been repudiated again and again by the Socialist Party." Spargo excoriated the *ISR* not only for advocating "anarchistic theories and policies of the crudest and most dangerous type," but also because it was also attempting to "control the Socialist Party through the election of its paid employees to the N.E.C." (Bohn was a member of the *ISR* staff.)[94]

This effort at intimidation ultimately failed when the investigating committee reported back to the 1912 Socialist Party convention that the staff members of the *ISR* were meagerly paid, and that Charles Kerr derived only a modest income from its publication, as well as the books and pamphlets issued under his name. Nevertheless, this incident clearly demonstrated the eagerness of the moderate leaders of the Party to initiate repressive measures aimed at stifling dissidents, especially those who challenged the concept of a labor party.[95]

The moderates' assault on the Left even extended to Gene Debs, the beloved symbol of the Socialist Party. During the first decade of the Party's existence, Debs had been chosen three times as the presidential nominee, either by acclamation or over token opposition. The 1912 convention proved very different. This time the moderate leadership presented two strong alternative candidates, Emil Seidel and Charles Edward Russell. Delegates were pressed to drop their support for Debs so that the SP could have a fresh look. In spite of this concerted opposition, Debs won a substantial majority, with 165 votes out of a total of 275. Nevertheless, a very clear warning had been sent.[96]

Debs did not take these maneuvers lightly. In a letter to a leading moderate, he decried the existence of a closed caucus of right-wingers that had met during the convention. This caucus, with the participation of most of the Party's leadership, worked hard to block Debs' nomination. The effort had failed, but it left Debs feeling embittered and angry.[97]

Once Debs was nominated, the moderate leadership sought to tighten its control over the presidential campaign. During the last hours of the convention, with the delegates exhausted and preparing to return home, Hillquit engaged in yet another duplicitous stratagem. As chair of the constitution committee, he proposed J. Mahlon Barnes for the post of campaign manager. Hillquit claimed, erroneously, to be speaking for the National Executive Committee on this issue, so, after a very brief discussion, Barnes was elected to the post. His appointment, and the manner in which it had been engineered, set off a firestorm of protest, once again exacerbating the divisions within the Party.[98]

Barnes had served as national secretary of the SP from 1905 to 1911. A staunch moderate, and a veteran union official in the Cigar Makers Union, Barnes appears to have been a competent functionary. He was also a womanizer. Indeed, after charges of sexual harassment by several members of the national office clerical staff began circulating, Barnes had been forced to resign.[99]

Debs took Hillquit's maneuver to ensure Barnes' selection as campaign manager as yet another move by the moderate leadership to isolate him, and to undercut his standing as a political leader. In a letter to Walter Lanfersiek, the newly appointed national secretary, Debs insisted that the "official bureaucracy and all its dependents" had done "everything in their power to defeat me and to elect Barnes." Those who had "held high office since they have been in the Party" had "come to think" that it was "their duty to run the Party."[100] Debs understood that this same group was also intent on promoting a labor party, and then submerging the Socialist Party within it.

At a joint meeting of the NEC and the national campaign committee held soon after the convention, Haywood and Kate Richards O'Hare distanced themselves from Barnes. Still, Hillquit and the rest of the moderate leadership held firm, and Barnes remained as campaign manager.[101]

For those on the radical Left, the Barnes incident provided a prime opportunity to challenge the same moderate leaders who were also eagerly preparing the way for a labor party. The July 1912 issue of the *International Socialist Review* featured an editorial on this unseemly dispute that focused on Hillquit's dishonest tactics. It declared that the issue was not the "character and the conduct of Comrade Barnes," but rather "the bossism of Hillquit," emphasizing that Hillquit had "procured" Barnes' approval as campaign manager through "trickery and evasion."[102]

When Barnes received word that this editorial was about to appear, he personally confronted Kerr, who assured him that the editorial did not constitute "a personal attack," but that it reflected "a consistent policy dating back to the Walling letter." Kerr advised Barnes that he and his fellow editors were "convinced" that Hunter and Hillquit "were both in with Simons," and that all three were working secretly to further the formation of a labor party. Kerr's suspicions were justified.[103]

HAYWOOD UNDER ATTACK

Of course, Big Bill Haywood was the primary target for the moderate leadership. Haywood exemplified the hardrock miner of the American West. Raised in Salt Lake City, Utah, he joined his father in the mines at the age of 15. Over the next twelve years, Haywood drifted from mining camp to mining camp, with brief interludes as a farmer and a cowboy.[104]

In the spring of 1896, at the age of 27, Haywood moved to Silver City, Idaho, one of the more permanent mining communities. That summer, he attended a rally featuring Ed Boyce, the president of the recently formed Western Federation of Miners. Boyce was a militant, a firm believer in industrial unionism, and a left-wing socialist. Inspired by Boyce, Haywood soon set out to build the fledgling WFM local in Silver City. Within five years, he was elected president of the local, a member of the union's executive board, and then, with Boyce's support, its secretary-treasurer.[105]

Although radicals seemed to be in firm control of the union, their influence would soon be challenged by union officials looking to pursue a more cautious strategy. Frustrated by the growing divisions within the union, Boyce resigned his post at its 1902 convention. His successor, Charles Moyer, was far more pragmatic.[106]

Under Boyce, the WFM had left the AFL, and had begun looking toward the formation of an alternative, radical federation of unions. In June 1905, the Industrial Workers of the World was founded in Chicago, with Haywood a leading presence, and with the Western Federation of Miners providing the organizational basis for the new organization. Then on December 30, 1905, Frank Steunenberg was killed by a bomb blast. Six years previously, while governor of Idaho, Steunenberg had crushed a strike of silver miners in Couer d'Alene by rounding up hundreds of WFM militants, and then holding them for months in a barbed wire bullpen. Two months after the bomb blast, Haywood and Moyer were kidnapped from Denver, union headquarters, by Pinkerton detectives, and then held for nearly a year and a half without bail on a charge of conspiring to assassinate Steunenberg. Haywood was acquitted in one of the most dramatic trials in U.S. history, but his legal victory was quickly followed by a serious political defeat.[107]

During the months that Haywood and Moyer shared a cell, their differing viewpoints crystallized into a bitter enmity. At the same time, the two officials named to replace them on an interim basis were committed moderates. The interim leadership began withdrawing the WFM from the IWW, and the swing to the Center continued when Moyer was released from jail. In April 1908, the executive board fired Haywood from his position as a union organizer.[108]

Thus, at the time of the debate within the Socialist Party on the merits of a labor party, Haywood was employed as a frequent writer for the *International Socialist Review*, and as a traveling lecturer on industrial unionism and the general strike. Haywood had been publicly identified with the SP while secretary treasurer of the WFM, and, indeed, he had stood as its candidate for governor of Colorado while still imprisoned in Idaho. Nevertheless, it was only after leaving union office that he became immersed in the internal debates of the Socialist Party. As an informal member of the *ISR* circle, he quickly allied himself with those who rejected the labor party perspective.

The campaign against Haywood was initiated by Hillquit with a letter to the *Call* that appeared only days after Haywood and Bohn had announced that they were seeking a position on the National Executive Committee. Hillquit's tactical purpose was obvious, to link Haywood to anarchist groups that engaged in acts of violence, while blurring the distinctions between nonviolent direct action and terrorism.

Hillquit focused his polemic on a few sentences selected out of context from the 60 pages of Haywood and Bohn's *Industrial Socialism*. Interestingly enough, Hillquit did not debate the validity of another section of the booklet that analysed the question of a labor party from a revolutionary perspective. There, Haywood and Bohn had argued that the "party of the workers" was "the Socialist Party." Although a "labor reform party might elect" its candidates to "offices very quickly, and, in a few years," could "control the country," nevertheless little would change. Inevitably, a labor party once in office would be "no better than any other capitalist party," since it was "not a Socialist party."[109]

Hillquit ignored this passage and instead zeroed in on a paragraph that lauded class conscious workers who retained "absolutely no respect for the property 'rights' of the profit- takers." Accordingly, workers who came "to know this truth" would "use any weapon" that would "win" their "fight." Indeed, "whatever action advances the interests of the working class is right, because it will save the workers from destruction and death."[110]

Hillquit condemned this argument, warning that whenever the working class movement had adopted the strategies of direct action, sabotage or anarchism it had "invariably served to demoralize and destroy the movement," for it had led "workers to needless and senseless slaughter." Socialists adamantly pursued an "incessant and aggressive struggle," but they did so with "clean weapons."[111]

In a second letter to the *Call*, written in response to a rebuttal from Haywood, Hillquit sharpened his critique. By calling for workers to break the law, Haywood and Bohn were implicitly holding that arson and robbery were effective tactics to be frequently "employed by the workers in their struggle against capitalism."[112]

Hillquit's critique could have been countered with an argument based on the actual experiences of trade unions. In fact, successful organizing drives have consistently had to overcome the repressive measures of the state, from violent assaults by police and private guards to sweeping injunctions from the courts. Indeed, as Haywood and Hillquit debated, Samuel Gompers, along with others in the AFL leadership, was appealing a conviction for contempt of court for engaging in a union boycott of scab goods. Furthermore, Hillquit served as legal counsel to the International Ladies Garment Workers Union (ILGWU), which had only recently organized the garment trades of New York City by militantly defying a judicial injunction that banned picketing during the confrontational strike of 1910.[113]

An unsigned foreword to the 1914 edition of *Industrial Socialism* skillfully parried Hillquit's critique. It rejected as "unfounded" Hillquit's charge that the cited passage "gave countenance to the use of physical force by the individual workers against the capitalists," insisting that this section of the book had been solely intended to "point out that class interest" was "the basis of class ethics."[114]

Unfortunately, Haywood took Hillquit's bait. In his response, he insisted on the necessity of violence as a critical aspect of the revolutionary process, and proceeded to chastize his critic for overlooking "the spirit of revolt animating the workers in every city of the world at the present moment." Haywood wondered if Hillquit would require the construction of "barricades on the asphalt pavement before the door of the building" where his law offices were located before being brought "to a realization that the fight" was "now on." Defiantly, Haywood insisted that he would "continue to appeal to the workers in the future to defend themselves at all hazards and with every weapon against the further encroachment of a common enemy."[115]

Yet for all of his strident rhetoric, Haywood understood full well that the United States was not poised on the brink of a revolutionary confrontation. Indeed, the IWW avoided violence in its organizing drives, and, instead, emphasized mass action and nonviolent civil disobedience. Haywood allowed Hillquit to set the terms of the debate, and, in doing so, he gave Hillquit an insurmountable advantage.

Nevertheless, the essential issues underlying the dispute were unrelated to the role of violence in the socialist politics of that time and place. Hillquit was intent on eliminating the influence of the militant Left in the Socialist Party, and Haywood provided a convenient target. The *International Socialist Review* made this point repeatedly, but, unfortunately, the message got lost in the heated debate on violence and sabotage that soon followed.

In spite of Hillquit's sallies, when the votes were tallied in January 1912, Haywood had been elected, the first radical to serve on the National Executive Committee (NEC). Moderate leaders were dismayed, convinced that Haywood's election would undermine the Party's credibility with the AFL. On the other hand, Haywood was buoyed by his victory, and adamant in his views. In a mass rally at New York's Cooper Union, he stressed the battles being fought by combative industrial unions. Still, these strikes were often defeated, crushed by police and militia units under state control. Independent political action, through the Socialist Party, could bring to power local and state governments that would refuse to side with the corporations during these bitter strikes. For Haywood, this was "as far as" he could "go on political action. But that" was "a long way."[116]

This strategic perspective consigned electoral activity to a position as a subordinate adjunct to the activities of militant industrial unions, rather than viewing it as an important forum for presenting a revolutionary socialist analysis of the global capitalist system. Furthermore, Haywood's perspective minimized the significance of every issue except those directly related to the workplace. These included questions of war and peace, issues that would soon enmesh the entire Left in a wrenching series of controversies.

As the divisions within the Party deepened, Debs intervened in the debate. In an article for the February 1912 issue of the *ISR*, he challenged the decision of the national committee to investigate Kerr and the *ISR*. The investigation was an effort "to punish" the *ISR* "for its advocacy of industrial unionism, and for opposing pure and simple craftism." Debs remained "opposed under all circumstances to any party alliances or affiliations with reactionary trade unions, and to compromising tactics of every kind or form."[117]

Having reiterated his belief in the core values of the radical Left, Debs proceeded to condemn Haywood and the IWW for its defense of sabotage and direct action. These were tactics that could only be undertaken by "stealth and suspicion," and could not "substitute for solidarity." The class struggle had to rely on mass action, and not on "the sling-shot, the dagger and the dynamite bomb." Debs was convinced that the advocacy of these tactics had "prevented the growth of the Industrial Workers of the World," for "sabotage repels the American worker." Finally, Debs urged the Socialist Party at its upcoming convention to "place itself squarely on record" against "sabotage and every other form of violence and destructiveness suggested by what is known as 'direct action.'"

These comments gave implicit support to the drive to remove Haywood from the NEC. Although Debs would later state his opposition to the imposition of sanctions on those who advocated sabotage, he still bore significant responsibility for the success of the recall initiative.[118] Debs could have legitimately criticized Haywood for his rhetoric, and yet he also knew that the IWW sought to avoid violence, and that it relied on mass struggle and nonviolent direct action. Furthermore, he understood that violent confrontations had frequently erupted during the course of strikes led by AFL unions, even during those led by Debs' own American Railway Union.

By the spring of 1912, the controversy had escalated to the point at which a substantial section of the Party was demanding Haywood's recall from the National Executive Committee. In February 1912, the Yuma, Arizona, local proposed such a recall, citing the anti-electoral bias of his speeches. This initiative was endorsed by the Bridgeport, Connecticut, local, a right-wing stronghold where Robert Hunter retained considerable influence.[119]

Recall motions were common in the Socialist Party, and many were directed against the moderate members of the NEC. The constitution required that such an initiative would only be brought to a referendum vote if locals or state committees representing 5 percent of the previous year's membership supported it. Hillquit initially urged the New York local to back Yuma, but then reversed his position, and the motion died for lack of support.[120]

Hillquit may have been dissuaded from moving further by Haywood's prominent role in the Lawrence strike, which was successfully concluded in March 1912. Certainly Lawrence provided a major boost to the IWW, while greatly increasing Haywood's stature and notoriety. Yet Haywood had already become a national celebrity. After all, he would not have been elected to the NEC over the determined opposition of the moderate leadership had this not been the case. More likely, Hillquit hesitated because he understood that Haywood's recall would trigger a huge furor within the Socialist Party, one that was likely to greatly damage it.[121]

HAYWOOD'S RECALL

In any case, when Haywood traveled to Indianapolis in May 1912 to attend the SP national convention, he did so as a delegate, and as a member of its National Executive Committee. Although radicals were a minority among the 293 delegates, they nevertheless wielded considerable influence over the convention's proceedings. Haywood urged the convention to initiate a call for a general strike should the United States deploy troops in Mexico, although such a motion never reached the floor. Later, the convention passed by acclamation a report from a special committee on labor that advised trade unions of "the vital importance of the task of organizing the unorganized, especially the immigrants and the unskilled laborers," and then urged "all labor organizations" to "throw their doors wide open to the workers of their respective trades." Haywood enthusiastically endorsed the report, commenting that its passage would make it possible to "talk Socialism from a Socialist Party platform to the entire working class." He then pledged that he would "urge that every working man use the ballot at every opportunity."[122]

Clearly, Haywood was assuming a leadership position within the Socialist Party. Furthermore, his political perspective was evolving, moving him closer to Bohn and the *ISR* editorial staff. His advocacy of a SP campaign of direct action around the issue of U.S. intervention in Mexico is a clear indication that Haywood was coming to see the role of a political party in terms that went well beyond the election of local sheriffs to make it easier for militant industrial unions to conduct strikes.

For the moderate proponents of a labor party, Haywood's political evolution made him even more of a threat than before. A caucus of moderates met at the 1912 SP convention and decided to launch a direct counterattack. Hillquit as chair of the constitutional committee then brought forward a constitutional amendment barring from the Party those members who opposed electoral politics or advocated violence. A heated debate ensued, during which Haywood refrained from speaking. The amendment was approved by the convention by a vote of 191 to 90, and then adopted by a membership vote of 13,000 to 4,000. In its final version, the amendment provided for the expulsion of any member engaged in "the advocacy of crime, sabotage or other methods of violence."[123]

Haywood appeared undaunted by the passage of this amendment, persevering as a radical critic of the Party leadership. At the June 1912 joint meeting of the National Executive Committee and the campaign committee, the moderate majority proposed that Keir Hardie be invited to the United States for a national tour. The proposal was approved despite Haywood's objections.[124]

Haywood then proceeded to criticize the proposed tour in the *International Socialist Review*, specifically attacking the British Labour Party for consistently acting as "the tail of the Liberal Party." Furthermore, the Socialist Party could not "afford to stand sponsor for anyone" who would use his influence to promote support for "the thought of establishing a Labor party in this country." Thus, Haywood firmly aligned himself with the radical Left in the Party in directly rejecting the labor party perspective.[125]

Until the fall of 1912, the question of whether or not Haywood would be the subject of a recall referendum remained in doubt. It would seem that Keir Hardie's intervention was influential in tipping the balance. During September and October of 1912, Hardie spent several weeks touring the United States under the auspices of the Socialist Party, addressing election rallies in dozens of communities. Although he spoke in favor of Gene Debs for president, he also indicated his belief that the future of working-class politics in this country depended on the AFL and the SP working together toward the creation of a broadly based labor party.[126]

While in the United States, Hardie met with AFL officials at every level, from local leaders to the very top of the bureaucracy. During a discussion with Gompers, he was given a tour of the AFL's headquarters. Hardie was impressed, convinced that the federation "as a business organization" came "as near perfection as anything of the kind well could be."[127]

At the same time, Hardie met with Socialist Party activists, from local militants to national leaders. He almost certainly advised them that Haywood, and the IWW, represented a dangerous threat. During his previous trip to the United States four years earlier, Hardie had already indicated that Haywood would have to be silenced before the Socialist Party could hope to become an integral component of a labor party. Since then, Haywood had become a spokesperson for the Party's left-wing, so the issue had become even more acute. While in New York, Hardie stayed with Hillquit, enabling the two of them to engage in extensive discussions.[128]

The issue of Haywood's role in the Party remained dormant during the last weeks of the election, an election in which the Socialist Party reached the zenith of its popularity, but soon afterward the New York local, at Hillquit's initiative, sponsored a recall petition aimed at Haywood. There is no written record of Hillquit's interchanges with Hardie, but there is every reason to suspect that Hardie was influential in convincing Hillquit to move forward with Hillquit's recall from the National Executive Committee.

The initiative to recall Haywood relied on the momentum generated by the approval of the sabotage amendment, which clearly stated the Party's rejection of violence and sabotage. Yet the New York local did not utilize the sabotage amendment, with its sanction of expulsion, as the procedural basis for its recall initiative. Instead, it relied on the long-standing provision providing for the removal of National Executive Committee members for inappropriate behavior. With the New York and New Jersey state committees seconding the proposal, the recall petition easily surmounted the 5 percent barrier, and the issue was submitted to membership referendum.[129]

Haywood was defiant. During a mass rally on December 1, 1912, with the referendum still in doubt, he stressed the need for "direct action," while insisting that he continued to "believe in sabotage." At the other end of the spectrum, Germer advised Hunter that the one victory "above all others" that had to be won by moderates was "to set Haywood outside of the party." In February 1913, the official count was announced, and Haywood was removed from the Party's National Executive Committee by a margin of 2 to 1 – 22,000 to 11,000.[130]

As the votes were being counted, Hardie wrote to Adolph Germer, whom he had met while touring the previous fall, that he was "waiting with much interest the result of the ballot on Haywood. The fellow is a bounder. Fortunately, all of his type on this side remain outside the [Independent Labour] Party, and, as a consequence, are quite powerless for evil." Hardie insisted that if Haywood "had any sense of honour, he would have cleared out long ago."[131]

Germer notified Hardie that the recall referendum would be carried. Thus, Haywood's "doom" was "sealed in the Socialist movement of this country." Indeed, "the quicker" the Socialist Party got "rid of him, the better" off it would be. Undermining Haywood would constitute only one facet of a broader transformation. According to Germer, the socialist movement was "undergoing a change." The Socialist Party was "being cleansed of that turbulent element" that had "marred its growth in the past." Haywood's recall "might result in a split," but "the constructive wing of our movement" would then be free to "build up an organization" that would "challenge the admiration of the world," or at least those aligned with Hardie's perspective.[132]

THE SOCIALIST PARTY IN DISARRAY

In the immediate aftermath of his recall from the NEC, Haywood clung to the hope that the SP would quickly repeal the sabotage amendment, thus making it possible for him to reclaim his leadership position. Debs soon realized his mistake in providing ideological cover for the attack on Haywood, and began working toward a reunified party. In an article for the *International Socialist Review,* Debs argued that the sabotage amendment "ought to be stricken from the Socialist Party's constitution." This would constitute an essential prerequisite to the unity of all of those interested "in establishing the economic and political solidarity of the workers." Since the "overwhelming majority of industrial unionists favor independent political action," and "an overwhelming majority of Socialists favor industrial unionism," it was necessary "that these forces" be "brought together in harmonious and effective economic and political cooperation."[133]

In spite of Debs' urgent plea, the sabotage amendment would remain in the Socialist Party constitution until April 1917, when the radical upsurge sparked by U.S. entry into World War I swept through the Party. By then, Haywood had allowed his membership to lapse and had moved away from any interest in electoral politics.[134] The split between the industrial socialists and the Debsian socialists undercut the potential for a strong revolutionary Left at the very moment when socialist ideas had their greatest appeal.

Haywood's recall from the NEC divided the Socialist Party, as thousands of activists tendered their resignations. During the last months of the 1912 campaign, the Party's membership soared, reaching 128,000 in October of that year. As soon as the New York local opted to pursue a recall, membership figures began a rapid decline, and the descent continued over the next months of turmoil and division. By June 1913, SP membership had fallen to 81,000, a precipitous drop of 37 percent. Over the next few months there was a slight increase, but after that total membership vacillated from 80,000 to 100,000, until the government's repression of World War I, and the Communist Party split, led to another drastic drop.[135]

Haywood's recall also had a devastating impact on the autonomous language federations that were affiliated with the SP. Divisions within the Finnish Socialist Federation, the largest of the federations, grew so bitter that several of its locals opted to secede. These locals, mostly located in Michigan and Minnesota, maintained an uneasy status for several years as IWW general membership branches.[136]

Haywood's recall from the National Executive Committee marked a crucial turning point for the Socialist Party. During the first decade of its existence, the SP had rapidly grown, generating a wave of optimism, a feeling that socialism was riding the current of popular opinion. After Haywood's recall and resignation, this sense of optimism faded. The Socialist Party had lost its initial dynamism. Nevertheless, the SP remained a small mass party, with solid roots in several distinct communities. For those on the Party's Left, the departure of tens of thousands of militants made it far more difficult to effectively challenge the moderate leadership. Although many of the more prominent radicals remained, it became considerably more difficult to gain a hearing within the Party.

For the moderates, the course of events during 1912 could not have seemed more propitious. With Haywood's recall, and the exodus of thousands of radicals, the moderates' domination of the Party's leadership seemed ensured. At the same time, unions open to socialist ideas were gaining in strength within the American Federation of Labor. When Max Hayes challenged Gompers for AFL president at the 1912 convention, he received more than 30 percent of the vote.

At every level, the path toward a labor party seemed open, and yet over the next five years a series of events would undercut any possibility of such a formation. In 1913, President Woodrow Wilson appointed William B. Wilson, a former secretary-treasurer of the United Mine Workers, to his cabinet as Secretary of Labor. Beyond this symbolism, Wilson did little to aid the cause of workers or trade unions, but AFL officials came to view themselves as insiders, with personal access to those in power. As World War I engulfed Europe, virtually every single union official, including most of the progressives, rallied behind the president. After April 1917, and U.S. entry into the war, the Socialist Party went from being a mass-based party with a significant electoral base to a hunted pariah. Gompers and most of the AFL leadership not only supported the war effort, they enthusiastically endorsed the federal government's draconian repression of the Socialist Party.

Only with the end of World War I would proposals for a labor party re-emerge. By then, the Socialist Party had split, with most of its left-wing members leaving to join the Communist Party. During the 1920s, as union officials flirted with the idea of forming a labor party, the SP could only join in as an enthusiastic cheerleader.

4
The Conference for Progressive Political Action: Labor Party or Pressure Group

The years immediately following the close of World War I in November 1918 were marked by intense conflict. Government repression of radical organizations remained pervasive, with hundreds of activists sentenced to lengthy terms in federal and state penitentiaries. At the same time, the gains achieved by organized labor during the war were reversed under the impact of a concerted offensive by powerful, and politically connected, corporations.

In this context, the prospects for a labor party began to gain support within the ranks of progressive AFL officials. The railroad unions, representing a critical sector of the economy, would be in the forefront of this incipient movement. For the moderate leadership of the Socialist Party, this tentative approach to independent politics constituted a validation of their labor party perspective. In February 1922, the SP eagerly joined with a coalition of railroad unions in creating the Conference for Progressive Political Action, certain that it would serve as an organizational vehicle for an independent labor based third party. Instead, the CPPA remained mired within the two party system, organizing support for progressive candidates nominated by the mainstream parties.

THE SOCIALIST PARTY SWINGS LEFT AND SPLITS

World War I transformed the Socialist Party. From the start of hostilities in August 1914, prominent intellectuals began justifying their support for Britain and its allies. Although most socialists firmly held to an anti-war position, the entire Party was stunned when the great majority of the German Social Democratic Party supported the Kaiser and the war. Socialist Party leaders had frequently cited the German Social Democrats as exemplars of orthodoxy, and yet the outbreak of World War I had exposed them as unprincipled careerists carried along by the hysteria of national chauvinism.[1]

In the United States, the entire liberal community rallied behind President Woodrow Wilson and his call for neutrality. Any hopes for a labor party were shelved as influential progressive unions such as the International Association of Machinists endorsed Wilson's re-election in 1916. Even after Wilson launched a "preparedness" campaign as a tentative step toward direct participation in the war, most progressive trade union officials continued to support him.

Throughout the first three years of the war, the entrenched leadership succeeded in maintaining its tight control over the Socialist Party's apparatus. The SP issued public statements condemning both combatants, criticizing preparedness, and demanding that the United States continue to keep its troops out of the European conflict. All of this collapsed in April 1917, when the United States declared war on Imperial Germany.

World War I was intensely unpopular in the United States. Spontaneous, unorganized resistance erupted throughout the country, most especially in the West. Working people saw no credible reason to send their sons into the grotesque and pointless slaughter of trench warfare. Although the pacifist movement provided a modicum of opposition to the war effort, the Socialist Party stood at the center of a mass movement. Yet President Wilson had not the slightest intention of modifying his policies in response to the popular resistance. On the contrary, he ordered a massive, coordinated effort to crush any and all who opposed the war effort.

When the SP's emergency convention assembled in St. Louis on April 7, 1917, only five days after Wilson's declaration of war, the radicals prevailed. The convention's proceedings focused on the Party's resistance to the war effort, with the delegates adopting a ringing resolution declaring entry into the war to be "a crime against the people of the United States and against the nations of the world." The Socialist Party pledged itself to "continuous, active and public opposition to the war, through demonstrations, mass petitions, and all other means within our power." Furthermore, the SP would join with others in organizing "mass action to shorten" the war.[2]

The radical left-wing saw a unique opportunity to transform the Party into a militant force for fundamental social change. For a start, the constitution was amended to delete the clause prohibiting the advocacy of sabotage, the same clause that had triggered Haywood's recall from the national executive committee in 1913, and the resignation of thousands of radical activists. At the same time, a con-stitutional provision was added affirming that no members could "under any circumstances vote in any political election for any candidate other than Socialist Party members" campaigning on the Party's own ticket. Any violation of this clause would "constitute party treason and [would] result in expulsion from the party."[3] Obviously, the SP could not monitor the voting patterns of its members, but the 1917 constitution is indicative of the Party's rejection of any alliance with progressive third parties.

With sentiment at the St. Louis convention swinging to the radical Left, Hillquit sought to divert the anger of the rank and file by vociferously proclaiming a radical rhetoric, while pursuing a tactical policy of caution and moderation. As a result, the National Executive Committee elected at St. Louis was still controlled by the moderate Center. This would prove to be of crucial importance during the next two years of conflict and repression. As the United States escalated its repression of the anti-war Left, the leadership of the Socialist Party retreated from the St. Louis manifesto, without formally repudiating it. In turn, the Party's radicals grew increasingly frustrated with the timidity of the Party's leadership, and the ideological gap continued to widen.

In New York, the debates became particularly heated. A new group of young militants came to the fore, prepared to unseat Hillquit and his group of insiders. Louis Fraina soon emerged as the most influential figure among these radical dissidents. An Italian immigrant, Fraina joined the Socialist Labor Party in his youth, and soon became a staff journalist for its newspaper, the *Weekly People*. Five years later, he quit the SLP and started writing for left-wing journals such as the *International Socialist Review* and the *New Review*. Soon after the U.S. decision to enter World War I, Fraina joined the Socialist Party, and quickly became the driving force in its left-wing. Fraina rejected the strategic desirability of a labor party model, holding that the British Labour Party was "hardly a credit to the Movement."[4]

Radicals within the Socialist Party were in contact with European anti-war socialists, most especially the Tribune group in Holland, which had been expelled from the Dutch Socialist Party in 1908. Connections were also established with Russian socialists, as political exiles sought refuge in the United States. In January 1917, Leon Trotsky arrived in New York, having already established a considerable reputation within the international socialist movement. For ten weeks, Trotsky worked closely with Fraina, as well as with other New York radicals, in an effort to cajole the Socialist Party into taking a more militant stance in opposition to the war. At the time, Trotsky expected to remain in the United States for an extended period, so he took his participation in the SP quite seriously.[5] He therefore had to be well aware that radical socialists in the United States were adamantly opposed to the formation of a labor party.

With the Russian Revolution of November 1917, the cohesion of the SP began to rapidly disintegrate. Enamored with the Bolshevik seizure of power, left-wing activists sought to mold the Socialist Party into a disciplined cadre formation. Locals controlled by the left-wing linked up into a nationwide caucus that began assessing dues, issuing membership cards, and even setting strict guidelines as to who could join.[6]

As long as the war continued, the SP maintained a tenuous unity as the federal government exerted tremendous pressure on the Party, forcing it into a virtual underground existence. With the armistice signed in November 1918, the deep-seated divisions within the SP reached breaking point. The rift came in May 1919, when Morris Hillquit insisted that the Party recognize the inevitability of an organizational split and proceed to "clear the decks." During the next few months, two-thirds of the members were expelled by the National Executive Committee, as the Party's rolls precipitously declined from 109,000 to 40,000. The NEC also set August 1919 as the date for an emergency convention to finalize the split.[7]

In June 1919, the left-wing caucus met in Cleveland, seeking to formulate a coordinated response to the continuing round of expulsions. Instead, the group divided, with a majority voting to attend the Cleveland convention, and a minority breaking away to form a new organization. The majority issued a manifesto, written by Fraina, rejecting the labor party perspective, holding that such a formation could not serve as "the instrument for the emancipation of the working class." Indeed, reformist organizations such as a labor party, or even the Socialist Party, represented "a danger to the revolutionary proletariat."[8]

THE FARMER-LABOR PARTY

The opposition caucus's rejection of a labor party was nothing new. Indeed, this position had been consistently raised by radical critics of the Party's moderate leadership. Still, in 1919 the issue was no longer a purely theoretical one. In the fall of 1918, the Chicago Federation of Labor (CFL) set into motion a series of events that, for a moment, brought the question of a labor party into the forefront of political debate.

Chicago was a major industrial center, with steel mills and stockyards establishing the basis for a militant working-class movement. Yet most of Chicago's industries remained unorganized. A journeyman blacksmith by trade, John Fitzpatrick would lead the Chicago Federation of Labor for four decades, starting in 1906. Fitzpatrick sought to democratize Chicago's AFL craft unions, and to prod them into being more open and inclusive. In doing so, he attracted a solid group of union militants and social activists. One of them, Robert Buck, had briefly served on the Chicago city council. Buck was a staunch progressive and an ardent supporter of the British Labour Party.[9]

Nevertheless, Fitzpatrick remained a Gompers supporter and a Democrat. He endorsed Woodrow Wilson in 1916, and then supported the decision to enter World War I. Yet Fitzpatrick became increasingly disillusioned with the government's repression of the radical Left, and the drastic erosion in civil liberties.[10]

Fitzpatrick soon realized that the economic boom generated by war production had created an excellent opportunity to organize the mass production industries. In 1917, he brought the CFL behind a drive to organize the stockyards, selecting William Z. Foster to head this effort. Foster had spent several years organizing for the IWW, before quitting the Wobblies to pursue a policy of boring from within the AFL.[11]

With prices soaring and wages lagging, Buck convinced Fitzpatrick to look at the potential for a labor party formation in the light of events in Britain. Once again, developments in Britain spurred third party efforts in the United States. The British Labour Party had rallied behind the war effort, serving as a junior partner in a national unity coalition cabinet. After the first Russian Revolution in March 1917, quickly followed by Wilson's decision to send combat troops to Europe, the tide of battle shifted to Britain and its allies. Within the British cabinet, heated debates unfolded, with Labour ministers opposing the imposition of onerous reparations on a defeated Germany. Arthur Henderson, an influential Labour member in the war cabinet, resigned and began exploring the potential for a negotiated surrender with Germany.[12]

In looking forward to the post-war period, Labour, with Henderson in the lead, decided to reinvent itself as a political party. At its annual conference in February 1918, it abandoned its previous organizational configuration as a federation of affiliated organizations, and opted for a new, hybrid structure. Individuals were permitted to join directly, rather than through a trade union, cooperative society or affiliated political party. Furthermore, local constituency parties were guaranteed a significant minority of positions on the national executive committee.[13]

The Labour Party also voted to amend its constitution. For the first time, Labour pledged "to secure for the producers by hand or brain the full fruits of their industry" through the "equitable distribution" of the social product by means of "the common ownership of the means of production." This rather hazy formulation gave a socialistic gloss to the Labour Party, although Clause 4 deliberately omitted any mention of workers' control as an essential element in an alternative society.[14]

In December 1918, a month after the armistice, Labour contested its first election as a fully independent party. With the Liberals hopelessly split on post-war policy, Labour gained 2.2 million votes, nearly a quarter of all those cast. By doing so, it became the principal opposition to the ruling coalition constituted by the Conservatives and Lloyd George Liberals.[15] The 1918 election marked the Labour Party's permanent displacement of the Liberals as one of the two leading parties in Britain.

Fitzpatrick and his circle of union officials were impressed by the success of the British Labour Party, and they hoped that the formation of a viable labor party could provide a counterbalance to corporate power in the electoral arena. On October 6, 1918, the Chicago Federation of Labor issued a call for an "independent labor party along [the] lines of the British Labour Party, but adapted to American conditions." (The Chicago Labor Party inspired similar formations in New York and Seattle.) A month later, the CFL presented a platform for the proposed new party, one based on 14 points. This statement of principles was written by Basil Manly, a leading progressive who had served on the National War Labor Board during World War I. (Manly would re-emerge as a key strategist in Senator Robert La Follette's independent presidential campaign in 1924.)[16]

The 14 points included the usual gamut of progressive reforms, such as an eight-hour day and government ownership of the railroads system and of the nation's natural resources. Yet the 14 points also moved a step beyond the limitations of the traditional tenets of progressive reform. Inspired by the Labour Party's Clause 4, the CFL program called for "the democratic control of industry" by "those who work with hand and brain." This revised and diluted the already imprecise wording in the Labour Party constitution.[17]

In January 1919, 750 delegates from an assortment of Chicago trade unions met to form the Cook County Labor Party. The new party nominated a slate of independent candidates for the municipal elections of April 1919, with Fitzpatrick leading the ticket, at the same time that it launched a new newspaper, *The New Majority*. With the Chicago Federation of Labor putting time and resources into the campaign, the Cook County Labor Party appeared to be solidly grounded. Fitzpatrick obtained 56,000 votes for mayor, or 8 percent of the total vote. For a first campaign, this would seem to be a credible showing, but the CFL's leaders were disenchanted. They had hoped to repeat the rapid electoral success of the British Labour Party, convinced that a new third party could rapidly become a credible electoral alternative to the Democratic and Republican parties. Nevertheless, the 1919 municipal campaign would stand as the high-water mark of the Chicago labor party experiment.[18]

Fitzpatrick saw the urgent necessity of moving beyond the local level to the formation of a nationwide third party. As a first step, an Illinois Labor Party was formed, with the support of the Illinois Federation of Labor, only a month after the Chicago municipal election. In November 1919, the CFL convened a founding convention for a nationwide party. In response, 1,200 delegates from 33 states assembled, although none of them represented the national leadership of an AFL affiliated trade union. Still, 50 local union federations were represented, including New York City, so the convention proceeded to set July 1920 as the date for a nominating convention to select an independent presidential ticket.[19]

When the July convention opened in Chicago, the national trade unions remained absent, although locals from several unions were represented, along with dozens of local union federations. In addition, the convention attracted an unofficial delegation from an important organization of progressive farmers, the National Nonpartisan League. In an effort to broaden the appeal of the new party, the convention adopted the name Farmer-Labor Party.[20]

Delegates hoped to nominate Senator Robert La Follette for president. La Follette had pushed through a series of social reforms as the progressive governor of Wisconsin, before being elected to the Senate, where he became the leading figure in a loose circle of progressive dissidents. Although he had endorsed the AFL's position on a series of controversial issues, his base of support was rooted in the small farmers of the Upper Midwest. Fitzpatrick hoped to convince Frank Walsh, a prominent liberal attorney, to campaign as the vice-presidential nominee along side of La Follette.[21]

The plan foundered when La Follette criticized the platform, a reworking of the 14-point program of the CFL, as "full of revolutionary language." In particular, he objected to the demand for "an ever increasing voice for the workers in the management and control of industry." When the FLP leaders refused to budge, La Follette declined the nomination. Walsh then backed out, and Fitzpatrick was left hanging.[22] Although La Follette focused on the platform as the basis of his decision to decline, it seems likely that he was also wary of embarking on an independent presidential campaign without the support of the American Federation of Labor, or at least a significant number of its more influential affiliates.

THE SOCIALIST PARTY LOOKS TO A LABOR PARTY

With La Follette's refusal, some of the delegates looked to Eugene Victor Debs as a potential presidential candidate. Since the local labor parties had been created as a political alternative to the Socialist Party, this would appear to have been an unlikely choice. Nevertheless, Debs commanded tremendous moral authority. Throughout the 1920 election, he remained a prisoner in the Atlanta federal penitentiary for a speech denouncing the U.S. entry into the war. The possibility of Debs emerging as the candidate of the Farmer-Labor Party forced the Socialist Party to more clearly define its position on the labor party.

The actions of the British Labour Party had reverberated within the SP, as they had in the Chicago Federation of Labor. In January 1919, the National Executive Committee reminded locals that the constitution prohibited the endorsement of candidates from another party. For the Chicago local, the point was moot, since it sharply condemned Fitzpatrick and the Cook County Labor Party, while advancing its own slate of candidates for the municipal election.[23]

Still, the NEC was far from hostile to the newly formed locally based labor parties. It advised Party members to "realize the futility of destructive criticism of the new Labor Party," and urged the rank and file to "maintain an open mind." After all, the British working class was "making strides toward socialism" under the aegis of the Labour Party. On balance, the NEC took a wait and see attitude, while holding out hope that the recent global upsurge in socialist activity might yet "give rise to a new party in this country, socialist in all but name."[24]

The NEC statement epitomized the Socialist Party position on the labor party effort initiated by the CFL. Without the backing of a significant section of the AFL, a nationwide labor party was bound to fail. The Party's leadership hoped to maintain good relations with Fitzpatrick and his allies, but they were unwilling to submerge the SP into the coalition represented at the Chicago convention, one comprised primarily of local union federations. Nevertheless, the NEC statement marked an abrupt break with Party policy. SP moderates had been lavish in their praise of the British Labour Party during the years prior to World War I, and yet publicly they had always insisted that the Socialist Party was and would be the only working-class party in the United States. In the aftermath of World War I, the Party's leaders were prepared to openly advocate the formation of a labor party. Still, they remained skeptical of Fitzpatrick and his call for a new party.

Thus, when Debs was nominated for president at the FLP convention, the SP's National Executive Committee rejected the idea. Otto Branstetter, the SP's national secretary who attended the Chicago convention as an observer, believed that the Farmer-Labor Party was "too uncertain as to its future plans and principles" to justify a joint ticket. Furthermore, Debs' nomination would have ignited "a bitter attack" on the Party from "some of the ex-Socialist leaders of the convention." One of those leaders, Max Hayes, would be nominated as the vice-presidential candidate on the Farmer-Labor Party slate.[25]

Debs agreed with the NEC decision. In a letter signed by his brother Theodore, Debs praised "the excellent judgment" of the NEC in rejecting the possibility of his standing as a candidate of the FLP, and commended the Party for moving forward in nominating its own candidates. In doing so, the SP had "maintained the integrity" of the Party.[26]

Ultimately, the FLP convention nominated Parley Christiansen, a relatively unknown Utah attorney, as its presidential candidate, while the Socialist Party rallied behind Debs. Imprisoned in the maximum security federal penitentiary in Atlanta, Debs was prevented from campaigning, and yet his candidacy gained momentum, while Christiansen's effort stalled from the start.[27]

As the 1920 campaign neared its end, Hillquit assessed the situation from the viewpoint of a labor party advocate. From this perspective, it was a matter "of comparative indifference" whether independent politics was "carried out" by an explicitly socialist party "or some other formation" such as a labor party. An independent party could well "take its starting-point in a large body of workers organized for the protection of their class interests, but without a definite program of ultimate social and political aims."[28]

Logically it would appear that Hillquit should have supported the FLP, an electoral formation that appeared to meet his minimal prerequisites for an independent, working-class party. Yet he continued to be skeptical, convinced that the FLP had failed "in attracting the support of the bulk of the organized workers in the United States." Hillquit remained committed to the example set by the British Labour Party. Only the official support of the AFL, or at least a sizable segment of its national affiliates, could provide the basis for a mass labor party along the line of the British model. The Farmer-Labor Party, with its base in the Chicago Federation of Labor and other local trade union councils, fell far short of this standard.[29]

Although Hillquit held back, waiting for a break with the two party system on a national level, Debs viewed the new formation as opportunistic in its conception. The Farmer-Labor Party sought to appeal to radicals as "sanely socialistic," while at the same time it "assured the conservative and reactionary elements" that it was "heading off Socialism." Furthermore, several FLP leaders had only recently quit the Socialist Party to support the U.S. war effort. To Debs, these former comrades had "deserted because they could not stand the Party's unpopular attitude toward the capitalist war."[30]

When the votes were counted, the SP presidential ticket had outpolled the FLP by the wide margin of 915,000 votes to 265,000. Even in Illinois, where most of the third party votes were drawn from Chicago, Debs drew substantially greater support than Christiansen. With the Farmer-Labor Party demoralized and in disarray, the prospects for a broadly based third party appeared bleak. Still, labor party advocates could focus their hopes on a promising development, the growing disenchantment of railroad union officials with the meager rewards of the two party system.[31]

THE RAILROAD UNIONS LOOK OUTSIDE THE TWO PARTY SYSTEM

Since railroads remained the dominant form of transportation into the 1920s, the entire economy depended on their efficient operation. On January 1, 1918, eight months after the United States had entered World War I, the entire railroad system was nationalized, with William McAdoo, the Secretary of the Treasury and President Woodrow Wilson's son-in-law, named as director general. Railroad employees had long been stratified into a multitude of crafts, with a distinct union for each craft. Only the most highly skilled workers, those who operated the trains, had succeeded in establishing viable unions. Their unions, the four railroad brotherhoods, had opted to remain independent of the AFL. Six of the non-operating unions covered the railroad shop workers, the crafts who repaired the trains and related equipment. These unions, as well as a few of the other non-operating craft unions, had affiliated with the AFL and its Railway Employees Department. Nevertheless, most railroad employees in the non-operating crafts worked without benefit of a union contract.[32]

McAdoo sought to preempt strikes by ensuring the cooperation of the railroad unions. On February 21, 1918, he issued General Order No. 8 establishing a policy of "no discrimination" against any railroad employee "because of membership" in any labor organization. Almost immediately, membership in the non-operating craft unions soared, with a million and a half railroad workers covered by union representation by the end of the war. This represented nearly 40 percent of all unionized workers in the United States. McAdoo also implemented a sizable increase in wages, with shop workers receiving additional increases, reflecting the wartime demand for their skills.[33]

McAdoo's executive orders had a tremendous impact on the railroad industry. Yet as World War I ended, the likelihood of the railway system remaining permanently under government control dwindled. Congressional Republicans argued for immediate privatization, while McAdoo called for a limited extension of government control. Initially, the president remained aloof from the controversy, but on May 20, 1919, he informed Congress that the railroads would "be handed over to their owners at the end of the calendar year." Even the railroad unions became considerably less enthusiastic in their support of public control after October 1918, when McAdoo issued another order prohibiting all railroad workers, as federal employees, from engaging in any partisan political activity.[34]

The railroad unions looked toward a new option, a third alternative to both continued government control and a return of the railroad system to corporate management. Glenn. E. Plumb, chief legal counsel for the four operating brotherhoods, devised a plan for a quasi-public, tripartite board that would own and control the railroads, with the right of workers to organize unions explicitly guaranteed. For the next several years, the Plumb Plan would become the highest priority of the railroad unions, gaining the support of a wide range of progressive organizations, including the Nonpartisan League. The

Plumb Plan served as a starting point for an emerging coalition of liberals and trade unionists, one that would quickly encompass the Socialist Party. The railroad unions also initiated and funded the Plumb Plan League, with the aim of sparking a groundswell of public support for the proposal.[35]

Railroad union leaders understood that they needed the advice and counsel of an experienced political strategist. In August 1919, they approached Edward Keating with an offer to become the coordinator of the Plumb Plan League. A liberal Democrat who had just completed three terms in the House of Representatives, Keating knew his way around Washington, and yet he was also aligned with the progressives within Congress, having sponsored legislation to create a minimum wage and restrict child labor. Keating accepted the offer, but, as a journalist, he also insisted on launching a weekly newspaper, *Labor*, which would serve as the voice of the railroad unions.[36]

Union officials quickly found themselves confronting a corporate and political establishment intent on reversing the wartime gains of the railroad workers. With bipartisan support, Congress passed the Esch–Cummins Act, returning the railroads to private ownership as of March 1920. Once signed into law by President Wilson, the same statute also created the Railway Labor Board, a tripartite body that was given the authority to seek judicial injunctions to enjoin strikes that challenged its decisions.[37]

From the start, the railway lines moved to undermine the wages and working conditions of their workforce. The leadership of the railroad craft unions was therefore confronted with a situation that bordered on the catastrophic. They had no desire to challenge the economic and political power of the railroad corporations, and yet the open hostility of the railways, and the ineffectiveness of the Railway Labor Board, left them with little choice. The industry thus stumbled into a decisive confrontation.

The railroad unions had always been tied to the two party system, and yet the return of the railroad industry to corporate control forced the unions to start questioning these ties. Keating began this reassessment in January 1920, with an editorial in *Labor* outlining a perspective that would soon move the railroad unions to the edge of the political mainstream. Progressives were being cast aside as "the forces of reaction" gained "control [of] both the Republican and Democratic parties," and yet those same progressives were "not prepared to embrace socialism." Marginalized and outcast, they were being boxed into "a most uncomfortable position." Ideally, "the

Republican Party would become the conservative party, and the Democratic Party the progressive party," but corporate power had "manipulated things" to prevent this from happening. Thus the need to bring those who were "neither reactionaries nor socialists" into "a party" that would "consistently represent their ideals."[38]

Keating's call for a new political realignment provided the Socialist Party leadership with the opening they needed. Keating spoke for the railroad unions, so his willingness to consider electoral campaigns outside of the two party system appeared to open the way to the formation of a nationwide labor party. In fact, Keating had no interest in forming a genuinely independent third party, although he was willing to support independent candidates in certain restricted circumstances. Furthermore, Keating's editorial had made it crystal clear that he was hostile to the socialist movement. In spite of these fundamental and deep-seated difficulties, the SP responded with enthusiasm to the railroad union initiative.

The railroad unions refused to support the Farmer-Labor Party during the 1920 elections. Still, the election results had reinforced the conservative wings of both mainstream parties, further convincing Keating of the value of a broad progressive coalition that would work within and outside of the two party system. Railroad union leaders saw no choice, and yet most of them fervently supported McAdoo's bid to become the Democratic Party's presidential nominee in 1924. Keating's effort to fashion the alliance of railway unions into an effective pressure group would alter the political landscape. Indeed, the railroad unions constituted a formidable force, with 1.5 million dues-paying members. Although the Socialist Party had remained aloof when Fitzpatrick and the Chicago Federation of Labor attempted to launch a farmer-labor party, this initiative was different in that key union officials at a national level were willing to consider some form of independent politics.

LAUNCHING THE CONFERENCE FOR PROGRESSIVE POLITICAL ACTION

Debs received nearly 1 million votes in 1920, thereby demonstrating that the Socialist Party still retained a significant electoral base. SP leaders were convinced that the Party could act as the catalyst in the formation of a broadly based labor party, thereby replicating the role played by the Independent Labour Party in Britain. In June 1921, Hillquit advanced a resolution at the Party's national convention holding that the restriction of civil liberties and the "securing of substantial measures of relief" could "be accomplished only through the united and concerted action of all progressive, militant and class conscious workers." Accordingly, the National Executive Committee was "instructed to make a careful survey of all radical and labor organizations" to ascertain their willingness "to cooperate with the Socialist movement" in a broadly based electoral coalition. In defending his resolution, Hillquit assessed the recently formed Farmer-Labor Party as "an awful failure." Nevertheless, socialists in the United States were viewed as "something of a joke in the world movement." The necessity for the rapid creation of a strong working-class party made it impossible to continue to "wait for the slow building up of the Party in the old way."[39]

Hillquit's motion passed overwhelmingly, to "thunderous cheers," thereby quashing an alternative motion that would have mandated the NEC "to enforce the provision in the party constitution prohibiting fusion, compromise or trading with any other political party."[40]

At its next meeting, the NEC implemented the convention resolution by issuing a call to more than 100 organizations, inviting them to participate in an initial conference on independent politics. The call insisted that should a "federation or working agreement be reached," the participating organizations, including the SP, would retain "complete independence" within the guidelines set by the coalition.[41]

Although the NEC invitation "met with quite a favorable response," there was also a pervasive belief that the call would prove more compelling if it came from another source. Accordingly, William Johnston, the president of the International Association of Machinists and a leading trade union progressive, informally wrote Hillquit suggesting that "a close and confidential conference" be held at the initiative of the railroad unions, rather than that of the Socialist Party.[42]

Formal invitations were then extended to the same array of organizations that had received the initial proposal from the SP. The railway union alliance proposed to convene "a conference of progressives" with the goal of "cooperation [in order to] bring about political unity." Still, the railway unions insisted that the conference would not "attempt to form a new political party." The conference would convene in Chicago on February 20, 1922.[43]

The railway union proposal was greeted with enthusiasm by the Socialist Party, which proceeded to send a delegation that included Hillquit, along with several other influential members. They were among the 150 delegates invited to attend the founding assembly of the Conference for Progressive Political Action (CPPA). Although many of the delegates represented farmer cooperatives, or farmer-labor parties, the railway unions comprised the dominant presence. Hillquit played a prominent role at the founding conference, where he was elected to the 15-person executive committee. Generally satisfied, Hillquit appraised most of the delegates as union officials of "the sound, solid type."[44]

In general, the sessions proceeded smoothly, but tensions rose when Hillquit proposed that the CPPA consider launching a new third party. His proposal was quickly sidetracked. Edward Keating informally approached Hillquit to question him as to whether the socialist contingent had traveled to Chicago "in the hope of forming an independent political party." Hillquit reassured him that although he believed the Conference had initiated a process that would "ultimately lead to the formation of a labor party," the Socialist Party had "no intention" or desire "to 'capture the conference.'"[45]

A month after its founding conference, the CPPA national committee issued a "call to action" urging the formation of state conferences to bring together "progressive farmers and labor organizations" within an electoral coalition. Nevertheless, "the organization of a new party should await developments." Indeed, in "many states the best result" would "be secured by nominating genuine progressives in the primaries of the dominant parties." Only when such "action within the old parties" proved "futile" should CPPA state affiliates "organize independently."[46]

Although the CPPA's founding conference had left it well within the parameters of the two party system, the SP leadership still held high hopes for the rapid formation of a genuinely independent labor party. Hillquit joined the four other Socialist Party delegates in issuing a joint public statement in which they noted that "the decision of the Conference to continue its work" held "great promise" for a more united organization.[47]

Those within the Socialist Party who sought to further the formation of a labor party understood that such a party could only become a reality if a significant segment of the AFL leadership embraced this position. Johnston, the president of the International Association of Machinists, was the only influential railroad union leader to back the labor party perspective, and he supported the concept as a long-range goal. In April 1922, Johnston, acting as chair of the CPPA, issued a circular in which he held out the hope that the Conference could "ultimately result in the creation of a new party."[48]

For Hillquit and the moderates within the Socialist Party, comments such as Johnston's were enough to reinforce the fervent belief that a labor party was on the horizon. In a letter to Frederic Howe, CPPA secretary and a leading progressive reformer, Hillquit concluded that "the organizations represented" in the Conference would quickly "discard" their current policy of working within the two party system "for straight-out independent political action after some practical experience." Still, Hillquit reassured Howe that he was "not trying to force" his views on the Conference since its members would "learn from experience."[49]

When the Socialist Party convened its national convention in New York City during the last days of April 1922, the question of the CPPA proved to be contentious. Hillquit formulated a constitutional amendment that urged state affiliates of the SP to "cooperate with the organizations of labor and working farmers" in the pursuit of "independent political action." Such efforts at joint electoral activity would only be undertaken with the understanding that the "integrity of organization and official political standing of the Socialist Party" remained "fully preserved."[50]

After a lengthy debate, the Hillquit amendment was adopted, with minor revisions.[51] Yet its implementation would inevitably undercut the integrity of the Party. After all, the railroad union officials who controlled the CPPA affiliates were closely tied to politicians from within the two party system. Thus, engaging in joint electoral campaigns with the CPPA necessarily led the Socialist Party to compromise its principles by blunting its commitment to a truly independent politics.

THE RAILROAD STRIKE OF 1922

As the Socialist Party joined the CPPA, the trade unions that served as its nucleus were dragged into one of the largest and most fiercely fought strikes in U.S. history. Divided and disoriented, the same union officials who flirted with independent political action failed to provide the leadership needed to conduct an effective strike, with disastrous results for hundreds of thousands of railroad workers.

In the immediate aftermath of railroad privatization, tensions soared throughout the industry as the railway lines moved to roll back the victories won by unionized workers during the war. The final trigger to a direct confrontation came in early June 1922, when the Railway Labor Board authorized the lines to institute a 12 percent decrease in the wages of shop workers. The impact of this pay cut was electrifying.[52]

Confronted with a crescendo of demands for militant action, the six shop craft unions polled their members, with 96 percent voting in favor of a strike. On July 1, 1922, the pay cut went into effect, igniting a walkout by the six railroad shop unions, with the support of the AFL's Railway Employees Department. Although the four brotherhoods of skilled operating crafts ordered their members to continue working, the strike held firm. Through the first weeks of the strike, 90 percent of all shop workers were off the job, a total of 400,000 workers. In addition, tens of thousands of workers in other crafts defied their union leaders and refused to act as strikebreakers. The railroad strike of 1922 represented a critical turning point in U.S. labor history. More workers joined the strike than in any previous industrial dispute in U.S. history.[53]

From the start, the strike was fiercely fought. Union officials understood that this was bound to develop into a long, bitter dispute, but they saw no choice, given the anger of the rank and file. They confronted a railroad management divided into two rival camps. Several of the largest railway lines, including the Pennsylvania Railroad, made it abundantly clear that they had no intention of negotiating an agreement with the striking unions. The other lines, led by the Baltimore and Ohio, insisted on devastating concessions before they would even consider a new contract. Strikebreakers were brought into shops under the armed protection of private guards, supplemented by police, state militia and federal troops. While the leaders of the striking unions scrambled for some way out of the impasse, the rank and file fought back, utilizing tactics from mass pickets and sit-downs to the destruction of railroad property. Railroad cars were burned, engines were sabotaged and tracks were ripped up and destroyed. The railroad strike of 1922 quickly snowballed into a pitched battle with no quarter given.[54]

For Gene Debs, the 1922 railroad strike was a bittersweet reminder of the 1894 Pullman strike, when federal troops had crushed a walkout of the American Railway Union, under Debs' leadership. The railroad workers were still divided along craft lines, still unable to unite against the common enemy. Furthermore, the railroad unions had enthusiastically supported World War I, and had endorsed the repressive measures employed by government agencies to silence anti-war dissidents, including Debs and the Socialist Party. In spite of the central role played by the railroad unions within the CPPA, Debs lashed out at the strike leaders.

Debs challenged the rank and file railroad workers to replace the current union leaders with more radical militants committed to industrial unions and independent political action. Railroad union officials had "stood with the Wall Street profiteers in holding for war" just a few years earlier. Furthermore, the striking workers had to "cut loose once and for all from the rotten political parties" of their "masters."[55]

Thus, Debs issued a public denunciation of the railroad union leadership only months after those same officials had initiated the CPPA. Obviously, those within the Socialist Party who advocated a labor party did not share Debs' viewpoint. On the contrary, they remained convinced that the alliance of railroad unions could serve as the organizational basis for a formidable labor-based third party. Although Debs was outspoken in his criticisms of the entire array of railroad unions, the SP official journal, *Socialist World*, ignored the role of the union leadership as it focused on the need to break with the two mainstream parties. With federal district judges issuing local injunctions throughout the country, the need for working-class control of the state had become all too obvious. From this perspective, the railroad strike had dramatically demonstrated that the time was "opportune for independent working class action."[56]

Needless to say, the railroad union leadership remained impervious to Debs' critique. Instead of improvising a militant campaign to win the strike, the union officials who had authorized it were anxious to bring it to a rapid conclusion. Only days after the walkout had begun, union leaders began meeting secretly with key railroad executives. The unions representing the shop workers were willing to order their members back to work at significantly lower wage rates. Thus, in effect, the unions conceded defeat from the start. The sole demand that the unions insisted on maintaining was an agreement that the strikers could return to work with seniority rights intact, thus pushing newly hired strikebreakers to the bottom of the hiring pool.[57]

By the end of July, continuing negotiations had left only one issue unresolved, the unions' insistence that a settlement be implemented on an industry-wide basis. Since the intractable railway lines, such as the Pennsylvania Railroad, rejected any agreement that allowed the strikers to return with their seniority intact, the talks quickly came to a stalemate. Although a few workers drifted back to their jobs, most remained off the job, as the strikers relied increasingly on acts of sabotage to disrupt service.[58]

On September 1, 1922, Attorney General Harry Daugherty, with President Warren Harding's approval, convinced a federal court in Chicago to issue one of the most sweeping injunctions in U.S. history. Railroad union officials throughout the United States were forbidden to discuss or advocate any action that might promote the strike. By then, the strike was winding down, with dozens of more limited, local injunctions having been issued, and with federal troops and state militia having been deployed to execute those injunctions. The Daugherty injunction was not strictly enforced, but it did represent a clear signal that the Harding administration would not pressure the more recalcitrant railway lines into accepting the tentative agreement.[59]

Less than two weeks later, on September 13, 1922, the striking unions reached an overall agreement with several key railway lines, including the Baltimore and Ohio. The agreement established general guidelines within which each line could negotiate its own contract. Strikers would be hired back with seniority, but a bipartite commission was established to screen out those who had "been proven guilty of acts of violence." Over the next weeks, more than 100 railway lines signed contracts in accord with these guidelines, permitting roughly half of the original strikers to return to work with their seniority rights intact.[60]

Nevertheless, the agreements represented a devastating loss to the railroad shop unions. The September 13 settlement left strikers on the hard-line railway lines entirely on their own. Ultimately, 175,000 workers were forced to return to work stripped of their seniority rights, with many of the most militant strikers fired and blacklisted. By 1924, a majority of railroad workers in the non-operating crafts were enrolled in company unions.[61]

The railroad shop workers strike of 1922 had been a total and unmitigated disaster. Debs was outraged at the narrow-minded myopia of the railroad union leadership. He felt certain that the strike could have been won, but "craft unionism with its consequent division and dissension [had] lost the day in ignominious defeat." For Debs, the decision of the skilled crafts of the operating brotherhoods to continue to work during the walkout constituted "the very climax of organized scabbing and strike-breaking."[62]

THE CPPA REJECTS INDEPENDENT POLITICAL ACTION

In spite of the craft divisions that had undermined the shop workers' strike, the alliance of railroad unions remained united in their support of the Plumb Plan, and of the Conference for Progressive Political Action as a means of furthering its implementation. Leaders of the unions representing the operating crafts continued to work closely with William Johnston as chair of the CPPA, while simultaneously ordering their members to cross the picket lines established by the Machinists and the other railroad shop unions.

In accordance with the plan of action adopted at its first conference, the CPPA dispatched organizers to form statewide affiliates around the country. Progress was so rapid that, by the end of 1922, the CPPA had chartered 30 state organizations. These state affiliates endorsed and supported progressive candidates of the two mainstream parties in the 1922 Congressional elections.[63]

The CPPA was pleased with the election results, with liberals defeating conservatives in several key contests. In addition, 15 AFL trade union members were elected, including Victor Berger from Milwaukee. Keating, in an editorial in *Labor*, contended that the 1922 election had "demonstrated" that a strategy based on backing progressive candidates in both parties could "'deliver the goods.'" Keating went on to specifically reject the idea of creating an independent party along the lines of the British Labour Party, arguing, instead, that "the party label counts for nothing. The character of the candidate and the principle he advocates count for everything."[64]

When the second conference of the CPPA convened on December 1922 in Cleveland, the underlying political disagreements remained as acute as ever. The railroad unions still supported McAdoo as the Democratic presidential nominee, and they remained adamantly opposed to any move that might orient the CPPA toward the creation of an independent third party. This left the Socialist Party in a quandary. Its leaders desperately sought to become an integral part of a genuine labor party, one that would command the solid backing of the railroad union leadership. They were thus opposed to any move that might antagonize those officials. Yet the SP wanted the CPPA to enter the electoral arena as an independent force. This was a dilemma without a solution. It reflected the underlying flaws at the core of the labor party perspective.

The December conference adopted a constitution establishing the CPPA as a coalition. Each affiliated national organization received one voting delegate per 10,000 members, with state and local affiliates receiving between one vote and three votes. Since the railroad unions had well over 1 million members, the structure was similar to that of a labor party, in that bloc voting by union officials dominated the proceedings. Yet the CPPA never became a political party, remaining instead a political current operating within the two party system.[65]

The delegates also approved an abbreviated platform, highlighted by the call for the "repeal of the Esch–Cummins railroad law and [the] operation of the railroads for the benefit of the people." When the railroad unions insisted on maintaining the CPPA's support for progressive candidates from within the two mainstream parties, John Fitzpatrick of the Chicago Federation of Labor countered with a resolution calling for an independent presidential campaign in 1924. Fitzpatrick looked to the Left for help in passing this resolution. Although the Socialist Party adhered to the principle of independent political action, it refused to challenge the policy guidelines set by the railroad union leadership. Yet the Communist Party, having followed a circuitous path since its formation, had arrived at virtually the same electoral policy as that adopted by the SP.[66]

THE COMMUNIST PARTY ORIENTS TOWARD A LABOR PARTY

By the autumn of 1919, there were two distinct and competing Communist parties jostling for Moscow's attention. Neither party showed much interest in any form of electoral politics, and both were hostile to the Farmer-Labor Party. Louis Fraina, as the international secretary of one of the factions, sent a report to the Communist International's executive committee dismissing the initial steps then being taken toward a labor party, arguing that such a formation would turn out to be "much more conservative than the British Labour Party."[67] Since Lenin and the Bolsheviks had been excoriating moderate social democrats in the harshest terms, there seemed little reason to doubt that this position would meet with Moscow's approval. American Communists would soon be in for a rude shock.

The Bolsheviks had seized power in November 1917 convinced that the Russian Revolution would inspire similar revolutions in Germany and throughout Europe. By the spring of 1920, the revolutionary upsurge that had followed in the wake of World War I was losing momentum. Lenin concluded that it was essential to develop a new set of policies that would enable the Bolsheviks to retain power in the Soviet Union, while waiting for the revolution to spread to the industrialized nations of Europe and North America. At the time, Britain was still the most powerful nation in the world, and yet the British revolutionary Left was small and fragmented. The situation in the United States looked even less promising.

In April 1920, Lenin signaled a new strategic orientation with his pamphlet *Left-Wing Communism: An Infantile Disorder*. Although he devoted most of this work to castigating certain political tendencies that he viewed as ultra-leftist, Lenin also reviewed the question of the British Labour Party. Most of the groups that were eager to affiliate with the Communist International adamantly rejected any effort to join the Labour Party, although the question remained a controversial one. At this point, Lenin was only prepared to concede that the question of affiliation was "highly complex," although he also stressed "the unique character of the British Labour Party, whose very structure" was "so unlike" that of the European social democratic parties.[68]

Ten weeks later, Lenin came out directly for "affiliation to the Labour Party," but only "given wholly free and independent Communist activities." When the Second Congress of the Communist International (Comintern) convened in July 1920, the new perspective proved to be contentious. Lenin personally led the argument in favor of affiliation, a strong indication of the importance he placed on the issue. Once again he stressed the "highly original type of party" structure that characterized Labour, making it possible for Communists to affiliate as an organization and yet to "freely and openly declare that the party leaders" were "social traitors."[69]

Lenin's argument was spurious at every level. First, relying on the federated structure of the Labour Party was hardly original. Indeed, Robert Hunter had relied on the same argument a decade earlier, but Hunter did so as a proponent of a labor party, and as one of the leading moderates in the Socialist Party of America. Second, the 1918 annual conference had significantly altered the Labour Party's constitution, so that it was no longer structured as a loose coalition of affiliated unions and socialist organizations, but rather it had been transformed into a hybrid organization of affiliates and individual members. Furthermore, the 1918 conference had adopted a distinctive, if nebulous, social democratic ideology, as embodied in Clause 4. Finally, the union officials who dominated the Labour Party would never permit the Communist Party to affiliate as an organization, nor would they tolerate the confrontational opposition that Lenin claimed was possible.

Lenin must have been aware of the actual situation, so his arguments were almost certainly specious. In his speech to the 1920 Comintern Congress, he provided a glimmer of insight into his actual reasoning. Since "progress in Britain" for the revolutionary Left would "perhaps be slower than in other countries," radicals would have to settle for a role as a left-wing tendency within a broadly based labor party, rather than forming an explicitly socialist party.[70]

Moscow also stepped into some of the controversies dividing the U.S. Communist tendencies. With Fraina representing the Communist Party, and John Reed representing the Communist Labor Party, the Comintern ordered the immediate fusion of both organizations into a single, unified party. Although the debate on the floor concerning the question of a labor party was limited to the situation in Britain, this did not extend to two lengthy and informal discussions that Fraina held with Lenin during the Comintern Congress. Lenin made it abundantly clear that he expected Communists in the United States to work toward the formation of a labor party, although he phrased his comments as advice rather than orders. Fraina continued to be wary of the labor party perspective, a point that may well have contributed to the Comintern's decision to dispatch him to Mexico as a secret agent.[71]

In the aftermath of the 1920 Congress, U.S. Communists focused on the Comintern's orders to merge rather than on the question of electoral politics. As the competing organizations melded into one, a bitter dispute developed on the need for an underground party. Once again, Moscow determined the outcome of the dispute, stressing the importance of open, legal work. Yet the merged party still ignored Lenin's advice on the need for a labor party. At the third Comintern congress in the summer of 1921, Lenin met informally with the entire U.S. delegation, chiding them for not backing Debs during the 1920 presidential campaign, and again emphasizing the need for a labor party. This time there could be no doubt as to where Moscow stood on the question.[72]

Still, the CP refrained from sending a delegation to the founding conference of the CPPA in February 1922. In May 1922, the Communist Party finally issued a statement endorsing the goal of a labor party, while questioning whether the current situation made it possible. Until this point, Moscow had limited itself to sending coded telegrams and instructing delegations to its congresses. With links between the Communist International and its U.S. affiliate tenuous and infrequent, the Communist Party was left, by default, with substantial leeway over its own affairs. In July 1922, the Comintern sent a three-person delegation to the United States, and all of this began to change. One of the three, Josef Pogány (John Pepper), would remain in New York until the spring of 1924, becoming the most influential voice in Communist politics.[73]

Pogány, a Hungarian journalist, had been a social democratic activist until World War I. After participating in Bela Kun's short-lived soviet government in 1919, he went into exile in Moscow and became a Comintern official. Pogány was then sent to Germany in 1921 as part of a delegation with orders to create a revolution. The result, the abortive revolt of March 1921, provided the Communist International with one of its most embarrassing moments.[74]

This was hardly an impressive list of accomplishments, but to U.S. Communists Pogány appeared to be the genuine article, a hardened revolutionary with direct contacts to the higher echelons of the Comintern. His orders were clear, the Communist Party was to help in the formation of a broadly based labor party. As Pogány came to terms with the political situation in the United States, he quickly reached the same understanding as that of the Socialist Party leadership: the CPPA provided the only possible vehicle for a labor party, so the CP had to make every effort to work within it.

A high level delegation was therefore dispatched to Chicago for the December 1922 CPPA conference. The Communists' request for affiliation was referred to the credentials committee, where Charles Ruthenberg, the Party's national secretary, declared that there would soon "be a labor party in the United States, a party of the unions," and that the CP would remain within the CPPA "until the time" came "to realize it." When Ruthenberg was informed that the CPPA was "committed to the policy of participation in the primaries of the old parties," he still insisted that the Communists intended to "stay in the Conference for Progressive Political Action."[75]

The CP was not only jettisoning the long-standing opposition of the SP left-wing to the creation of a labor party, it was also significantly diluting a fundamental principle of the entire socialist movement: total opposition to electoral activity within the confines of the two party system. Needless to say, the entire Left understood the irony of this drastic switch. J.B. Salutsky had been a prominent member of the SP left-wing, before joining the Communist Party in the fall of 1921. As a delegate to the December 1922 convention from the Amalgamated Clothing Workers, he was ordered by the CP leadership to raise the question of seating the Communist delegation from the floor. His refusal to do so led to his expulsion.[76]

In his defense, Salutsky pointed out that many of those at the CPPA conference had come through the socialist movement. These former socialists were bound to raise "the embarrassing question as to whether" Salutsky "had helped split the opportunist SP in order to organize another even more opportunist [party]." The decision to support the formation of a labor party, and to seek affiliation with the CPPA, left the Communist Party aligned with "the muddle-headed leadership of the gentlemen who made the SP famous."[77]

Since the railroad union leaders who controlled the CPPA were adamant in their opposition to Communist participation, the CP was denied affiliate status. Indeed, the credentials committee screened out most known Communists as delegates. As a result, Pogány was confronted with a hopeless quandary. Excluded from the conference, the Communist Party gave its moral support to Fitzpatrick's resolution calling upon the CPPA to initiate a new third party. The motion failed by a vote of 62 to 54, with the Machinists' delegation, and the Socialist Party, voting with the majority. Instead, the majority of delegates reiterated the CPPA's commitment to "securing the election of progressive" candidates to Congress and the state legislatures.[78]

For Fitzpatrick, this vote represented the final straw. He had assumed a considerable risk in 1920 in initiating the Farmer-Labor Party, only to see it fizzle. In fact, the Cook County Labor Party was virtually moribund by the fall of 1922, having nominated only three candidates for the state legislature in the November elections. These campaigns would mark the last time that the CFL promoted an independent electoral campaign in the Chicago area. Nevertheless, Fitzpatrick was still not prepared to totally abandon his hopes for a labor party, although he was becoming increasingly restless. In March 1923, he decided to leave the CPPA and to initiate a call for a conference to form a nationwide farmer-labor party in July 1923.[79]

His Communist allies were reluctant to join him, arguing that "if the militant elements would stay in the Conference for Progressive Political Action, they would sweep along ever greater masses against the officials." Pogány understood the thrust of the Comintern's directions. The CP was to aid in the formation of a labor party based on the American Federation of Labor, the official union structure, and yet Fitzpatrick's base remained limited to the CFL and a few local union federations. In spite of the Communist Party's advice, Fitzpatrick moved ahead with the plans for a national conference to be held that

July, and the CP, excluded from the CPPA, decided it had little choice but to join him.[80]

A RADICAL CRITIQUE OF THE LABOR PARTY POSITION

The decision of the CPPA's December 1922 conference to remain within the two party system sparked a heated debate within the Socialist Party as well. William R. Snow, a member of the National Executive Committee and the state secretary for Illinois, presented the left-wing position. Snow pointed out that among "the most severe critics" of the Communist Party for its "efforts to copy the Russian Revolution" in the United States were those who insisted that the SP "must go to the other extreme of modeling" itself after the Independent Labour Party of Britain. Snow was dismayed by the way that "the former extreme radicals" within the CP were "joining with those of the extreme right" of the Socialist Party "in demanding a respectable, middle-of-the-road" labor party, one that would function as yet another "milk-and-water-reform-party."[81]

Snow warned the SP to avoid any effort to become "more respectable" by attempting "to get away from that dreadful word SOCIALISM." Instead of looking toward a labor party, Snow urged the Party to stand firm, for he was "proud of the name Socialist Party, proud of its traditions, and of the enemies" it had made. In any case, it was futile to "try to ape England," since the United States did not possess "the material conditions to build a labor party."

Snow's article built on the tradition of the Party's left-wing. Unfortunately, as Snow fully realized, most of the members of that left-wing had joined the Communist Party, and were therefore lost to a genuinely radical politics. Within the SP, Snow reflected a significant current of opposition, but a distinctly minority one. When the Party's national convention met in New York City in April 1923, the delegates were confronted with two conflicting motions on electoral politics. Labor party proponents recommended that state affiliates be advised to "cooperate" with other CPPA affiliates with "the purpose of forming independent political labor parties in their respective states." The delegates approved the motion, which ignored the fact that the CPPA remained steadfastly within the two party system.[82]

Radicals advanced an alternative resolution urging the Socialist Party to "sever its connections" with the CPPA, and to restore the provisions of the 1920 constitution that had prohibited "all forms of fusion or cooperation with other political parties or organizations." The alternative motion was tabled by the SP convention without debate.[83]

This still left open the question of the Party's attitude to Fitzpatrick's call for a farmer-labor party conference. The convention decided to decline an invitation to attend, viewing the Chicago conference as a threat to the CPPA. An open letter by a designated subcommittee made the political basis for the rejection crystal clear. The formation of a "really powerful" labor party required "the active support of at least a majority of the great trade unions." Thus, "it would be a mistake to force the issue prematurely."[84]

A CONVENTION DISINTEGRATES

As the date for the July 1923 Farmer-Labor Party conference drew near, Fitzpatrick realized that his decision to leave the CPPA had left him isolated. None of the larger unions affiliated with the AFL were willing to send delegates to a conference committed to the creation of a new third party. Fitzpatrick sensed a disaster, and he began retreating. The convention would be limited to the discussion of the potential for third party activity, leaving any definitive decisions to the indefinite future.[85]

Pogány was dismayed. The Communist Party had been vociferous in its denunciations of the CPPA, so there seemed no way back. Yet for Fitzpatrick, a return to the CPPA remained a viable option. The Communist Party leadership opted to press forward with the July conference, and mobilized its members to become authorized delegates from a bewildering variety of front groups. As a result, Fitzpatrick was marginalized and defeated, as the Communists created the Federated Farmer-Labor Party, a shell from the start.[86]

This maneuver proved to be a tactical disaster. By May 1924 Fitzpatrick had dropped any support for independent politics, and had returned to the AFL orthodoxy with its support for the lesser evil.[87] The FFLP was stillborn, serving as yet another CP front group. Within the CP, the decision to take over the July 1923 conference acted as the launching pad for a bitter factional dispute that would divide and demoralize the CP for several years.

William Z. Foster had traveled to the Soviet Union in the summer of 1921 to attend the congress of Communist unions, the Red International of Labor Unions or Profintern. Although he came to Moscow as a sympathetic observer, Foster was so impressed that he secretly joined the Communist Party. By 1923, he had emerged as one of its leading members. Foster had equivocated on Pogány's decision to take over the FLP convention, but he soon turned against this maneuver as it became clear that most progressive trade unionists were so incensed that they would no longer work with Foster on efforts to revitalize the AFL structure. Foster then joined with James P. Cannon, a former IWW activist and CP leader, to form a dissident faction. The Communist Party thus entered the 1924 election campaign as a deeply divided organization, with acrimonious personal disputes intertwined with a serious factional debate.[88]

HILLQUIT DEFENDS THE LABOR PARTY

In spite of the CPPA's reluctance to move beyond the constraints of the two party system, the Socialist Party leadership remained doggedly committed to it as a precursor of a mass labor party. In the aftermath of the 1923 Socialist Party convention, Hillquit presented a theoretical justification for this perspective in two articles that appeared in the Party's press. He began with the provocative claim that "the recent development of the British Labour Party" was "a more thoroughgoing revolution than the Bolshevik coup d'état in 1917." Furthermore, the Labour Party, "starting on conservative lines" had "gradually evolved to a clear understanding and unreserved acceptance of the Socialist program." As proof of this acceptance of a socialist perspective, Hillquit referred to the nebulous formulation in Clause 4 of the revised Labour Party constitution.[89]

The question was not one of purely theoretical interest. Indeed, Hillquit maintained that no one could "read the history of the early phases of the British Labour movement without being struck with their similarity to the modern American movement." Thus, "with the example and ready methods of England" as a guidepost, a coalition of unions, progressives and socialists could proceed to "form a powerful Labor Party in this country today."[90] Hillquit's assessment of the British Labour Party was far too favorable. This is painfully clear with the hindsight of the twenty-first century, and the sordid political opportunism of Tony Blair, but it should have been obvious even in 1923. After all, the Labour Party had zealously supported the war as a junior partner within Lloyd George's war cabinet.

Yet more fundamental was the complete misunderstanding of the U.S. political context. The British experience could not be slavishly emulated in the United States, a point made by Snow a few months earlier. Hillquit responded by reverting to a mechanical economic determinism. The course of the U.S. working class was "being determined by the same forces" that had pressured the British trade unions into abandoning the Liberals and forming the Labour Party.[91] This was exactly the kind of shallow, fatalistic, and unconvincing argument that so discredited the "orthodox" Marxism of the Second International.

LOOKING TO 1924

As the summer of 1923 drew to a close, the prospects for an independent campaign in 1924 seemed dim indeed. Fitzpatrick's Farmer-Labor Party had disintegrated, with the residual shell taken over by the Communist Party. Furthermore, there seemed little reason to believe that the Conference for Progressive Political Action would ever be more than an organizational framework for those interested in working for progressives within the two party system. Although the Socialist Party leadership remained convinced that the CPPA would soon be transformed into an independent labor party, the union officials who dominated it held firm to their commitment to the Democratic Party, and to their hopes for William McAdoo as its 1924 presidential candidate.

At this critical juncture, the most explosive scandal in U.S. history burst into view, temporarily shifting the fixed parameters of mainstream politics. The CPPA was pushed into support for the independent presidential campaign of Robert La Follette, as hopes for a permanent labor party seemed to be coming to fruition. The 1924 campaign would put to the test the political strategies that had been evolving during the crisis-filled years following the end of World War I.

5
The Octogenarian Snail:
The La Follette Campaign of 1924

The 1924 independent presidential campaign of Senator Robert La Follette marked the zenith of progressive third party politics in the United States. La Follette received 16 percent of the total vote, while carrying his home state of Wisconsin. Although his base of support came from Midwestern small farmers, his campaign depended on the support of the Conference for Progressive Political Action, which had been initiated by an alliance of railroad unions. Indeed, Samuel Gompers and the American Federation of Labor even endorsed La Follette.

Thus the 1924 campaign represents a critical test of the labor party perspective. Although La Follette attacked the two major parties for their subservient dependence on corporate interests, he never definitively broke with the two party system. Throughout the campaign, he urged his supporters to vote for progressive candidates from both mainstream parties. Under pressure from the AFL leadership, La Follette even acted behind the scenes to stifle the Socialist Party from putting forward its own candidates.

In spite of these fundamental underlying problems, the SP gave its enthusiastic and uncritical support to the La Follette campaign. Party leaders were certain that the campaign would provide the springboard for a nationwide labor party. Yet these hopes soon proved to be illusory. Gompers returned to the tenets of lesser evil politics as the ballots were being counted, and the railroad unions were not far behind.

Left-wing dissidents within the Socialist Party resisted the drive to the third party politics of the La Follette campaign, but they were only able to rally a small minority of members to their views. Gene Debs, who had always been allied with the radical opposition, saw the SP as fragile and demoralized. Unwilling to confront the Party's leaders, he went along with the majority in supporting La Follette, although he did so with an obvious lack of enthusiasm. Afterward, when the unions had retreated back to the Democratic Party and the SP had left the third party coalition, Debs publicly aired his misgivings.

He remained convinced that the socialist movement could only move forward through the building of a vital democratic socialist party.

PARALLEL CONVENTIONS

Throughout 1923, the potential for independent political action remained uncertain. Railroad union leaders not only maintained their loyalty to the two party system, they continued to avidly support McAdoo as the Democratic candidate in 1924. Indeed, McAdoo was widely perceived as the likely nominee, with Al Smith, the governor of New York, a distant long-shot. Thus, the CPPA continued to delay a decision on the 1924 presidential campaign.[1]

As a result, the initiative for the creation of an electoral vehicle for an independent La Follette campaign passed to the Minnesota Farmer-Labor Party, which had been formed as an offshoot of the National Nonpartisan League (NPL). From 1915 to 1922, the League burgeoned into a mass movement, shaking the political structure of the northern plains state, and then rapidly disintegrated. The NPL began as a split from the Socialist Party of North Dakota, where a significant number of poor farmers had been won over to the socialist cause. One of those farmers, Arthur Townley, left the Party in 1915, convinced that only a more broadly based electoral formation could gain the support needed to begin implementing important social reforms. The North Dakota SP had been on the Party's right-wing, emphasizing a platform with planks such as state ownership of the grain elevators. Townley took over this program, but he stripped it of any connection to a vision of a socialist future. Furthermore, he decided to work within the constraints of the two party system, backing only those candidates pledged to the implementation of the League's program.[2]

The NPL grew exponentially, and it was soon spreading into Minnesota, a state with a large population of farmers, as well as a militant trade union movement centered in the Twin Cities of Minneapolis and St. Paul. In 1918, the NPL presented a slate of candidates in the Republican Party, and lost. A quickly formed coalition of NPL clubs and trade union activists nominated a list of independent candidates as a progressive alternative. The list did well, although none of its nominees were elected. Townley then blocked a similar coalition effort in 1920.[3]

By the fall of 1922, the National Nonpartisan League was in disarray, making it easy to revive the Minnesota coalition. This time it would come together as a permanent alliance. A year later, the Minnesota

Farmer-Labor Party was formally launched, evolving into a hybrid organizational structure. Farmer-labor clubs from around the state could send delegates to the statewide conference, but trade unions could also affiliate their entire membership on an organizational basis. Although union delegates dominated decision-making bodies in the Twin Cities, the rurally based membership clubs tended to hold a majority of the votes at the statewide level.[4]

From the start, the Minnesota party was an electoral success. The Republican Party dominated Minnesota politics, with the Democrats a marginalized minority. Drawing progressives from both mainstream parties, the party quickly established itself as the main electoral alternative to Republican conservative policies. In Minnesota, voters interested in a third party did not confront the usual dilemma. No one could feel that their vote was "wasted," or that they were dividing the liberal constituency, by backing an FLP candidate.[5]

In North Dakota, the NPL emerged directly from the Socialist Party, and "the overwhelming majority" of its organizers were former socialists. This held true in Minnesota as well. Henry Teigen had been state secretary of the North Dakota SP before becoming the NPL secretary. After moving to Minneapolis to staff the League's national office, Teigen was drawn into Minnesota politics, coordinating the Farmer-Labor clubs around the state. In contrast to Townley, Teigen still believed in third party politics. No longer a socialist, he still hoped the Minnesota Farmer-Labor Party could spark the formation of a nationwide progressive party.[6]

Teigen worked closely with William Mahoney, another former SP member. Mahoney was a typographer and a local union leader. After leaving the Party in World War I, he began looking to the possibilities for a progressive third party. Mahoney acted as the primary link between the FLP and the Minneapolis-area trade unions.[7] He and Teigen provided much of the direction for the new party.

In the summer of 1923, Mahoney and Teigen convinced the Minnesota FLP to host a nationwide meeting of progressive and socialist activists, with the aim of providing La Follette with the organizational basis for a presidential campaign. The conference was scheduled for St. Paul that November. In publicizing the conference, Mahoney sent Eugene Debs a circular promoting it. Eighteen months after his release from prison, Debs remained in frail health, having been incarcerated for two and a half years, from April 1919 to Christmas Day, 1921, for resisting the war effort. While in jail, Debs had avoided any discussion of the Party's decision at its 1921 convention to explore the possibilities for a labor party.

After his release, Debs spent much of his time in a sanitarium, in a futile effort to recover from the liver and heart ailments that had brought him to a state of "utter exhaustion." He was reluctant to return to the tensions of ideological disputes, and, indeed, he had warned Otto Branstetter, SP national secretary, that his physical and emotional problems made it impossible for him to enter the "factional dogfight" that had erupted between the Socialist Party and the Communist Party.[8]

By the fall of 1923, Debs' morale had improved, but his health remained precarious. Understandably, Debs was hesitant to enter the debate on the labor party, especially since he viewed the Party as weak and divided. Nevertheless, his response to Mahoney was decidedly tepid. Although he was in "principle favorable to the proposed coalition" that would soon convene in St. Paul, he was also convinced that this was not "a favorable time for the Socialist Party" to participate in such a coalition. After all, the SP had been "practically wiped out in most of the states during and since the war," so the immediate task was "the reconstruction of the Socialist Party."[9]

Although Debs was not prepared to challenge the underlying assumptions of the labor party perspective, he was still willing to argue that, at least for the foreseeable future, the Party should be spending its time advocating socialism, and not the progressive reforms of a farmer-labor party. Of course, both Debs and Mahoney knew that Debs had opposed the creation of a labor party when the SP was far larger, during its heyday. Thus, Debs' explanation for rejecting SP participation at the St. Paul convention could only be understood as a polite rejection.

On November 15, 1923, 150 progressives and socialists met to discuss the potential for independent politics in 1924. The conference issued a call for a nominating convention to be held in St. Paul the following summer for the purpose of nominating an independent presidential ticket.[10] Of course, without La Follette's agreement to stand as an independent candidate, the conference was bound to founder.

The November conference jolted the CPPA out of its somnolent complacency. William Johnston, its chair, issued a call for a third conference, to be held the following February.[11] Although the call left the question of the 1924 campaign unresolved, most railroad union leaders were still hoping that McAdoo would be selected as the Democratic presidential nominee. Tea Pot Dome would transform the political landscape.

A Senate investigating committee, initially proposed by La Follette, had been probing the sale of oil leases on government land, with the trail pointing to high officials in the Coolidge administration. Interior Secretary Albert Fall had accepted sizable bribes from oil interests in return for releasing petroleum holdings previously withdrawn from production for a naval reserve. One of these reserves was at Tea Pot Dome in Wyoming, while the other was located in the Elk Hills range in California. Word began circulating that Edward Doheny, an oil baron and a leading Democratic Party contributor, had hired key officials from the Wilson administration to facilitate the lease transfer at Elk Hills. On February 1, 1924, Doheny testified that he had retained McAdoo as an attorney since 1919, soon after he left government office. Doheny mentioned a figure of $50,000 a year, while McAdoo insisted it was only $25,000. Although there was no evidence that McAdoo had directly participated in the illicit payoffs to Fall, and McAdoo insisted that he had been hired to defend Doheny's oil interests in Mexico, his reputation had been destroyed.[12]

As the Tea Pot Dome scandal rocked the nation, railroad union leaders were left stranded. They had been counting on McAdoo as the Democratic presidential nominee, but his candidacy had been reduced to shambles. Edward Keating advised McAdoo to withdraw, but he pressed ahead nevertheless. Tea Pot Dome created the space for a La Follette campaign, a fact that Hillquit fully understood.[13]

Thus, on February 11, 1924, when the CPPA convened in St. Louis, the political climate had undergone a seismic shift. This time the meeting went smoothly, with the 200 delegates approving a call for a nominating convention to select an independent presidential ticket. The convention was scheduled for Cleveland on July 4, two weeks after the Democratic convention opened, by which time it was expected that La Follette would be prepared to announce his intention of standing as an independent candidate for president. The CPPA had set the stage for two parallel conventions, both of them designed to become the organizational starting point for an independent presidential campaign.[14]

LA FOLLETTE PREPARES TO RUN

An editorial by Keating in *Labor* succinctly summarized the situation in the spring of 1924. Should "both the old parties select reactionaries," the CPPA would "name Robert M. La Follette" as its presidential nominee at the July 4 convention, assuming "the great Wisconsin Senator" would "consent to run."[15] This made it clear that the railroad unions were not breaking with the two party system, but rather they were prepared to support an independent campaign as a means of demonstrating their disenchantment with the conservative drift of the Democratic Party, and as a means of pressing the Democrats to nominate more liberal candidates in the future. The analogy to Ralph Nader's campaign in 2000 is striking.

In the same editorial, Keating declared that progressives could "not afford to be partisan" when it came "to electing Senators and representatives." Those Congressional incumbents who could be "relied on to defend the people's interests should be supported without regard to their party labels." Thus, Keating explicitly stated that the railroad unions would remain within the framework of the two party system, even if they felt constrained to back La Follette for president. Keating went further, holding that it was "extremely important that the Progressives in each Congressional district should get behind one candidate. Nothing should be permitted to divide the Progressive vote."[16] This point would come back to haunt the Socialist Party during the 1924 campaign.

Keating functioned as the chief political advisor to the railroad unions. His editorial made it apparent that the railroad unions rejected the underlying postulates of independent political action. Nevertheless, the SP continued to ally itself with the CPPA, and the Party's leadership continued to delude itself into believing that an independent labor party would soon be formed.

With Tea Pot Dome dominating the headlines, an independent presidential campaign appeared increasingly likely. Still, La Follette remained elusive, unwilling to commit himself as a candidate. Although La Follette was edging toward a decision, he had no intention of initiating a presidential campaign on a purely educational basis. Before making a final decision, he wanted a significant indication that he could organize a credible, nationwide campaign. This could only happen with the endorsement, and the resources, of AFL unions. He therefore met with key union leaders, who pledged to publicly support him and to provide him with three million dollars in union funds.[17] Of course, all of this was contingent on McAdoo not receiving the Democratic nomination.

As La Follette edged toward an independent presidential campaign, the Socialist Party enthusiastically pledged its support. Norman

Thomas, who would become the Party's candidate for governor of New York, wrote an opinion piece for the *New York Times*, confirming that the SP stood "ready to endorse third party candidates." While conceding that the railroad unions were prepared to back La Follette only "as the very last resort," he insisted that "the elements of a constructive revolt are nearer coalescing" than ever before.[18]

Thomas' views represented those of the Socialist Party leadership. As the Party's revered spokesperson, and perennial presidential candidate, Debs came under growing pressure to swing behind a La Follette campaign. In an article appearing two months prior to the July 4th convention, Debs voiced his doubts, without totally rejecting the process. He stood "heartily in favor" of joining in a broader alliance, but only if the convention determined "that there must be a complete and final break" with "the two old capitalist parties," and that the 1924 campaign would be conducted on the basis "that the working class must strike out boldly for independent political action, along the lines of its class interests." Should the CPPA convention "fail to take such advanced grounds," Debs was "opposed to unity or cooperation," insisting that the SP instead opt for "nominating its own candidates" as it had "done in all previous years."[19]

As the convention date approached, and it became clearer that La Follette would stand as an independent candidate, and that the Socialist Party moderate leaders would enthusiastically endorse him, Debs muted his misgivings. In an article appearing in June 1924, immediately prior to the CPPA convention, Debs accepted the labor party perspective. He "earnestly" awaited the formation of a "united labor party," after which the SP would "be in a position to carry forward" its "educational work," acting in the same role as the Independent Labour Party had "in developing and building up the British Labour Party."[20]

This was the essence of the labor party perspective, and yet Debs proceeded to add provisos that reflected his underlying doubts. Even should a labor party emerge out of the CPPA, it would be essential "to preserve strictly the identity and guard rigidly the integrity of the Socialist Party as the uncompromising revolutionary political organization" of the working class. Debs also placed the discussion of the labor party in the context of the dire condition of the Party and the urgent need for unity. The SP had been "sadly crippled" by government repression, and the Communist split, and yet "the loyalty of the remaining members" had "not been impaired."[21]

GOMPERS BLASTS COMMUNIST PARTICIPATION

Torn by conflicting pressures, Debs found himself stuck in a painful and awkward situation. He was not the only one. William Mahoney and Henry Teigen, the Minnesota Farmer-Labor Party leaders responsible for organizing the St. Paul convention, were anxious to work closely with the CPPA, and yet the convention soon developed a life of its own. The Communist Party had been invited to St. Paul, and it had accepted with enthusiasm. Communists were actively involved in organizing the June convention. Yet the FLP leadership was eager to smooth over the differences with the CPPA, and the CPPA was adamant in excluding any Communist participation in the 1924 campaign.[22]

Well before the CPPA had initiated its own call for a conference for July 4, Mahoney was hoping to mollify the CPPA. In January 1924, he assured Hillquit that Communist sympathizers would be swamped by the turnout of progressives, and that it was "quite probable" that a coalition of progressives and socialists could "altogether eliminate" the Communists from the upcoming convention. Three months later, Mahoney assured Johnston that the Communists were "few in numbers, but very noisy and active." On balance, they were "of minor importance" and could be kept "busy doing practical work." Needless to say, these reassurances did not mollify the railroad union leaders or the CPPA, which proceeded with its own convention plans.[23]

The situation became even more volatile when Gompers made it clear that he would publicly denounce any third party effort that tolerated the presence of the Communist Party. As a growing number of local unions opted to send delegates to the St. Paul conference, Gompers decided to forcefully intervene. In the latter part of May, he convened a large, informal meeting of leading Congressional progressives and top union officials, including William Johnston. Gompers insisted that the St. Paul conference represented "nothing more nor less" than a ruse to enable the Communist Party "to capture the entire effort of labor, farmers and progressives."[24]

Gompers then informed the group that he would soon be issuing a public statement to union members "advising them of the trap" that had "been laid for them." He promised that he would briefly postpone the release of this statement to allow La Follette "the opportunity to disentangle himself" from the Communist Party and the Farmer-Labor Party conference. This was a very real threat, since La Follette was counting on the AFL for resources and visible support.

Gompers followed up this meeting by dispatching AFL secretary Frank Morrison to La Follette with a similar message.[25]

Gompers was not alone in his intense distrust of the Communist Party. The railroad union leaders who had initiated the CPPA had been clear from the start that Communist participation would not be tolerated. In the middle of May, La Follette's closest advisor, Gilbert Roe, had urged him to write an open letter to Herman Ekern, the attorney general of Wisconsin and a close ally, denouncing Communist participation in the FLP. La Follette was staying in Atlantic City at the time, recuperating from a bout of pneumonia. He was reluctant to undertake this maneuver, holding that such a statement should "come from the labor leaders themselves, or others interested in the progressive movement." Still, La Follette agreed to meet with Johnston and the CPPA leadership to discuss the issue. La Follette was coming under intense pressure from union officials to openly disassociate himself from the Communist Party.[26]

THE COMMUNISTS FLIP-FLOP

As La Follette pondered his options, political divisions within the leadership circles of the Soviet Union were undermining the basis for a Communist presence in the third party campaign of 1924. Both of the major caucuses within the CP rallied behind the effort to build the FLP conference. Yet the disagreements remained, and with them the personal bitterness. Josef Pogány, the Comintern representative unofficially guiding one of the factions, understood that La Follette could hardly be termed a labor party candidate, and yet he would certainly be chosen as the nominee of the June conference. Pogány and his supporters, including Charles Ruthenberg, resolved this contradiction by insisting that the Communists did not support La Follette, and would not vote for him at the conference. At the same time, the CP would not seek to block his nomination. Once La Follette was nominated, the CP would support the ticket, with criticisms.

Ruthenberg developed this tortured argument in the *Daily Worker* in April 1924. La Follette had gained the fervent support of "masses of farmers and workers," as well as a significant sector of the middle class. The CP recognized this fact, and was "endeavoring to fit its policies so as to meet the situation." Nevertheless, the Communist Party was not and could "not be for La Follette," since, should he be elected, he would "serve capitalism," rather than the "workers and the exploited farmers." Even so, the CP would "unquestionably support" La Follette once nominated by the FLP, as would "the masses of workers and farmers."[27]

The other CP faction, the Foster–Cannon caucus, rejected these Machiavellian maneuvers, and argued that the CP instead should simply endorse La Follette and work for the FLP ticket. There can be no doubt that Pogány's stratagem would have accomplished little, while irritating everyone. Yet Pogány was not primarily concerned with the Minnesota FLP, just as a few months earlier he had not been particularly concerned about the Chicago Federation of Labor. Pogány realized that Moscow would be reviewing U.S. developments in the light of factional disputes that were raging within the Soviet Union, and he hoped to be able to cover his flanks.

Deeply divided on the tactics to be followed at the June conference, the CP once again took its problems to Moscow. In the spring of 1924, Pogány and William Z. Foster traveled to the Soviet Union to attend the Fifth Congress of the Communist International to be held in June. Initially, the Comintern reinforced the decision to work within the Farmer-Labor Party, without determining the exact tactics. It hailed the June conference as of "momentous importance," urging the Communist Party to "utilize every available force" to aid the St. Paul conference in becoming a "great representative gathering [of] labor and left-wing."[28] This verdict, rather than settling the question, sparked a volatile debate, as the question of La Follette and the labor party quickly emerged as a political football at the apex of the Soviet hierarchy.

When Lenin died in January 1924, no one doubted Leon Trotsky's ability to succeed him. Nevertheless, he soon found himself on the outside, marginalized and on the defensive. Abrasive, arrogant, and a Jew by ethnic background, Trotsky had joined the Bolshevik Party in August 1917, only a few weeks before the revolution. Dislike and distrust of this charismatic figure proved to be enough motivation to bring together a loose coalition that included most of the other influential Bolshevik leaders. Trotsky knew that he was being pushed aside, and he responded with a withering attack on the new Soviet leadership. Central to this critique was the belief that the regime was opening the door to a capitalist restoration by encouraging the richer peasants to accumulate wealth.[29]

Communists in the United States understood very little of what was taking place in the Kremlin, and most of them sought to avoid being caught in the crossfire. Pogány was the sole exception. An experienced Comintern functionary, he understood that Trotsky was becoming isolated within the Soviet elite. Pogány sought to avoid being caught in this factional warfare, while utilizing his connections to win a favorable decision from the Comintern. He began circulating his views of U.S. political developments among top Soviet officials, including Trotsky. In doing so, he walked into a hornets' nest.[30]

Trotsky was appalled by Pogány's views. It appeared to him to represent yet another instance of an unwarranted blurring of class lines. Working-class independent politics were being submerged into a loosely defined farmer-labor party that cut across class lines. On May 20, 1924, Trotsky circulated a position paper within the Politburo, the most powerful decision-making body in the Soviet Union, attacking the decision to work within the progressive coalition as "monstrous opportunism." To support La Follette, even critically as the Pogány–Ruthenberg faction proposed, was "to head toward the dissolution of the [Communist] Party in[to] the petit bourgeoisie." Furthermore, La Follette presented "quite a hopeless figure," a politician who had "not yet found the time to leave the Republican Party."[31]

Trotsky's critique sparked a bombshell. When the issue was presented to the Politburo, Trotsky's rivals hesitated, unsure of how to proceed, until Lev Kamenev, a close ally of Lenin's before the revolution, moved to accept Trotsky's position. With the Politburo agreed, the decision of the Comintern executive committee was a foregone conclusion. A telegram was promptly dispatched to New York, ordering a "sharp campaign" against La Follette. Furthermore, Communist delegates were told to insist that La Follette would have to agree to cede "control [over] campaign funds" as a prerequisite to becoming the nominee of the St. Paul conference. Foster was ordered to return immediately to the United States with a detailed set of instructions on implementing the newly determined line.[32]

A CONVENTION DISINTEGRATES

With the Communist Party leadership in New York awaiting Foster's return, and a clear delineation of Moscow's new line, La Follette moved to publicly assail the Communist Party. Acting in accord with Roe's advice, La Follette wrote an open letter to Herman Ekern clarifying his views on the Communist role in his campaign. The letter was released to the press on May 28, with dramatic effect.[33]

La Follette denounced the Communists as "the mortal enemies of the progressive movement." Indeed, their presence provided a cloak for "reactionary interests" to "plant their spies and provocatory agents." On the same day this letter was released to the press, Gompers issued a public statement urging union locals to boycott the St. Paul convention, since the Communist Party would be in "control [of] the machinery." Gompers insisted that Communists sought "first of all to destroy opportunities for genuine progressive action," so that "reaction and radicalism [could then] hold the stage."[34]

Communist leaders, almost certainly in receipt of the Comintern telegram, took the opportunity presented by La Follette's public letter to implement the new position. Accordingly, the CP's executive committee released a statement attacking La Follette as "the enemy of the Farmer-Labor movement." When Foster returned from Moscow on June 1, he immediately presented the CP's top leaders with a detailed report on the proposed campaign against La Follette. Both of the competing factions readily accepted the new directives from Moscow.[35]

La Follette's letter destroyed the St. Paul convention as a credible framework for the 1924 presidential campaign. Mahoney and the Minnesota Farmer-Labor Party leaders were left in an impossible situation. The June 17 convention went forward, with a much smaller participation than expected, and with many of the delegates in attendance either Communist Party members or sympathizers. La Follette had not yet declared his candidacy, so Mahoney proposed that the convention nominate a token slate of national candidates, who would withdraw once the Wisconsin Senator officially declared. Foster, speaking for the CP, agreed, but he also made it clear that the Communists would only accept La Follette if he were prepared to run as a candidate of the Farmer-Labor Party, accept its control over campaign funds and stand on its platform. Since La Follette had publicly declared his unwillingness to be associated with a coalition in which the CP held a prominent position, this was pure posturing.[36]

Nevertheless, the convention proceeded to nominate a ticket headed by Duncan McDonald, a former SP member and an activist in the United Mine Workers. As soon as La Follette formally announced, the Minnesota Farmer-Labor Party enthusiastically endorsed him, leaving the national farmer-labor organization a shell. The national committee of the FLP, with a Communist majority, then withdrew its own presidential slate and endorsed the Communist ticket of Foster and Benjamin Gitlow.[37]

The St. Paul convention had been a complete fiasco, but then it was bound to be given the La Follette letter. Still, the sectarian posturing of the Communist Party had made a bad situation even worse. Mahoney was furious, and he would remain a committed opponent of Communist participation in the Minnesota Farmer-Labor Party. A decade later, when the CP was once again fervently advocating the creation of a nationwide labor party, Mahoney's enmity would prove costly.[38]

THE CPPA CONFERENCE

With the FLP convention doomed to failure, the focus of attention shifted to the CPPA convention to be held on July 4. In the weeks leading up to this convention, La Follette and his closest advisors developed the underlying guidelines for the campaign. Roe proposed that La Follette declare himself as an independent candidate standing on his "own platform, and let the action of the convention take the form of an endorsement rather than a nomination." Thus, the candidate would be ensured of total control of the platform, so that if the convention sought to amend or revise it, La Follette "would not be responsible" for the changes. La Follette would proceed to act in accordance with these recommendations.[39]

La Follette's presidential hopes soared when the Democratic Party convention held in New York a week after the disastrous FLP convention quickly descended into a shambles. The convention rules required a two-thirds majority to gain the presidential nomination. Discredited by Tea Pot Dome, McAdoo could not gain enough votes to carry the convention, while his leading opponent, Al Smith, could not overcome the hostility aroused by his support for the repeal of Prohibition. The convention deadlocked for two and a half weeks of endless roll calls. Even as the CPPA convention prepared to assemble in Cleveland, a significant section of the railroad union leadership remained in New York in a futile effort to round up delegates for McAdoo. A few days after the CPPA convention had concluded, the Democrats finally nominated John W. Davis, a Wall Street corporate lawyer.[40]

Everything had now fallen into place for a La Follette campaign. On July 2, the national committee of the CPPA met to make sure the convention proceeded without discord. La Follette had already made it clear that he would only campaign as an independent candidate, and not as the nominee of an independent party. This accorded with the views of the railroad union leaders, as well as those of Gompers and the AFL leadership, all of whom remained tied to sections of the Democratic Party. Only Hillquit argued for the immediate formation of a new party. Instead, the CPPA national committee sent an open letter to La Follette urging him to campaign as an independent candidate.[41]

The following day, Robert La Follette Jr. addressed the opening session of the CPPA convention, and delivered his father's acceptance speech, which would set the basis for the campaign. Tea Pot Dome and the pervasive corruption of the Harding administration had established incontrovertibly that "both party organizations" had "fallen under the domination and control of corrupt wealth." It was therefore essential for progressives to break with the two party system. Only in this way would it be possible to overcome the "private monopoly system," which could not have consolidated its wealth and power if "either the Democratic or the Republican parties [had] faithfully and honestly enforced the law."[42] (Senator La Follette was a staunch believer in the efficacy of anti-trust laws.)

La Follette proclaimed the need "for an honest realignment in American politics," through the formation of a new party "in which all Progressives may unite." Nevertheless, he adamantly opposed the immediate creation of a third party, since there was "not sufficient time before the elections in November for the adequate organization of such a party." This was a flimsy excuse, particularly since La Follette had held back for months before finally declaring his candidacy, waiting to observe developments in the two mainstream parties before making a final decision.[43]

La Follette sought to reconcile these conflicting positions by pledging his support for the formation of a third party in the near future. He was confident that the November election results would be so encouraging that they would "ensure the creation of a new party."[44] La Follette was interested in the potential for a new third party, but only if and when several stringent conditions had been met. Furthermore, the third party he proposed to form would not have been genuinely independent, but rather would have continued to endorse progressive politicians from within the two party system. This was a very tepid version of independent politics, and yet it was more than enough to satisfy the leadership of the Socialist Party, which uncritically and enthusiastically supported the La Follette campaign.

La Follette also insisted that he was "unwilling to participate in any political campaign at this time" that might "diminish the number of true Progressives" in Congress or in state legislatures. He admonished the CPPA that he would only campaign for president if it did not contribute to the defeat of Congressional progressives, a "defeat that would inevitably result from the placing of complete third party tickets in the field."[45]

As the campaign evolved, it emerged that La Follette would not only endorse progressive candidates within the two party system, but he would also actively discourage independent candidates in districts in which the election was closely contested. La Follette's acceptance speech made it crystal clear that the Wisconsin senator hoped to initiate an electoral formation that would function as a pressure group on the two mainstream parties, rather than acting as a genuinely independent party.

Socialist Party delegates to the Cleveland CPPA nominating convention found that key decisions had been made before the convention even opened. Along with many other rank and file delegates, socialists hoped to see the convention formalize the creation of an independent party, only to discover that the national committee had worked out an arrangement with La Follette to permit him to run his own independent campaign. Still, there remained one controversial issue that had been left unresolved, the choice of a vice-presidential candidate. A range of possible candidates had been mentioned, including Supreme Court Justice Louis Brandeis, several railroad union leaders, and an assortment of Congressional progressives.[46]

Frustrated in their desire to move the CPPA to a clear break with the two party system, the SP caucus at the convention discussed a proposal to bring to the floor a motion calling for the selection of a vice-presidential candidate by the convention. A motion along these lines might well have been approved, but the Party's leadership, most probably Hillquit, "argued that it might cause irritation." In other words, the SP's labor party advocates were so anxious to remain a subordinate component of the La Follette coalition that they were completely unwilling to publicly challenge the personal authority of the candidate, in fear of antagonizing the alliance of railroad union leaders. Interestingly enough, the proposal to call for a democratic process to select a vice-presidential candidate originated with Jacob Panken, a New York City municipal judge and a labor party advocate.[47]

With the SP throttled and the La Follette forces and the railroad unions working in close harmony, the convention moved rapidly, with little dissent. The platform adopted by the convention came unchanged from a draft submitted by La Follette. The Organizing Committee of the convention brought a resolution to the floor endorsing La Follette and instructing the national committee to make the final selection of a vice-presidential candidate in consultation with the La Follette campaign committee. After a boisterous celebration, the resolution was passed by acclamation.[48]

The Organizing Committee also submitted a resolution, which was overwhelmingly approved by the delegates, calling for the holding of another convention within three months of the November elections. The primary purpose of this convention would be "to consider and pass upon the question of forming a permanent independent political party for national and local elections."[49] Given the record of the CPPA, and of La Follette, the "independence" of such a formation would have been highly questionable, but the resolution did seem to set the groundwork for the possible formation of a new third party.

The scheduling of another convention, as well as La Follette's contingent support for a new party, were enough to sway the SP leadership. Hillquit would later write that the Party had participated in the La Follette campaign because the promised convention "could not possibly fail to launch" an independent party on a "permanent basis."[50] This was wishful thinking at its worst.

THE SOCIALIST PARTY ENDORSES LA FOLLETTE

Once the CPPA convention concluded, the Socialist Party held its own convention in the city. The convention was marked by heated debates over the La Follette campaign, with two distinct tendencies presenting sharply diverging positions. A 15-member committee was formed to report back to the convention on relations with the CPPA. The majority report began by praising the Conference's recent convention as "the most significant gathering of American labor for common political action" in U.S. history. The CPPA had taken "an important step" toward cutting "loose from the old political parties." By actively participating in the La Follette campaign, the SP would further "facilitate the formation of a genuine labor party" at the next CPPA convention. The majority report endorsed La Follette, and urged the convention to delegate the decision as to a vice-presidential candidate to the national committee, which would consider the matter after La Follette and the CPPA had made their decision.[51]

The minority report, which William R. Snow introduced to the convention, started from a radically different approach to independent politics. It pointed out that the recent CPPA convention had "failed to launch an independent Party of Labor, or even an independent third party." Instead, it had endorsed a campaign built "around the personality of one man, and that man was a life-long Republican." In addition, the campaign's platform was "vague and indefinite," and "so meaningless that it might have been written by W[illiam] J[ennings] Bryan thirty years ago."[52]

The minority urged the SP to reject the CPPA's decision to support La Follette, and its "hazy, indefinite promise that seven months from now a labor party may be formed." Instead, the Socialist Party should nominate its own national ticket, and it should proceed to launch its own campaign based on a socialist platform that formulated "distinctly the fundamental problems that confront modern society."[53]

The decision to undertake a socialist presidential campaign in 1924 would have been a difficult one, given the popular enthusiasm for La Follette. Nevertheless, it was a principled position, one to which the SP should have adhered. The minority's position correctly analysed the weaknesses in the La Follette campaign. By lining up behind La Follette, the Party was compromising its commitment to independent politics, while diluting its vision of a socialist transformation of society.

The Socialist Party convention proceeded to approve the majority report by a vote of 113 to 19. A few days later, La Follette chose Senator Burton Wheeler, a Montana Democrat, as his running mate. Wheeler had no intention of severing his ties to the Democratic Party, and indeed he returned to mainstream politics at the conclusion of the 1924 campaign. The CPPA quickly concurred with La Follette's choice, and the SP National Executive Committee then unanimously endorsed the La Follette–Wheeler ticket.[54]

For Gene Debs, the CPPA convention and the SP's support for La Follette posed a series of vexing questions. Debs, in ill health, was confined to a sanitarium during the Socialist Party convention, but he sent a telegram urging all members to "unite loyally in carrying out the program adopted by the convention." Although he relied on the judgment of the delegates, he suggested that it might be "wise" for the SP "to make no nominations," but "at the same time to hold the Socialist Party intact."[55]

Given the Party leadership's fervor for the La Follette campaign, Debs sought to avoid a bitter faction fight, and a possible split, by accepting the majority position. Still, his lack of enthusiasm frequently surfaced. His ambivalence is evident in an open letter he issued when accepting his selection as the Party's chair. Debs began by arguing that the option of running a distinctly socialist presidential campaign "would have proved [to be] a dismal failure." He had come to the realization that socialists could not "lay down hard and fast rules," but rather they had to adapt fundamental principles to "the exigencies that arise from time to time in the development of the labor movement."[56]

Debs thereby implicitly conceded that support for the La Follette campaign ran counter to the underlying tenets of independent political action. Nevertheless, he felt that there was "genius in a wise compromise and in a masterly retreat." The CPPA convention had constituted a "historic gathering of labor's forward-moving forces," and it represented "in embryo the American Labor Party." It was "at least a beginning," perhaps even "a very promising one."

Debs supported the majority position, but he went out of his way to defend the members of the minority, who had remained "absolutely loyal to the Party according to their light." Although he was convinced "that the logic of events" would validate the majority perspective, he admitted that he too had been skeptical of the CPPA. Indeed, he conceded that he had only recently reversed his position, persuaded by "the unprecedented and extraordinary situation" that was currently unfolding.

LA FOLLETTE CAMPAIGNS

While Debs transmitted conflicting signals, most Socialist Party leaders were unabashed in their fervent endorsement of the La Follette campaign. Yet there were a variety of disturbing signals that should have given pause to even the most zealous of labor party advocates. For one, the campaign was focused on the personality and charisma of the presidential candidate. Not only did La Follette stand as an individual, and not as the nominee of a party, but his closest advisors were also drawn from a closely knit circle of friends and relatives. Yet La Follette was a sick man, having been hospitalized with pneumonia during the spring of 1924. Furthermore, he suffered from a chronic heart ailment that would be the cause of his death less than a year later. As a result, La Follette was forced to limit his campaign swings during the final weeks of the election.[57]

La Follette hammered away at the coercive power of large corporations as the central focus of his campaign. Indeed, the "great issue before the American people" was "the control of government and industry by private monopoly." The concentration of industrial power was destroying the market economy, since monopoly "crushed competition [and] stifled private initiative." His election would bring the "use of the power of the federal government to crush private monopoly, not to foster it." The federal government could counter the power of the corporate giants by regulating key industries and taxing excess profits and wealth. La Follette also called for the repeal of the Esch–Cummins Act and the "public ownership of railroads." He also argued for "public ownership of the nation's water power," and the "strict control" of "all natural resources."[58] This was not the program of a radical, let alone a committed socialist. Although La Follette's critique of corporate power was insightful, his calls for social change were cautious and tentative.

La Follette also established a Joint Executive Committee to assist him in determining overall policy. As campaign manager and chair of the Executive Committee, La Follette turned to Representative John Nelson of Wisconsin, a trusted friend and advisor. Hillquit and Norman Thomas were two of the twelve chosen for this committee. Hillquit was eager to be seen as a loyal and useful member of this committee, even if this meant downplaying his socialist politics. When the committee sought a publicity director, Hillquit suggested Charles Ervin, a former editor of the *Socialist Call* who had taken a job as public relations director with the Amalgamated Clothing Workers. Although Ervin remained a socialist, Hillquit vouched for him, since "like some others of his political creed," he was "not aggressive" in asserting his own position. Indeed, Hillquit promised that Ervin would "keep himself in the background."[59]

La Follette believed that a credible third party could only be launched by drawing prominent progressives away from the two party system. He therefore discouraged CPPA affiliates from fielding complete slates, concerned that this might lead to the defeat of his allies in Congress. During the campaign, both La Follette and Wheeler endorsed several leading liberals, including Senator George W. Norris of Nebraska. Yet only one of their Congressional allies was prepared to openly support the Progressive ticket. Republican Senator Smith W. Brookhart of Iowa denounced President Calvin Coolidge, while praising La Follette as the progressive alternative. Most Congressional progressives either remained silent or publicly endorsed the presidential candidate of their party.[60]

THE UNIONS AND LA FOLLETTE

While La Follette sought to protect his links to those who remained within the two party system, his erstwhile trade union allies followed an even more cautious policy. The railroad unions publicly supported the Progressive campaign from start to finish. Union resources were directed to mobilizing members to vote for La Follette, and, indeed, Edward Keating wrote a series of articles for *Labor*, the newspaper of the railroad union coalition, praising La Follette and urging union members to vote for him. Nevertheless, Keating was clear that this support did not imply union backing for an independent third party, a possibility that La Follette continued to hold open. Furthermore, the railroad unions enthusiastically endorsed those Congressional candidates from within the two party system who criticized the Esch–Cummins Bill, the legislation that had returned the railroad industry to private corporate control.

Gompers and the American Federation of Labor were even more circumspect in their endorsement of La Follette. Until Tea Pot Dome, Gompers had no interest in an independent presidential campaign, and, indeed, attacked any prospects for a labor party. As the ripple of corruption spread, leaving McAdoo engulfed in its wake, Gompers began reassessing his position. In early 1924, he warned Democratic Party leaders that the AFL would bolt unless the Democratic platform made significant concessions to union concerns.[61]

The executive committee of the AFL's Political Campaign Committee then issued a public statement setting forth a set of minimal demands. A revised, and more nebulous, version of these demands was then presented to the Democratic and Republican conventions. These demands were very limited in their scope, and, indeed, were significantly more moderate than La Follette's campaign platform. For instance, instead of demanding the public ownership and control of the railroad system, the AFL stood for the repeal of the labor relations sections of the Esch–Cummins bill. In particular, the AFL called for the abolition of the Railway Labor Board and the termination of those provisions that prohibited strikes on the railways. The most controversial plank in the AFL program called for legislation prohibiting the courts from issuing injunctions limiting peaceful protests during strikes.[62]

Needless to say, neither mainstream party was prepared to revise the Esch–Cummins Bill or curb the power of the judiciary. When the Democrats rejected the AFL program, Gompers warned that the Federation was being "forced to turn to La Follette." His disenchantment was further exacerbated when the Democrats nominated John W. Davis, a conservative corporate lawyer. Gompers concluded that there was "no other way" but to endorse the La Follette ticket.[63]

The AFL immediately opened up negotiations with the CPPA, and with Senator La Follette. By 1924, Gompers was nearly blind, and chronically ill. Indeed, he was hospitalized for six weeks during June and early July of 1924, recovering from a life-threatening heart condition. Gompers therefore delegated Frank Morrison, the AFL's secretary, and Matthew Woll, a Federation vice-president, as his "confidential representatives" to these talks.[64]

Morrison and Woll met with William Johnston, as chair of the CPPA, to express two primary concerns. The AFL pressed the CPPA to agree that it would endorse Congressional candidates who accepted the limited reform measures embodied in the AFL demands. This was a key concession, since the CPPA had been initiated by the railway unions for the express purpose of promoting the Plumb Plan for quasi-public control and ownership of the railway industry, and this point was conspicuously lacking in the AFL program. Johnston pledged that the CPPA platform would be "binding only upon the Presidential and Vice-Presidential candidates," and that Congressional candidates would be supported "on a non-partisan basis, similar to that followed by the American Federation of Labor."[65]

The AFL leaders also sought clarification on the purpose of the next CPPA conference to be held soon after the election. Johnston advised Morrison and Woll that "no one could definitely say what might take place," but in any case its direction "would likely be determined by the results of the pending" campaign. Should there be "large defections from both the Democratic and Republican parties," the CPPA "would then be in the position to amalgamate these forces and assume leadership." Without such a development, Johnston informed the AFL leaders, the prospects for a third party remained doubtful.[66] Since there were no indications that such large-scale defections were about to occur, Johnston was implicitly promising that the CPPA would not initiate a new third party at its next conference. Nevertheless, the ambiguity could have only reinforced Gompers' doubts as to the entire project.

This meeting was followed up by further informal discussions between AFL officials and CPPA leaders. As a result, both sides agreed that the AFL would "assume the leadership in the Congressional campaign, while cooperating in the Presidential campaign under the leadership of the CPPA." Woll also met with La Follette who expressed his "complete accord with the idea that the AFL should lead in the Congressional campaign."[67] La Follette's willingness to accede to AFL policy guidelines for Congressional campaigns would directly impact the Socialist Party as it attempted to reconcile its position within the progressive alliance with its commitment to a truly independent politics.

In early August, the AFL executive committee formally endorsed La Follette. Gompers insisted that this decision remained "in strict accordance with our long-established policy of non-partisan political action." In evaluating the three main presidential candidates, the AFL had determined that La Follette was "distinctly preferable." Since the United States was "seething with protest against the machinations of Big Business," it was "no fantastic thing to look for" a La Follette victory.[68]

As the campaign moved into high gear, Gompers was hopeful that La Follette would make "a good showing," since this would "make the two political parties sit up and take notice." Although Gompers viewed the Republicans as "beyond hope," the Democrats stood at a crossroads, confronting "the reorganization of that party with a constructive, progressive program, or else its entire elimination and making way for some other party to take its place."[69] This is an interesting formulation. Gompers would soon abandon it in order to beat a hasty retreat back into the Democratic Party, but Ralph Nader, seven decades later, would voice remarkably similar sentiments during his 2000 presidential campaign.

Gompers' enthusiasm diminished as it became increasingly clear that La Follette's enormous popularity could not counterbalance the powerful forces arrayed against him. Gompers continued to endorse the Progressive presidential ticket, but his tone became increasingly perfunctory. In an article written just prior to the election, Gompers declared that the AFL had backed La Follette because it had been presented with "no other choice."[70]

Although union leaders differed in the enthusiasm with which they related to the La Follette campaign, all of them were adamant in their resistance to the formation of a permanent independent party. Accordingly, they were unwilling to directly contribute to the campaign, since these funds might be used to launch a new party after the election. The AFL gave $25,000 to the campaign committee, a modest sum even then. Even the railroad unions were wary. Total campaign receipts from all sources came to $229,000, much of it from wealthy donors. Union contributions fell far short of the $3 million that had been promised.[71]

LA FOLLETTE PRESSURES THE SOCIALIST PARTY

Although the union leadership approached the La Follette campaign with cautious skepticism, the Socialist Party enthusiastically threw its resources into the effort. In a confidential letter to convention delegates, J. Mahlon Barnes, the Party's campaign coordinator, stressed that the SP was giving its "whole-hearted support" to La Follette, having "offered the supreme sacrifice, even to the life" of the Party, "for unity on the political field."[72]

The National Executive Committee issued an open statement setting guidelines for state affiliates during the campaign. For state elections, the guidelines provided that SP affiliates should endorse candidates backed by the CPPA when those candidates were independent of the two mainstream parties. In the many states where the CPPA endorsed Democrats or Republicans, the Party should proceed to field its own candidates.[73]

On the federal level, the guidelines directed state affiliates in a very different direction. Since La Follette and Wheeler had placed "special stress on the election of progressive members to Congress," the National Executive Committee directed state affiliates to "abstain from making nominations" in those cases where the CPPA endorsed a candidate from the mainstream parties. This left most SP locals in the position of tacitly aiding in the election of liberal politicians who remained within the two party system.[74]

In its eagerness to mollify La Follette and, indirectly Gompers and the AFL, the national leadership went even further in softening its commitment to independent political action. State affiliates were pressured to withdraw candidates who could potentially swing an election where both Democratic and Republican candidates held to the corporate mainstream. In West Virginia, the Socialist Party had established a solid presence in the decade prior to the draconian government repression of World War I. By the 1920s, its organizational structure had been greatly weakened, and yet the Party still retained its ballot status and significant popular support. In accordance with the guidelines established at the 1924 convention, the SP's state organization deferred to the Progressives in nominating a slate of third party candidates. Since the Progressive Party was an unknown factor in West Virginia, most of those on the Progressive ticket turned out to be SP members.[75]

Matthew S. Holt, the candidate for U.S. Senate, was a well-known personality throughout the state. As a Socialist Party activist, he had opposed the U.S. entry into World War I, holding firm to his vocal opposition in spite of the vitriolic hostility of some of his neighbors and local officials. Holt had campaigned as a socialist for statewide office in several previous elections. In addition to his courage as a political dissident, he was widely admired for his service as a socially conscious physician.[76] At its state convention held in March 1924, the Progressives selected Holt as their candidate for U.S. Senate. Once the slate was adopted, with La Follette and Holt featured as candidates, the Socialist Party endorsed the Progressive ticket and placed it on its ballot line. Thus, West Virginia was one of the few states where La Follette campaigned under the Socialist Party designation.

The Senate seat was hotly contested, so Holt had the potential to act as the swing factor. Both mainstream candidates were prominent members of the corporate establishment. William E. Chilton, the Democrat, had already been elected to a term in the Senate from 1911 to 1917, before returning to private practice as a corporate lawyer. His Republican opponent, Guy D. Goff, had recently served as assistant attorney general during the administration of President Warren Harding.[77]

In accordance with the secret agreement made between La Follette, the CPPA and the AFL, the AFL would set the direction for the coalition's effort in the Congressional elections. Chilton was a solidly entrenched member of the corporate mainstream, but for Woll, and Gompers, he was still the lesser evil candidate. La Follette acceded to this decision, so in August 1924 his eldest son and alter ego, Robert La Follette Jr., "appealed" to Bertha Hale White, Socialist Party national secretary, "to effect the withdrawal" of Holt from the Senate campaign. White referred the issue to the state organization, but West Virginia refused to comply since Chilton was, "in the opinion" of the West Virginia "comrades, a rank reactionary." White then brought the issue to the attention of the National Executive Committee, but the issue remained unresolved.[78]

Since the CPPA had also agreed to follow the AFL in the determination of the progressive coalition's policy in Congressional elections, William Johnston, as CPPA chair, wrote to Hillquit, once again urging the Socialist Party to ensure Holt's withdrawal from the campaign. Hillquit forwarded the letter to White for immediate action.[79]

In responding to Johnston, White pointed out that Holt had been nominated by the Progressive convention, and only then been endorsed by the SP. Nevertheless, she had written directly to Holt, conceding that the Party could not endorse or support a candidate of either of the two corporate parties. Furthermore, Chilton's record did not "make it easier to advocate Dr Holt's withdrawal." Still, and in spite of all that, Goff's conservative positions, and his hostility to granting amnesty to Debs and other political prisoners while a member of the Harding administration, led White to suggest to Holt that the SP would greet Goff's "defeat with lively satisfaction."[80]

In spite of the pressure from the national office, the West Virginia Socialist Party did not accede to Holt's withdrawal. Instead, the state Party made only a token effort to promote his candidacy. As a result, Holt received less than 1 percent of the total vote, a nominal result that lagged far behind La Follette's showing in West Virginia. In the end, Goff gained a majority of the total votes cast for Senator, defeating Chilton by a substantial margin, as the Republicans swept the state.[81]

As a tactic in realpolitik, the pressure on Holt to withdraw was pointless, but that hardly constitutes the essential point. La Follette's campaign was drawing the Socialist Party away from its previous commitment to independent political action and toward a pragmatic acceptance of the lesser evil. The Party's leaders should have been supporting those locals that fielded candidates committed to socialist principles and a total opposition to the two party system. Instead, in a futile effort to appease La Follette and the CPPA, the SP leadership acted to undercut committed activists such as Matthew Holt and his West Virginia comrades.

Indeed, the Socialist Party leadership never wavered in its uncritical enthusiasm for the La Follette campaign. Hillquit was certain that a labor party would be founded soon after the election. In September 1924, he informed Friedrich Adler, a noted Austrian social democratic leader and the general secretary of the Labor and Socialist International, that La Follette's independent presidential campaign was "of unusual importance to the Socialist Movement of the United States," and that the outcome of the campaign would "very largely determine" the SP's future. The Socialist Party believed that "a permanent political unity" would be forged between socialists and trade unions.[82]

As Hillquit and the Socialist Party leadership lavished praise on the La Follette campaign, Debs remained quiet. During the last two months of the campaign, he issued only one public statement, on the occasion of Labor Day, in which he avoided any mention of La Follette. Since the Socialist Party had opted to endorse independent progressive candidates, it would "in good faith" provide "unqualified support" through the end of the campaign. In doing so, it would resolutely "maintain the absolute autonomy of the Socialist Party."[83]

Debs looked forward to the formation of an independent labor party, but such a party must be formed "by the workers themselves," rather than by a political candidate, no matter how popular. Of course, the Socialist Party's leadership clung to a very different perspective, relying on La Follette to lead the way to a new third party.[84]

For his part, La Follette acted to distance himself from the Socialist Party, while utilizing the party's ballot status where necessary. In New York, where the Socialist Party retained a solid electoral base, La Follette campaigned on both the SP and Progressive tickets. Ultimately, he received more votes on the SP ticket than on the Progressive line. Yet Norman Thomas, as the Party's candidate for governor, had to promise to avoid any mention of his own candidacy before being permitted to speak at La Follette campaign rallies.[85]

THE COALITION UNRAVELS

For all the problems with the campaign, La Follette proved to be an extremely popular candidate, especially in the Midwestern plains states and the Pacific West. The final tally gave him nearly 5 million votes, more than 15 percent of the total. La Follette came in second in eleven states, and carried Wisconsin, his home state. By any realistic standard, the La Follette campaign had been enormously successful.[86]

Nevertheless, from the moment the campaign came to an end, the coalition that had come together during the campaign began to disintegrate. Virtually every union that had backed La Follette quickly retreated back to the Democratic Party as the final results were still being tallied. In reviewing the results of the 1924 election, Gompers concluded that the "non-partisan political policy" of the AFL had once again been proven to be "the only sound political policy for American workers and American farmers." La Follette's showing had conclusively demonstrated "that a labor political party would be a suicidal venture." The U.S. working class had indicated that it did "not want a separate political party, and [that] as a matter of practical politics" it was "far too wise to indulge in any such futility."[87]

These views reflected those of most union officials, not just Gompers. The railroad unions were wary of any further participation in the CPPA, and Keating's *Labor* dropped any further mention of third party politics. The only leading union official to oppose this perspective was William Johnston, who continued to support labor's engagement in electoral activity outside of the two party system, although only in certain circumstances. Yet Johnston had lost much of his authority as president of the International Association of Machinists (IAM). Dissidents within the union had successfully challenged Johnston and his supporters, in part on the basis of the union's inept leadership of the 1922 railroad strike. Although Johnston had been re-elected by a narrow margin in June 1924, his opponent charged him with election fraud, leaving the union virtually paralyzed. As the CPPA attempted to resolve its future, Johnston clung precariously to his position within the IAM.[88]

With AFL unions in retreat from independent politics, La Follette reassessed his future direction. The Senator remained within the Republican caucus, at the cost of his seniority. Yet La Follette had not foreclosed the possibility of a second campaign as an independent presidential candidate. Still, the next campaign, should it occur, would be significantly different from the last one. Days after the election, La Follette's advisors informed the *New York Times* that organized labor was the key to a future campaign. Furthermore, the progressives looked forward to the departure of the Socialist Party, "convinced that the Socialist affiliation [had] injured La Follette" during the 1924 campaign.[89]

In the wake of the 1924 campaign, only the Socialist Party steadfastly insisted on the need to take the next step forward. Hillquit advised Friedrich Adler in December 1924 that La Follette's showing had provided "a definite indication" that there was "enough sentiment" to "justify the immediate organization" of a third party. Furthermore, Hillquit continued to believe, contrary to all the evidence, that the next CPPA conference would "prove the existence of sufficient forces definitely committed to the organization of a new party to make the experiment worthwhile."[90]

Hillquit was engaging in pure fantasy. On December 12, 1924, the National Committee of the CPPA met in Washington, ostensibly to set the time and place for the next national conference. The railroad union leaders, led by Keating, argued for a delay to allow time for a survey to determine if there was sufficient support for a new third party. With Robert La Follette Jr.'s support, the majority overrode these objections and voted to proceed, setting the national conference for Chicago on February 21, 1925.[91]

With the end of the campaign, and the fragmenting of the coalition that had come together during the La Follette campaign, Debs shifted to a more vocal and open criticism of progressive politics. In an article that appeared in January 1925, Debs began with the prediction that the evolution of U.S. politics would "inevitably lead to and result in the formation of an American labor party."[92] This accepted the essential theoretical premise of Socialist Party strategy as it had been articulated since the 1921 convention. Yet Debs went on to undercut the arguments embedded within this premise.

The electoral formation that Debs envisioned would be a genuine working-class party, not a "middle-class party, *not* a reform party, nor even a progressive party." Indeed, Debs insisted that "if a bona fide labor party" could not "be organized at Chicago," it would be preferable "that no party at all" would "issue from that conference." Debs thus implicitly rejected the La Follette campaign, which had epitomized the politics of progressive, middle-class reform. Furthermore, a working-class party would have to be built from below, since the "present leaders of the unions" were "almost to a man opposed to a labor party." As a result, the "hope for an American labor party" lay "not in the official labor leaders but in the rank and file."[93]

Debs was using the terminology of the labor party proponents, while turning their entire argument upside down. The Socialist Party had looked to the British Labour Party as a model, a party based directly on the mainstream trade union structure, but Debs explicitly rejected this argument. A break with the two party system could only come when the ranks were "aroused" and prepared to "insist upon and compel independent political action," over the objections of the union bureaucracy.[94]

On February 20, 1925, officials from the 16 railroad unions met in caucus in Chicago, prior to the CPPA national conference. Only Johnston spoke for the formation of an independent third party, but he had been "specifically enjoined" by the machinists' executive board from serving as the union's representative to the CPPA. Every other union leader confirmed their commitment to working exclusively within the constraints of the two party system. By a narrow margin, the majority of officials agreed to attend the next day's conference, but only to announce their decision to withdraw from further participation.[95]

DEBS AND THE LABOR PARTY

Thus, the prospects for a labor-based third party had already vanished before the CPPA conference had even opened. On the following day, the railroad union leaders publicly announced their intention of leaving the CPPA and of returning to the pragmatic politics of the lesser evil. Debs then gave a lengthy and impassioned speech to the delegates. It would be his only address to a conference of progressive political leaders.

Debs began by restating his belief in the necessity of a class-based politics, insisting that in an industrialized capitalist society a political party is "either a capitalist party or it is a labor party." Those who believed that a party could be formed with an "appeal broad enough to embrace small capitalists and workers" were embarking upon "an impossible undertaking." Inevitably, these irreconcilable forces would come "more or less in conflict with each other," and then such a broadly based electoral formation would "soon begin to disintegrate," going "the way that all third parties have gone during the last fifty years."[96]

The analysis is as insightful now as it was 75 years ago. Debs went on to deride the idea of a progressive party, this to the Conference for Progressive Political Action, pointing out that there was "not a term in our vocabulary" that had "been more prostituted in the last few years than the term progressive." Indeed, the word had come to mean "absolutely nothing."

Debs then came close to discarding the entire concept of a labor party. It was essential to organize a social movement that could wrest "power from the autocracy" by "taking from them the private ownership of the instruments of production." Furthermore, the "fundamental question" remained whether or not to be "in favor of the nation owning and controlling its own industries." Thus, Debs had returned to the same position he had adhered to during the heyday of the Socialist Party prior to World War I. The party of the working class must of necessity be a socialist party. Needless to say, this argument represented the antithesis of the labor party perspective.

As soon as Debs finished speaking, the conference accepted the proposal of the railroad unions to dissolve the CPPA. An hour later, the remaining delegates reconvened, with the La Follette progressives in the overwhelming majority. Johnston was the only railroad union officer to remain. With the union officialdom having departed, the Socialist Party delegates had little interest in remaining. When Hillquit's motion to structure the new party on the basis of a federated coalition of organizational affiliates was defeated, the SP withdrew from further participation. The La Follette supporters proceeded to create a new organization, the National Progressive Headquarters, which soon fell into oblivion.[97]

In justifying its decision to leave, the SP insisted that the railroad unions had "constituted the great bulk of membership represented by the Conference" and had provided it with "prestige and promise to the movement." Once these unions had withdrawn, any political party emerging from those who remained could not possibly succeed as "a militant political organization of the toiling and producing masses."[98]

In the wake of the CPPA convention, the SP held its own convention, also in Chicago. Although there was general support for the decision to remain aloof from the new nationwide progressive formation, the majority still held to a labor party perspective. State organizations were permitted to affiliate with statewide parties such as the Minnesota Farmer-Labor Party, and to help in the formation of new ones.[99]

Although the party's moderate leadership maintained tight control over the convention, Debs articulated a very different strategic outlook. The 1925 convention constituted a "rebirth and reorganization" after "the terrible ordeal through which the Socialist Party" had "been required to pass." Indeed, Debs felt as if he had "been delivered from a nightmare." As long as the SP had remained an integral component of the "so-called Progressive movement," he had "felt like an octogenarian snail just crawling along." With the decision to withdraw, the Party was "out in the clear again. The shackles" had "fallen from us; the unholy alliance" having been "broken."[100]

Debs was relieved that the Party had decided to walk out of the recent convention of progressives because he had already determined during its first hours that "there must be a separation." (The February 1925 CPPA conference was the first one that Debs had attended.) He was so convinced of this that he had decided that he "would stand for withdrawing the Socialist Party from that alliance" even if he "had to stand alone."[101]

Debs' speech incisively countered every tenet of the labor party perspective. His critical perspective was further delineated in a letter sent by Theodore Debs to a veteran Party stalwart, Joseph E. Cohen, two weeks after the convention.[102] Theodore Debs served as his brother Gene's personal secretary, confidant and alter ego. He frequently answered his brother's correspondence, writing in his stead.[103] In the letter to Cohen, Theodore referred to his brother, implicitly underscoring that he was writing for both of them.

Theodore Debs admitted that he had never felt "just right" about the Socialist Party "being hooked up" with some of the middle-class elements and some of the wholly reactionary labor unions represented in the CPPA. As a result, it had come as a "positive relief when the ties were severed completely." Theodore Debs had not been able to attend the recent convention, but Eugene had informed him that it had been "an inspiration," and that the Party would "rapidly regain lost ground."[104]

THE AFTERMATH

La Follette died in June 1925, succumbing to the heart ailments that had hobbled his efforts throughout the presidential campaign.[105] Without La Follette as a rallying point for popular support, the progressive movement floundered as an independent electoral formation. For the Socialist Party, the 1924 campaign had proven to be an unmitigated disaster. They had submerged their own distinctive identity into that of a liberal electoral formation, which had then disintegrated, leaving nothing. Trade unions close to the SP, especially those in the garment trades, had previously provided the Party with resources and funds. During the 1924 campaign, these unions had supported La Follette, and they were reluctant to return to a policy that linked them to the electoral fortunes of the Socialist Party. Unions such as the International Ladies Garment Workers Union (ILGWU) drifted into the Democratic Party, leaving the SP even more isolated than before.

Norman Thomas, an enthusiastic booster of La Follette in 1924, would later concede that the SP had been "disorganized and discouraged" by the collapse of the CPPA. Indeed, the Party had thrown all of its "energies behind the national ticket," to the point of "neglecting" its organizational base. The La Follette campaign had therefore "left the Socialist Party in pretty bad shape."[106] In spite of the La Follette debacle, Thomas still believed in the concept of a farmer-labor third party. A decade later, when the issue returned as a vital prospect, he would again support the submersion of the Socialist Party into a labor-based third party formation.

Debs did not comment publicly on these issues after the SP convention of February 1925. During the last year and a half of his life, much of it spent in convalescent homes, he limited the expression of his views to private letters. Debs continued to defend the Party's policy during the 1924 campaign to those outside of the SP. When a liberal reformer queried him on his estimate of recent events, he held that although La Follette's program had not been "at all a socialist platform," the Socialist Party had been "enfeebled and decimated by the war." Given this, Debs remained "satisfied" that future generations of socialists would "vindicate the wisdom" of the Party's strategic retreat.[107]

Debs was far more critical of the progressive alliance in a letter to William H. Henry, the SP's newly appointed national secretary.[108] In June 1926, when Henry proposed to the National Executive Committee that W.S. Hutchins, an official of the Locomotive Engineers, one of the elite railroad brotherhoods, be disciplined for his public endorsement of a Democratic Party candidate, Debs was reluctant to proceed. Still, Debs also believed that Hutchins had to choose where he stood, since he was trapped between "conflicting obligations" that were "in conflict" and that could "not be harmonized."[109]

Decades of experience with the perils of lesser evil politics should have convinced the working class "of the utter futility of depending upon" the "old party politicians" for "anything but the crumbs that are brushed contemptuously from the tables of their masters." Hutchins, therefore, had to decide, either quitting his post as a union official or resigning from the Socialist party. Only in this way could he avoid being "placed in a position that would subject him to party discipline."[110]

In laying out this dilemma, Debs referred to the SP's recent experience within the progressive alliance. For it had been "precisely upon the issue here involved" that the CPPA had gone "to pieces at its last meeting." The decision of the railroad unions to go "off in one direction" had left the Party with "no other alternative [but] to take the opposite direction."[111]

Debs died four months later, so this represents his last recorded comment on the question of a labor party. The Socialist Party would put forward its own candidates for the next decade. With La Follette no longer on the scene, calls for a nationwide labor party ebbed, and progressive reformers returned to the Democratic Party, hoping to reform it from within. Only the Great Depression, and the rise of the Congress of Industrial Organizations, would bring the issue of independent political action again to the forefront of debate.

CONCLUSIONS

On one level, the La Follette campaign had proven to be an enormous success. With a modicum of financial resources, La Follette had presented both major party candidates with a credible challenge. His candidacy could not be dismissed as isolated and irrelevant. Instead, he had brought a sharp anti-corporate message into the mainstream of political discourse, and won nearly 5 million votes.

Yet the La Follette campaign had been presented as the starting point for a genuinely independent politics. On this basis it had been an abysmal failure. La Follette had maintained his links to progressive politicians within the two corporate parties. He had deliberately chosen to campaign as an independent candidate rather than the nominee of a democratically controlled third party. Finally, his coalition had disintegrated only a few months after the election.

For the Socialist Party majority, which had been unwavering in its support for La Follette, these failures should have led to a searching reassessment of the labor party strategy. The AFL unions were not one whit closer to breaking with the Democratic Party after the election than they had been before it. Indeed, less than a decade after the election the New Deal would bind the unions to the Democrats as they had never been before. Nevertheless, despite the lessons of the La Follette campaign, the labor party question would be a focal point for debate throughout the turbulent years of the Great Depression.

6
The Labor Party Question in the 1930s: Trotsky, Thomas and La Guardia

The economic collapse of the 1930s brought with it a profound disillusionment in the capitalist market system. Millions of working people were open to a radical political alternative. For the Socialist Party, the decade of the Great Depression appeared as one of tremendous opportunity, and yet popular enthusiasm for the New Deal undermined the potential for a major break with the two party system.

During the first years of the Depression, the entire range of tendencies within the Party held firmly to the goal of an independent party, one with strong ties to organized labor. Still, despite the economic crisis, President Franklin Delano Roosevelt remained enormously popular. Workers continued to vote for New Deal Democrats, and the few efforts at locally based independent electoral formations either failed or were coopted into the Democratic Party.[1] This disjuncture between the extreme volatility of the economic system and the relative stability of the political structure left socialists frustrated and confused. Within the Socialist Party, these tensions led to bitter debates, ideological fragmentation and organizational splits.

New York City provided the primary venue for these controversies. The Socialist Party retained a significant electoral base within New York's working class. In a strategic maneuver to divert this constituency into the ranks of the New Deal, unions based in New York City's large garment industry launched the American Labor Party in support of Roosevelt. A year later, in the fall of 1937, the ALP endorsed Fiorello La Guardia for re-election as mayor. When Norman Thomas opted to withdraw as the Party's candidate for mayor, the SP entered into an acrimonious debate, one that still sheds light on the question of the labor party and its implication for a socialist politics.

THE OLD GUARD WITHDRAWS

New York City held a unique position within the Socialist Party. The largest local, it was also one of the very few localities where the Party remained a significant electoral force. Although socialists could no longer elect candidates to the State Assembly or Congress, they still had the potential to become the swing vote in a close election at both the municipal and state levels.

New York City politics was dominated by a municipal patronage machine enmeshed in a dense web of corrupt connections. The Democratic Party machine, and most especially its Manhattan unit, Tammany Hall, controlled City Hall. Tammany Hall had been soliciting bribes and rigging elections well before Henry George's 1886 campaign for mayor. Politics in New York turned on the issue of "good government," with a loose coalition of middle-class reformers seeking to unseat the Democratic political hacks and to replace them with liberal politicians pledged to the administration of an honest, efficient government. Norman Thomas was an influential figure within this coalition.

In 1929, Thomas campaigned for mayor on the Socialist ticket, castigating the blatant venality of the Democratic machine. His appeal to progressive reformers attracted a receptive audience, with Thomas polling 175,000 votes, 12.4 percent of the total, a very respectable showing. Nevertheless, Thomas' increasing stature left the Old Guard, the older, entrenched leaders of the New York local, uneasy.[2]

The Old Guard was deeply rooted in the needle trades unions, especially the International Ladies Garment Workers Union (ILGWU) and the Amalgamated Clothing Workers Union. Many of its most prominent members were middle-level officials, integral components of a highly bureaucratized apparatus that sought to develop cooperative arrangements with garment industry employers. The needle trades unions employed many of the leading lights of the Old Guard, including Morris Hillquit, who acted as legal counsel to the ILGWU.[3] Politically, the Old Guard looked toward the formation of a traditional labor party, one that would be based directly on the trade unions.

During the first years of the Great Depression, the Socialist Party recruited a new generation of activists. These newly radicalized youngsters entered the Party, and its youth group, the Young People's Socialist League (YPSL), only to become increasingly dissatisfied with the timid and uninspiring policies of the Old Guard. Starting in New

York in April 1930, these dissident elements coalesced into a nationwide caucus, the Militant Caucus, and began pushing for a newly revitalized Party. They insisted that SP members who were active in unions should act in accord with socialist principles, specifically that they should actively challenge the close ties between most unions and the Democratic Party.[4] This argument brought them into direct conflict with the Old Guard, with its intimate ties to the leadership of the needle trades unions. Thus, the ensuing debate was far from theoretical.

The Militant Caucus brought together a broad and divergent coalition unified in their distrust of the Old Guard leadership. Some of its most active members viewed themselves as revolutionaries, intent on propelling the Party toward a more radical politics. Others were committed to a social democratic perspective, but were still dismayed by the reluctance of the Old Guard to challenge the devious maneuvers and undemocratic practices of the needle trades unions. Initially, Norman Thomas remained distant from the Militants, but he clearly identified with its more moderate elements.[5]

The battle lines were sharply drawn at the 1932 national convention in Milwaukee, when a loose coalition challenged Hillquit's election as the Party's chair. Norman Thomas joined with the Militants, and with Mayor Dan Hoan of Milwaukee, in opposing Hillquit. This was a formidable alliance, and the Old Guard knew it. Although Hillquit triumphed, the older leadership group was clearly on the defensive.[6]

That fall, the "good-government" forces finally succeeded in unseating the incumbent mayor of New York City, Jimmy Walker, for his blatant ties to the corrupt Tammany machine. In November 1932, Hillquit campaigned for mayor in the special election called to fill the vacancy. He received 250,000 votes, or 13 percent of the total, a high point for the Party's electoral success in New York City.[7]

With the advent of the Roosevelt administration in March 1933, progressives felt confident of their position, an influential component of a powerful nationwide movement. That November, Fiorello La Guardia, a liberal Republican, was elected mayor, running ahead of two Democratic rivals, one a candidate chosen by Manhattan's Tammany Hall and the other a candidate slated by the outer borough machines, with the tacit approval of the president. Norman Thomas was so disaffected by the Old Guard's tight control over the New York local that he declined the socialist nomination. Instead, the Party put forward Charles Solomon, a labor lawyer and an Old Guard stalwart, as its candidate for mayor. Solomon gained only 65,000 votes, a quarter of the number tallied by Hillquit during the special election a year earlier. La Guardia ran as a Republican, but he also benefited from the endorsement of the City Fusion Party, a shadow party created to make it easier for liberal Democrats to support La Guardia without voting on the Republican line.[8]

La Guardia won the election as the candidate of a broad progressive coalition. As mayor, he provided an honest municipal administration, a rarity in the long history of New York City. He also cultivated close relations with organized labor, and curtailed the harsh repressive tactics used by the police during militant strikes. Yet La Guardia was hardly a radical, endorsing a number of Republicans for local offices, some of them conservatives. In addition, he pushed through a municipal sales tax, a regressive tax that Norman Thomas condemned as a "disaster."[9]

By the June 1934 convention in Detroit, the Socialist Party had become a bitterly polarized battleground. Ostensibly the point in dispute concerned a Declaration of Principles written by Devere Allen, a political ally of Norman Thomas. The declaration, written in the aftermath of the failure of German social democracy to effectively resist the rise of the Nazis, affirmed that the SP sought to "attain its objectives by peaceful and orderly means." Nevertheless, should democratic rights be abrogated, and should a clear majority of the people support a socialist alternative, the Party reserved the right to engage in militant actions, including the "recourse to a general strike," that would "not merely serve as a defense," but could lead to a revolutionary transfer of power.[10]

The declaration triggered a lively and interesting debate, with the Old Guard insisting that the declaration represented the acceptance of an insurrectionist perspective. This represented a gross distortion of the text, but the entire debate remained of purely academic interest for socialists in the United States. Roosevelt's New Deal reforms constituted the cutting edge for U.S. politics in the 1930s. Union officials flocked to the Roosevelt bandwagon, especially those in the more progressive trade unions. Sidney Hillman, president of the Amalgamated Clothing Workers, and David Dubinsky, president of the International Ladies Garment Workers Union, were pivotal figures in the formation of the Congress of Industrial Organizations (CIO). Both came out of the socialist movement, and yet both were ardent supporters of President Roosevelt. Indeed, Dubinsky tendered his resignation from the Socialist Party in May 1936.[11]

In the aftermath of the 1934 convention, the factional disputes within the SP reached the point of open warfare. In New York, the two caucuses nominated distinct slates of delegates for the May 1936 convention in Cleveland. Since the Socialist Party remained an official ballot-certified party, the contest was determined by means of a statewide primary, with the Militant slate winning handily. When the Old Guard's New York delegates were rebuffed at the convention, they walked out and the split was official.[12]

TROTSKY REJECTS THE LABOR PARTY

As the Old Guard left the Socialist Party, a whole new political tendency entered. In the fall of 1934, Thomas proposed that the Party serve as the organizational framework for those on the Left who were critical of the Communist Party. The National Executive Committee agreed, and proceeded to issue a statement urging independent radicals to join the SP. Only a few dozen did so, most of them from the group around Jay Lovestone that had been expelled from the Communist Party in 1929.[13]

Albert Goldman was the exception. A Chicago attorney, Goldman left the Trotskyists to join the Socialist Party in November 1934. In February 1935, he began publication of the *Socialist Appeal* as an internal newsletter of the SP's left-wing. The *Appeal* would become a focus of controversy within the Party.[14]

The Trotskyists constituted the largest group of radicals to challenge the Communist orthodoxy. In December of 1934, they merged with another small group of radicals, the American Workers Party, to form the Workers Party US. James Burnham, who had been an influential figure within the AWP, would play a critical role within the Trotskyist movement during the next years. Still, even within the constraints of a disciplined cadre party, Burnham remained an independent thinker. A professor of philosophy at New York University, he would become the focal point for those dissatisfied with Trotsky's incessant tactical and strategic maneuvers.[15]

Once having merged with the AWP, the Trotskyist leadership looked to the Socialist Party. This orientation corresponded with Trotsky's perspective as it had already evolved in France. In July 1934, the French Communist Party had entered into a strategic alliance with the Socialist Party, thereby creating a "united front" of left-wing parties. Trotsky then urged his adherents to join the Socialist Party in order to present a left-wing alternative to Stalinism. The Communist

League of France dissolved in August 1934, with the Trotskyists reforming soon afterward as a distinct tendency within the SP. This was the "French turn," a political maneuver that set the pattern for Trotskyists in the United States.[16]

For the French Communist Party, the alliance with the Socialist Party was merely a first step. Fearful of a fascist takeover, the CP sought to consolidate links to the parties of the moderate Center. With the support of the SP leadership, these links were crystallized into the Popular Front, a coalition of forces that extended beyond the CP and the SP to the Radicals and other, smaller, moderate parties. In June 1935, the French Socialist Party ratified this agreement at its national conference in Mulhouse, with the Trotskyists leading a small minority of dissidents. Within weeks of the Mulhouse conference, the SP leadership began expelling the Trotskyist tendency, citing its polemical opposition to the policies of the Popular Front.[17]

The French experiment lasted a brief period of months. By the time consultations between the Workers Party and the Socialist Party USA had begun in earnest, the French Trotskyists were already being ousted. Nevertheless, the Trotskyists in the United States continued along the same course. For months, negotiations continued between James P. Cannon and Max Shachtman, two leading Trotskyists, and Norman Thomas on the terms for admission. Thomas insisted that the Trotskyists could only join as individuals. As members of the Socialist Party they would be prohibited from acting as a tightly disciplined faction, and, furthermore, they would have to dissolve their own publications and rely solely on the Party's publications for the distribution of their views. Ultimately, Cannon and Shachtman agreed to Thomas' conditions and the 300 members of the Workers Party joined the Socialist Party as individuals in May 1936, shortly after the Old Guard's decision to quit the Party. Once inside of the SP, the Trotskyists regrouped around Goldman's newsletter, the *Socialist Appeal*.[18]

The Trotskyists rejected the Socialist Party's position supporting the creation of a labor party, a position upheld by the entire range of tendencies already within the SP, and by the Old Guard as well. In the ensuing debates, their presence substantially widened the scope of the debate. Nevertheless, the issue had been a controversial one within the Trotskyist movement prior to its entry into the Socialist Party, with Trotsky advocating a series of conflicting positions over the years.

While still in the Soviet Union, Trotsky's comments on the question of a labor party were limited to a series of criticisms of the Communist Party for participating in a cross-class political party, the Farmer-Labor Party. In 1928, in a document that would spark the formation of a Trotskyist organization in the United States, he lashed out at Josef Pogány (John Pepper), the Communist International's representative to the United States, for having led "the young and weak American Communist Party into the senseless and infamous adventure of creating a Farmer-Labor party around La Follette." Yet Trotsky left unchallenged the arguments advanced by Lenin in directing the Communist Party to enter into the British Labour Party.[19]

Only after Stalin had exiled him from the Soviet Union in February 1929 did Trotsky begin to grapple with the fundamental underlying issues. Expelled to Turkey, he took up residence in Prinkipo, an island off the Turkish mainland, where, in March 1930, he received his first visitor from the United States, Max Shachtman. Throughout the next decade, Shachtman would function as a leading member of the Trotskyist movement in the United States, as well as its primary envoy to European Trotskyist organizations.

Shachtman came with news from the United States, where a fledgling organization, the Communist League of America (CLA), had been formally launched in May 1929. With fewer than a hundred members, the new group looked for guidance on the critical issues confronting the Left. The founding convention had approved a platform holding that the "perspective of a labor party as a primary step in the political development of the American workers" remained valid. Nevertheless, in accordance with Trotsky's critique of 1924, the CLA insisted that support for a farmer-labor party must be rejected, since it promoted the "basically false policy of a two-class party."[20]

To Shachtman's surprise, Trotsky objected to the CLA's perspective, although it took as its starting point Lenin's formulation of 1920. Instead, Trotsky advised Shachtman that "the stage of a labor party" was "by no mean inevitable." It could well be that "the tempo of development" would soon be "enormously accelerated."[21]

Trotsky followed up these observations with a more detailed analysis. In a letter to Shachtman in June 1930, he pointed out that "a labor party, if it has a definite, independent program – independent with respect to communism – is the tool of another class," that is it could not be viewed as a truly working-class party. Affiliation with such a party would be "as much out of the question" as a merger into a party within the social democratic mainstream. Nevertheless, Trotsky did not rule out "temporary ties" with a newly formed labor party that still had "no definite program."[22]

As usual, the Trotskyist movement in the United States adjusted its political perspective to Trotsky's latest position. The second convention of the League, held in September 1931, jettisoned the position taken by the Communist Party in the 1920s, and by the CLA at its first convention. The League no longer believed that the labor party represented "an unavoidable and necessary 'reformist' stage through which the American workers had to pass." Accordingly, the CLA would oppose the formation of a labor party, although should a "mass movement" opt to "organize a labor party," Trotskyists would reassess their perspective at that time to see if entry made sense.[23]

Trotsky did not address these issues again until March 1932. During an interview in the *New York Times,* he was quoted as insisting that the "emergence of a labor party" was "inevitable." Needless to say, this comment caused a furor among his partisans in the United States. Trotsky quickly clarified his views, insisting there had been "an accidental misunderstanding" based on confusion in the translation. He had been merely restating the fundamental belief of socialists that a "workers' party," but not necessarily a labor party, would constitute a crucial step in the development of a class-conscious working class.[24]

Although Trotsky was willing to concede that the formation of a labor party would constitute "a progressive step" in the context of the United States, nevertheless it did not represent a goal toward "which the Communists must strive." Throughout the next five years, Trotskyists would consistently argue that socialists should not be in the forefront of those advocating a labor party.[25]

Trotsky still believed that socialists could participate in an already existing labor party, although he limited this tactic to carefully circumscribed circumstances. Looking back to Lenin, he insisted that this was "not a question of principle but of circumstances." Nevertheless, the "possibility of participating in a labor party movement" would "be greater in the period of its inception," when it remained an "amorphous political mass movement." Even this limited exception did not extend to a farmer-labor party, since entry into such a party could only represent "a treacherous mockery of Marxism."[26]

When the Communist League of America fused with the American Workers Party in December 1934 to form the Workers Party USA, the new organization's founding statement reflected Trotsky's position as defined two years before. The "task of the revolutionists" was "to build their own party, [and] not to engage in building up any party of reform." Furthermore, a third party that sought to "represent two or more classes on an equal footing," such as a farmer-labor party, was "doomed to irresolution and surrender to the big capitalists in every decisive test." The Workers Party did not entirely rule out the possibility of working within an already existing labor-based political party, but it had established a very strict set of preconditions to any such participation.[27]

THE AMERICAN LABOR PARTY

As the Old Guard left the Socialist Party, and the Trotskyists entered it, significant sections of the trade union movement opted to create their own interlinking network of electoral formations. As a result, the labor party question zoomed to the forefront as a critical issue, since the stance one took had immediate implications for political practice.

In early April 1936, John L. Lewis, the president of the United Mine Workers Union and the head of the newly formed CIO, initiated the formation of Labor's Nonpartisan League (LNPL), with the approval of President Roosevelt. Although, George Berry, the president of the Pressmens Union, an AFL affiliate, served as its president, CIO unions dominated the LNPL, with Lewis serving as chair and Hillman as treasurer.[28]

The LNPL was primarily created to further Roosevelt's re-election bid, but it was also intended as the structural expression of union pressure on the Democratic Party. To maximize its leverage, the League's leaders issued nebulous threats warning that they would bolt the two party system should the Democrats continue to ignore their concerns.

Berry, a Democratic Party stalwart, carefully left open the option of an independent party. At a press conference announcing the formation of the LNPL on April 1, 1936, he deflected a reporter's query on the issue of independent politics by advising that the League might "want to cross the stream later." Hillman was even more specific, promising the executive board of the Amalgamated Clothing Workers Union that the League would be "laying the foundation for a labor party."[29]

The vague threats to bolt the Democratic Party represented an idle bluff. CIO leaders had not the slightest intention of breaking with the New Deal. On the contrary, they viewed President Roosevelt as a vital ally. In May, the LNPL leadership met with the president to discuss the election campaign. Afterward, the three union leaders, Lewis, Hillman and Berry, issued a public statement insisting that their "sole objective" was to "re-elect Franklin Delano Roosevelt to the Presidency."[30]

With the LNPL having been launched on a national level, officials in the needle trades unions sought to address the unique situation of New York City. Although most states prohibited fusion, the state of New York permitted a candidate to accept the nomination of more than one political party in a given election. La Guardia had been elected on ballots he had received from voters who would have never voted for him as a Republican, but who were willing to back him as the nominee of a fusion party. A progressive party in New York, one nominally independent of the Democratic Party, could provide liberal politicians with a crucial base of support.

Sidney Hillman was at the center of the secretive talks that led to the formation of such a party. He reached the president through his wife, Eleanor Roosevelt. At the same time, he sought out Mayor La Guardia, who quickly understood the virtues of another line on the ballot, particularly one that could rely on union resources. David Dubinsky and other key needle trades union leaders were also brought into the early planning meetings. It would be these unions that would provide the organizational resources for the new party.[31]

The president was readily convinced, so he ordered his two chief political lieutenants in New York, Jim Farley and Ed Flynn, to aid the needle trades unions in overcoming the many obstacles to the creation of a new political party. (Farley was the chair of the Democratic National Committee and Flynn controlled the Bronx machine.) New York state law mandated that a new party collect 12,000 signatures from around the state, with at least 50 coming from each of New York's 62 counties, as a prerequisite to ballot access. Since the needle trades were primarily located in New York City, collecting signatures in every county in the state represented a daunting barrier. Both Farley and Flynn objected to the president's decision, but both followed his mandate. Thus, a nominally independent party relied on the apparatus of the Democratic Party to gain its initial standing as a certified political party.[32]

On July 16, 1936 the New York affiliate of Labor's Nonpartisan League formed the American Labor Party. Initially, the new party permitted the direct affiliation of supporting organizations, as well as trade unions. The Old Guard had created the People's Party upon leaving the SP, and the People's Party quickly became an ALP affiliate. During the 1936 elections, the ALP endorsed Roosevelt for president and Herbert Lehman for governor. These were the same two candidates heading the Democratic ticket, but ALP leaders insisted that fusion was only a temporary tactic, and that the new party would soon field its own independent ticket. In late May, Hillman had reassured the delegates to the Amalgamated Clothing Workers convention that he still "believed" in "independent political action for labor."[33]

NORMAN THOMAS WAVERS

With the departure of the Old Guard, and the entry of the Trotskyists, the center of gravity within the Socialist Party shifted substantially to the Left. Norman Thomas, who had previously represented the political center, soon became the focal point for a newly reconstituted right-wing that sought to prod the Party toward a more pragmatic position. He began working closely with key members of the Militant Caucus, and in particular with Harry Laidler and Jack Altman.

Laidler held an important post within the socialist movement, executive director of the League for Industrial Democracy, which served as the educational wing of the Party. A prolific author, Laidler was chosen to be the Party's nominee for governor in the 1936 election. He also held the post of chair of the New York state party. In the coming months, Laidler would act as the Party's primary liaison with the ALP.[34]

Altman was a prominent member of the younger generation that had reinvigorated the SP during the first years of the Great Depression. He had been instrumental in forming the Militant Caucus in direct opposition to the Old Guard, but he moved toward an increasingly moderate position during the 1930s. An effective organizer, Altman served as the secretary of the New York City local, where he played a crucial role in the factional disputes. Thomas relied heavily on both Laidler and La Guardia, although he also directly participated in the intense debates that followed the Old Guard's decision to leave the Party.[35]

Without the Old Guard, the Militants had little to bind them together. With Thomas, Laidler and Altman working closely together to bolster the moderates, the Militant Caucus began to fissure. A new left-wing tendency began to emerge, the Clarity Caucus, presenting Thomas and his allies with a significant challenge. The labor party question, and in particular the strategic ramifications of the American Labor Party, stood at the core of this process of fragmentation.

The Trotskyist position was unequivocal. The ALP was merely a ruse to draw independent voters into the Democratic Party. Indeed, Cannon referred to the ALP as the "Roosevelt labor party."[36] Yet the Trotskyists maintained a more general opposition to the formation of any labor party, even one that was independent of the two party system. This put them on the extreme left-wing of the Socialist Party.

For the radical tendency of the Militant Caucus, the formation of the ALP posed a difficult problem. Its leaders zealously advocated the idea of a labor party as an immediate strategic goal. Furthermore, the ALP seemed to fit this mold in its organizational structure. Yet Clarity also insisted that such a party could only gain the support of socialists as long as it maintained its complete independence from the two mainstream parties. Clarity leaders therefore attacked the ALP as a phony labor party, as indeed it was.

The Clarity Caucus and the Trotskyists thus shared a similar critique of the ALP, and yet they began with two very different theoretical perspectives. This was one underlying factor that made it difficult to develop a cohesive opposition to the position taken by Norman Thomas and the Militants as it evolved over the next months.

Initially, during the summer of 1936, both wings of the Militant Caucus reacted to the formation of the ALP with critical disinterest. The New York state executive committee, which included both radical and moderate Militants, insisted that the SP would be "unable to give support" to the ALP as long as it continued to endorse New Deal Democrats. Although the state executive committee reaffirmed that the "formation of a genuine labor party" would constitute "the next step for American workers," it also warned that a "labor party must sever all ties with [the] capitalist parties" in order "to survive."[37]

At first, Norman Thomas was also critical of the ALP. He dismissed the new formation as "an unsatisfactory type of labor party," while publicly condemning its endorsement of the president.[38] Yet as he campaigned around the country, and contended with the president's vast personal popularity, he began to waver. The problems confronting the Socialist Party were even more daunting in New York, where the ALP sharply cut into the socialist vote. Perhaps of even greater weight, Thomas could see that the needle trades union officials who had been a mainstay of the SP in New York were abandoning it for the American Labor Party.

Thomas would later confess that he had come to the conclusion during the 1936 campaign that Roosevelt and the New Deal had "completely knocked the support out from under the Socialist Party." In fact, the final election results would show that the SP vote for president, both nationally and in New York City, had declined by 75 percent from 1932. Thomas carried on with the campaign, but privately he admitted that he was "more depressed" than he had "expected to be" the previous spring. A week before election day, Thomas was ready to concede that given the SP's "weakness and the vague sentiment" for "a labor party," socialists would "have to make terms" with organizations such as the ALP. At a mass rally in New York City, Thomas admitted that he had discovered that the prospects of a labor party aroused "little enthusiasm." While sternly disapproving of the ALP for its ties to the New Deal wing of the Democratic Party, Thomas still held out the hope that the ALP would "learn and become a genuine labor party."[39]

In private, Thomas was preparing to negotiate a working arrangement with the ALP for the 1937 municipal election even before the votes had been cast in the 1936 presidential campaign. His terms were minimal. Any agreement had to "preserve" the "identity and purpose" of the Socialist Party, making it possible to "hold together and finance" the organization. As vague and undefined as these goals were, the final understanding between the ALP and the SP would fail to meet them.[40]

A few days after the election, Thomas circulated a memorandum to key members of the SP leadership more fully delineating his perspective for the next period. In New York, the ALP had done reasonably well, and yet the Socialist Party retained a significant electoral base. Accordingly, the SP was "in a fairly good position to reach a satisfactory agreement on the 1937 campaign." Such an arrangement would allow for the ALP and the SP to "nominate all, or most, of the same candidates" on both tickets. In this way, the SP could work in close cooperation with the ALP without losing its own ballot status. This presented a limited, and yet specific, guideline for the coming negotiations. Nevertheless, even this basic prerequisite for an independent party was ultimately abandoned.[41]

Thus, in November 1936, a year before the New York municipal elections, Thomas was already preparing the way for an arrangement with the ALP that would lead to his withdrawal as the socialist candidate for mayor. Although La Guardia was certain to seek re-election, the coalition of parties that would endorse him remained uncertain. As the political situation became clearer, the SP grappled with the broader issues of third party politics.

THE CAUCUSES CRYSTALLIZE

Informal discussions between the ALP leadership and Socialist Party moderates began shortly after the presidential election. The Socialist Party was prepared to accede to the ALP's request that it not nominate a socialist candidate for mayor. In addition, the SP would cross-endorse progressive candidates for borough president and city council who were campaigning on the ALP ticket. In return, the ALP would place one or two socialists on its ticket for city council. Although Thomas and the moderates within the Militant Caucus were eager to cooperate with the ALP, they were unwilling to slate those ALP candidates who were nominated by either mainstream party. La Guardia could only be endorsed if he did not campaign on the Republican ticket.[42]

The talks were lengthy and contentious, especially since Alex Rose, the state secretary of the American Labor Party and the vice-president of the Hatters Union, was wary of bargaining with the SP as a distinct organizational entity. Negotiations became even more difficult when the ALP executive committee decided shortly after the elections that only trade unions would be permitted to affiliate on an organizational basis. This meant that the Old Guard would no longer be granted direct representation on the ALP state committee. Although the ALP directive was primarily aimed at the Communist Party, which had begun to steer community groups it dominated into the ALP, it was also designed to block the organizational affiliation of the SP. Until then, Thomas had consistently argued for organizational affiliation as an essential basis for a continuing working relationship. After the November ALP meeting, the negotiations resumed within new parameters, fixing the terms under which SP members could join the ALP as individuals.[43]

In response to the ALP decision, the Old Guard dissolved the People's Party and became the New York affiliate of the Social Democratic Federation, acting as an educational current within the ALP. The CP reacted by sending cadres into the ALP, cadres who insisted that they were merely progressives and not Communists. Yet the SP confronted a more complex set of issues, while negotiations continued with ALP leaders in a search for a formula that would prove to be satisfactory to both sides.[44]

As news of the discussions began circulating, left-wing members of the Militant caucus were appalled by Thomas' eagerness to reach an accommodation with the American Labor Party. The political differences that had been deepening since the Old Guard split reached breaking point, as the Militant Caucus fissured. In the months following the 1936 election, the two wings of the Militant Caucus moved further and further apart. By early 1937, a new caucus had emerged, the Clarity Caucus, with Herbert Zam and Gus Tyler as its most vocal members.[45]

Tyler was one of the young radicals attracted to the left-wing of the Socialist Party during the first years of the Great Depression. A journalist, he worked as a staff member of *Vorwärts*, the Yiddish daily newspaper with close ties to the SP. In the summer of 1936, Tyler was named the editor of the *Socialist Call*, the Party's weekly newspaper. In this role, he antagonized Norman Thomas with his editorials calling for a more radical politics.[46]

Tyler and Zam came from very different backgrounds. Zam had been a leading member of the Communist Party's youth group in the 1920s, aligning himself with the group around Jay Lovestone. In 1929, when the Lovestone group was expelled, Zam joined the Communist Party (Opposition). By the fall of 1934, when the Socialist Party opened its ranks to the anti-Stalinist Left, Zam was ready to leave the sectarian environment of the Lovestoneites for the more open setting of the SP. He quickly became one of the Party's most influential ideologues, and a leading member of the Clarity Caucus.[47]

Clarity quickly became a focal point for radicals in the Party. In spite of the substantial ideological differences between the Appeal Caucus and the Clarity Caucus, the two groups began cooperating to resist the rightward drift of the Militants. Arne Swabeck, one of the three members of the clandestine Trotskyist leadership committee, the Club, informed Vincent Dunne, the leader of the Minneapolis Trotskyists, that the two groups had begun working together in New York. In typical fashion, Swabeck informed Dunne that the Trotskyists were "separating" the "left centrists," that is the Clarity Caucus, from the "right centrists," the group around Norman Thomas. In any case, Swabeck was convinced that a unified left-wing formation would have to "be broad enough to include the left centrists."[48]

This is not to minimize the doubts that both groups felt for the other. Clarity leaders were concerned that the Trotskyists would quickly move to mold the Socialist Party into a tightly knit vanguard party should they become a dominant force within it. Clarity had good reasons to be wary. The Trotskyists were functioning as a sectarian cadre group within the SP. Furthermore, confidential letters between Trotsky and key members of the Appeal Caucus provide convincing evidence of the scorn with which the Trotskyists viewed Clarity's leaders. On the other hand, the Trotskyists doubted the commitment of Clarity's leaders to a radical politics. Since many prominent members of Clarity would be enrolled in the Democratic Party within three years of the La Guardia controversy, the Trotskyists had considerable grounds for their skepticism.

Nevertheless, in spite of all of these obstacles, the two groups slowly developed close working relations in the face of the Militants' obvious desire to subordinate the SP to the ALP. In February 1937, the Appeal Caucus convened a national conference in Chicago. A hundred delegates attended, including the entire Trotskyist leadership with the exception of Cannon. Clarity leaders were invited, with Zam presenting a 45 minute address on the internal debates within the SP. Burnham gave the main political statement, warning that the Party was "threatened with a split." He insisted that the Trotskyists stood for "a united party," and that the "unification of the left-wing forces into one united left-wing" required "unity between the Appeal and Clarity groups." A motion in support of this position was carried by the conference participants without opposition.[49]

As the Clarity Caucus and the Appeal Caucus looked to the formation of a coordinated left-wing opposition, the Party's most moderate members began calling for the mass expulsion of Trotskyists. Most of the Wisconsin SP had objected to the entry of the Trotskyists from the beginning. They were joined by a sizable section of the New York Militants, led by Jack Altman. Nevertheless, most Party members were staunchly determined to avoid another bitter split. After all, the Socialist Party was still reeling from the divisive struggle with the Old Guard, with membership in a free-fall.

By the end of 1936, Norman Thomas had come to regret his support for an all-inclusive party. He viewed the Trotskyists as a disruptive element, although he still opposed any move to instigate mass expulsions.[50] Instead, Thomas pushed for greater central control on key ideological questions. Clarity's leaders had always urged a more cohesive and unified party, so they welcomed Thomas' initiative.

The National Executive Committee responded to Thomas' initiative by setting March 1937 as the date for a special convention in Chicago, with the agenda limited to internal discipline and the labor party question. At the convention, Thomas successfully pushed for a resolution that brought all Party newspapers under the direct control of the NEC. The resolution was clearly aimed at the Trotskyists, who were utilizing *Socialist Appeal* as a factional organ. Yet the impact was also felt by the Clarity Caucus, which had just begun issuing its own journal, *Socialist Clarity*.[51]

The March 1937 convention also sought to heal the widening differences within the Party. Calls for the expulsion of the Trotskyist tendency were overwhelmed by the popular demand for unity. A single unified slate for the National Executive Committee passed overwhelmingly. The slate maintained a rough balance between the supporters of the Clarity and Militant caucuses, while the Trotskyists were excluded from representation. The composition of the NEC would prove to be of crucial importance as the SP polarized over the La Guardia campaign.

Only a few of the convention delegates voted for a motion critical of the labor party perspective. Instead, Thomas worked with Clarity leaders in jointly composing a resolution emphasizing the need for a nationwide labor-based electoral formation, while insisting that the Party would only work within such a formation if it maintained a total independence from the two mainstream parties.

For the Trotskyists, the Chicago convention had resulted in a series of ideological and organizational defeats. Nevertheless, Clarity delegates had been vocal in their rejection of any move toward further expulsions. Cannon therefore concluded that the convention had been "marked by" a "healthier atmosphere."[52] A strong, unified left-wing caucus remained a significant possibility, permitting the Trotskyists to further develop as a significant factor within the Socialist Party.

Within days of the Chicago convention, Thomas embarked on a six-week European voyage. Before his departure, he authorized Harry Laidler to act as his "deputy" in further discussions with ALP leaders. Although Thomas believed that the SP could not endorse the mayor if he accepted the Republican nomination, he also held that La Guardia had given New Yorkers "on the whole the best administration" the city had experienced in many years.[53]

Despite his misgivings, Thomas was "inclined" to believe that the Party should refrain from nominating its own candidate for mayor. Thomas had concluded that a socialist campaign in opposition to La Guardia "would incur a great deal of labor wrath," and "would complicate" the SP's "relations with labor." Needless to say, Thomas was referring to relations with Dubinsky, Hillman and Rose, the needle trades union leaders who controlled the American Labor Party.[54]

TROTSKY ORDERS A SPLIT

At this crucial moment, Trotsky decided to execute yet another sharp turn by pulling his supporters out of the Socialist Party. Just as the La Guardia campaign was acting as a wedge sharply dividing the Militant and Clarity caucuses, the Trotskyists provoked a split, virtually ensuring a victory for Norman Thomas and the Militant Caucus.

In early April of 1937, Albert Glotzer, a young Trotskyist militant, was dispatched to Mexico City, where Trotsky lived in exile, to aid in the preparations for the Dewey Commission, the tribunal headed by John Dewey that looked into Stalin's charges that Trotsky was a fascist spy and found them to be specious. Glotzer was also sent as an intermediary to bring Trotsky up to date and to return with the latest advice from the "Old Man."[55]

Upon his arrival at Trotsky's armed villa, Trotsky shocked Glotzer by notifying him of a drastic shift in policy. Although Glotzer had initially opposed the decision to enter the Socialist Party, once inside he was committed to carrying it through on a serious, long-term basis. Nevertheless, Trotsky informed Glotzer that events in Spain had made it essential to regain total freedom of action. Tensions within the Loyalist forces battling Franco were coming to a head, as relations between the Communist Party and the revolutionary Left deteriorated to the point of armed hostilities. Indeed, a month later, on May 3, 1937, troops loyal to the central government would seize the telephone exchange in Barcelona, which had been previously occupied by anarcho-syndicalist militants. Fierce battles erupted throughout the city, resulting in hundreds of casualties, and a crushing defeat for the radical Left. The clash in Barcelona marked a crucial turning point in the Spanish Civil War. Experiments in workers' control of industry and peasant collectives began to unravel, as a coalition of moderate socialists and Communists sought to make the Loyalist regime more palatable to Western democracies.[56]

Glotzer brought back informal word of the new turn, but Trotsky soon made it explicit. At the end of May, Trotsky dispatched an open letter holding that "the whole line" being pursued within the Socialist Party had been "an opportunistic one." Since the March 1937 convention had not addressed the question of the Spanish Civil War, or the Moscow Purge trials, it had been of "not the slightest revolutionary value." Indeed, the convention had prepared the SP "to enter [into] a bloc with the Stalinists." Thus, there was an urgent need for "a new policy."[57]

In less than three years, the small core of committed U.S. Trotskyists had merged with the American Workers Party, had then entered the Socialist Party, and was now being told to engineer a quick departure. Cannon quickly adhered to the new directives, but those in the New York leadership were far more resistant. Initially, Shachtman objected to the decision to provoke a split, but he soon swung into line; Burnham proved far more resistant.[58]

NORMAN THOMAS PREPARES TO WITHDRAW

As the Trotskyists debated the necessity of an immediate split, Norman Thomas returned from his European trip in early June 1937. He immediately pressed the Socialist Party to withdraw its own candidate for mayor, knowing that such a maneuver would precipitate a bitter and divisive debate within the Party. Yet Thomas understood that merely withdrawing his own name for consideration would not fully resolve this issue. Dissidents within the SP might well advance their own candidate for mayor as a credible alternative. Only an explicit decision by the Party could forestall such a possibility by placing New York City members under organizational discipline.

Thomas began his effort to sway the Party with a lengthy statement to Party members, in which he called for a "formal or informal conference with the ALP" to develop a joint ticket of independent candidates for the municipal election. The SP would "not endorse" La Guardia, should he accept the Republican nomination, but it would "be ready to withdraw" a socialist "mayoralty candidate against him." Thomas argued that the American Labor Party had been following a more independent policy over the previous year. It was no longer "an experimental local party," but rather, "with all its shortcomings," it had been transformed into "a mass labor party." Furthermore, although a socialist candidate for mayor would only attract "a very small vote," such a tally might prove to "be enough to defeat La Guardia." Such an outcome would leave the trade union officials who led the ALP "very bitter," so that Party members who were union officials would be forced "to choose between their union office and the SP." Instead, Thomas urged the Socialist Party to accede to "labor's reasonable desires to defeat Tammany [Hall]" by re-electing a mayor who, "with all his faults," had "given the city" four years of an "unusually good administration."[59]

Thomas followed up this statement with a supplementary memorandum that would seem to have been intended for a narrower audience, activists within the Militant Caucus. He warned his supporters that "a small group of enrolled socialists," perhaps tied to "Trotskyist extremists," might put forward a socialist candidate for mayor, thus undercutting the potential for a working arrangement with the American Labor Party. To forestall such a possibility, Thomas suggested that it might "be necessary to plan for a full ticket until the last minute [so as] to make such a maneuver more difficult." Thus, Thomas opted to leave his name in nomination as the Party's candidate for mayor, although he had already decided to withdraw, even if the SP decided to proceed with the campaign.[60]

These two documents are indicative of how far Thomas had moved by June 1937. Underlying the two documents was a strategic perspective that placed a premium on maintaining a close working relationship with prominent union officials such as David Dubinsky and Sidney Hillman, even though these union leaders remained locked into the Democratic Party. This was a strategic perspective that could only lead away from independent political action and toward the liberal wing of the Democratic Party.

CLARITY RESPONDS

The arguments put forward by Thomas in justification of his withdrawal as a candidate for mayor could only be seen as flimsy rationales by those committed to an independent, radical politics. Still, Thomas did advance one incisive point in his assessment of the New York situation. The strategic analysis presented by the Clarity Caucus was inherently contradictory. Clarity insisted on the need for a nationwide labor party, and yet it rejected every one of the actually existing labor parties. Thomas pointed out that once having accepted a labor party perspective, the Socialist Party could not "strain at a gnat," since it had already "swallowed a camel." Once having approved of "a labor party in theory," the SP could not then "refuse to take any steps" to put this "theory into practice."[61]

Both Thomas and the Trotskyists would attack Clarity for this apparent inconsistency, and with good reason. Nevertheless, the Clarity Caucus, from the ranks to the leadership, was genuinely determined to resist Thomas as he wheedled and cajoled the SP into implicitly supporting La Guardia. Two key leaders of Clarity, Herbert Zam and Max Delson, wrote a lengthy article for *Socialist Review*, the Party's theoretical journal, countering the initial memorandum by

Thomas. Dismissing the ALP as "bureaucratic," they condemned its leaders for refusing to allow the SP to join as an affiliated organization.[62]

Delson and Zam then addressed the core of the controversy. They insisted, contrary to Thomas, that the American Labor Party had "not come over to" the SP position on independent political action, but rather that it was still "hindering the movement" toward an independent working-class party by luring those who had broken with the two party system back into the mainstream. Indeed, in a period of economic decline, progressive labor leaders were stymied, "incapable of fighting aggressively for the formation of a Labor Party – an independent Labor Party."[63]

This point would seem to be even more relevant now, seven decades later, than it was then in the 1930s. Nevertheless, Zam and Delson did not carry the argument to its logical conclusion. In such a historical context, where the working class is on the defensive, and where reforms become increasingly difficult to win, the creation of a labor party becomes a virtual impossibility. As hopes for structural reforms of the type gained by European social democratic parties during the post-war boom vanish, union officials respond by clinging even more tightly to the Democrats as the lesser evil.

For all of its limitations, the article by Zam and Delson represented a significant step toward a genuinely radical politics. They explicitly rejected Thomas' primary reason for entering the ALP. Thomas had warned that a socialist campaign for mayor would "embitter relations" with powerful union officials. The Clarity leaders countered that to "give up the struggle" because it would incur "the enmity of labor leaders" was "tantamount to calling upon the Party to surrender to the trade union bureaucrats because they demand it." Zam and Delson condemned Thomas' position as a call for "the Socialist Party to turn traitor to socialism."[64]

These were strong words. Clarity was prepared to resist the maneuvers of Norman Thomas and the Militant Caucus, even at the risk of an organizational split. Yet forming a majority coalition that could defeat the turn to La Guardia was certain to be difficult. The Trotskyist decision to split undermined the potential for a left-wing defeat of Thomas and his allies.

In mid-June, the Appeal Caucus convened a mass meeting of its New York City members. The meeting issued a public statement that emphasized the repression of the Barcelona uprising, but the assembled Trotskyists also insisted on the need for "an independent socialist mayoralty campaign," while "rejecting any form of support of La Guardia and the American Labor Party." Although the Appeal Caucus statement represented a significant step toward a formal split, Clarity made yet another concerted effort to build a coordinated left-wing. Clarity leaders, including Gus Tyler, met with leading Trotskyists in New York, presumably Burnham and Shachtman, to explore the potential for a common program. The Trotskyists insisted that Clarity support the demand for a harsher condemnation of the Spanish Loyalist government for its repressive actions in Barcelona.[65]

The Trotskyist leaders apparently also demanded that Clarity should reverse its strategic perspective on the labor party question as a prerequisite to coordination. Although Clarity declined to join the Trotskyists in their vocal opposition to the formation of a nationwide labor party, Tyler, in an open letter describing this meeting, argued that while the need for a labor party "remained one of the lessons to be drawn from events," the "need for a revolutionary party" had emerged as "the basic lesson."[66]

Given the drive by Norman Thomas and the Militant Caucus to submerge the Socialist Party into the ALP, there was an obvious and compelling need to forge a broad alliance to resist this push, and to present a cohesive alternative. Within such a tactical coalition, each component tendency could have presented its own distinctive perspective on the theoretical question of the labor party, while acting in unity on the immediate issues at hand. Instead, the Appeal group, following Trotsky's directives, spurned the Clarity offer of "a voluntary truce."[67] Indeed, the Trotskyist critique of Clarity became increasingly polemical, leaving Thomas free to relentlessly pursue the ALP option.

The Clarity leadership understood that the Trotskyist move toward an immediate split undermined the potential for a Socialist Party committed to a radical politics. At first, Clarity hoped to deflect the efforts of Jack Altman and other Militant Caucus leaders to initiate a rapid expulsion of the entire Trotskyist contingent. Tyler warned that such mass expulsions "would place the Party in the hands of the 'right-wing.'"[68]

With Clarity and the Trotskyists unable to forge a unified opposition, Thomas and the Militant Caucus pressed forward with their plans to link up with the ALP and La Guardia. The New York City local's Municipal Election Committee approved a resolution by Altman and Laidler under which the SP would work for a common slate with the ALP, except for those offices where the ALP endorsed "candidates on any old party ticket." Furthermore, the SP would endorse Norman Thomas for mayor, but would agree to his withdrawal should discussions with ALP leaders indicate that such a move would "strengthen the labor movement" or the effort to establish "a national labor party." The resolution passed by a large majority, with only Zam and Delson opposed.[69]

On July 7, the Municipal Election Committee, with Norman Thomas leading the delegation, met with Mayor La Guardia for more than an hour. The details of this discussion remain unknown, but the SP was eager to gain endorsements for its nominees to the city council. Some time after this meeting, the City Fusion Party, which was closely linked to La Guardia, placed Harry Laidler on its list of recommended candidates to the council.[70]

In spite of the public moves to initiate an alliance with La Guardia, the issue remained very much in doubt within the Party ranks. A key confrontation came on July 13, 1937, when the New York City central committee met to determine the local's official policy. Zam and Delson presented an alternative motion to that of the Election Committee majority, holding that the SP should proceed "to run an independent candidate for mayor." Indeed, the Party would "not under any circumstances" withdraw its own candidate, thereby providing tacit support to the La Guardia campaign.[71]

After a contentious debate, in which Norman Thomas spoke for withdrawal, the central committee affirmed the decision of the Election Committee by a vote of 35 to 18. Having received more than a third of the total vote, the Clarity minority initiated a binding membership referendum.[72]

The New York Times of July 14 carried the gist of an SP press release announcing the Party's decision to put forward a slate of candidates for the municipal election, including Thomas for mayor. Yet the press release also stated the Party's willingness to withdraw from the mayoralty campaign, thus undercutting any leverage in the forthcoming negotiations with the ALP. Furthermore, the issue had still not been definitively determined within the New York City local, pending the results of the referendum. Nevertheless, the July 13 vote represented a critical turning point in the La Guardia debate. It was clear to all that Thomas was intent on reaching an agreement with the ALP for the 1937 election no matter how divisive the debate.[73]

As the divisions within the SP deepened, the Appeal Caucus moved ahead with its plans for a split, in accordance with Trotsky's directives. On July 19, the Trotskyists convened a closed meeting of the Club, the leadership of the caucus. Most of those present at the closed meeting agreed to provoke an immediate split, but Joe Carter (Joseph

Friedman), one of the leading younger Trotskyist activists, argued for the "perspective of an indefinite tenure in the SP." Mysteriously, a letter sent by a leading Trotskyist, Martin Abern, to a comrade in Massachusetts, and containing a brief description of this meeting, found its way to the SP's New York headquarters.[74]

A few days later, on July 24, a secret plenum of Trotskyist activists from around the country met in New York, and came to the same conclusion. The plenum decided to revive the *Appeal* in direct violation of the convention resolution requiring all Party periodicals to be authorized by the National Executive Committee. Although Burnham and Carter held out against the majority position, they found little support. Instead, the plenum voted to orient toward an immediate split from the SP, and the formation of a distinct and separate Trotskyist organization.[75]

At the same time, Clarity, realizing that it had to go it alone, called for a mass meeting of its New York supporters for July 20. The Trotskyists, having made the explicit decision to leave the Party, made a conscious decision to boycott the meeting. From the other side of the debate, the Militant Caucus held a competing rally the same night as a counter-attraction. In spite of these difficulties, the Clarity Caucus event drew 350 enthusiasts, including "many rank and file members of the Altman and Appeal groups." Sentiment at this meeting ran overwhelmingly opposed to any arrangement with La Guardia, although no formal vote was held.[76]

The Clarity leaders understood that they had been trapped, with no way out. Zam informed Arthur McDowell, the Party's national labor organizer based in Chicago, that the Abern letter demonstrated that "a very substantial section of the Appeal group" had adopted "the perspective of leaving or quitting the Party." Zam had "hoped to be able to win the support of a substantial number" of the Appeal Caucus for the Clarity position, but Altman and the Militant Caucus had stymied this possibility by pushing for the rapid, mass expulsion of Trotskyists.[77]

At the same time, the Militants had initiated "secret negotiations" with the Old Guard, as organized in the Social Democratic Federation. These negotiations, in which Laidler once again served as intermediary, eventually stalemated, with the coming war a crucial point of division. Nevertheless, Zam believed that a more positive outcome was a genuine possibility. After all, the political perspective of Norman Thomas and the Militants did "not differ substantially from [that of] the Old Guard." This convergence of views held "especially on the La Guardia question."[78]

The debate over the Party's attitude to La Guardia had been bitterly divisive within the New York local, and it became even more so after La Guardia accepted the Republican nomination. La Guardia's liberal policies had antagonized influential conservatives, so his endorsement was vehemently contested. Nevertheless, the Manhattan Republican organization decided in the last week of July that it would place La Guardia at the head of its ticket, but only after the mayor consented to endorse key Republicans for city office.[79]

By August 1937, the New York local was ready to move the issue of the La Guardia campaign to the national level, and yet the final resolution to this volatile controversy remained very much in doubt. First, the decision of the New York City central committee would have to be approved by membership referendum. Given the large and enthusiastic response to the Clarity Caucus meeting, it appeared quite possible that a majority vote would confirm the Party's earlier commitment to a mayoralty campaign. Second, the National Executive Committee would have to approve the New York decision. Clarity retained a strong position within the NEC, leaving that body evenly divided.

A CLANDESTINE OPERATION

At this point, the labor party debate of 1937 descended from the level of political controversy into the murky and secretive world of covert operations. As the Socialist Party heatedly debated its role in the municipal elections of 1937, powerful political forces paid close attention. Although the creation of the ALP as a nominally independent party had succeeded in diverting many socialist voters into the ranks of the New Deal, the SP still retained a substantial electoral base, votes that might determine a close election, at both the city and state levels.

As the divisions within the New York City local widened, a group of Militant activists secretly met to devise strategies to counter the Clarity Caucus, while speeding the mass expulsion of the Appeal Caucus. Upwards of 25 members of the Militant Caucus met frequently, with Norman Thomas and Jack Altman in attendance. At one of these meetings, held at Thomas' house on August 3, 1937, the group concluded "that [the] Trotskyists must be expelled in whatsoever manner the action could be taken." Thomas joined in this decision, further conceding that "he had made a mistake in approving the entry of the Workers Party into the Socialist Party." Less than a week later, the New York City central committee expelled 54 members of the Appeal group, with 70 more brought up on charges. These actions constituted a first step toward the mass expulsion of the entire Appeal Caucus.[80]

During this same closed meeting on August 3, Girolamo Valenti, an Italian socialist exile and a journalist and union organizer, proposed "that a committee be formed to approach the Amalgamated Clothing Workers Union and the ILGWU [International Ladies Garment Workers Union] for funds to finance the Altman group." Valenti "was certain that five to ten thousand dollars could be raised" through these channels. His proposal "was unanimously accepted" by the entire caucus, including Norman Thomas, with Valenti authorized to act as the group's representative in working out the specifics of this clandestine transfer of funds.[81]

Valenti's proposal profoundly altered the context of the debate within the Socialist Party. Five to ten thousand dollars was a great deal of money in 1937. Allowing for inflation, an equivalent sum would currently exceed $60,000–120,000, and yet even this underestimates its impact.[82] Money was very tight during the Great Depression. Furthermore, although Valenti posed the issue in terms of union financial aid, the garment-industry trade unions were the linchpins of the American Labor Party.

In fact, neither union could have readily delivered this kind of money into a clandestine effort to swing the Socialist Party into the orbit of the ALP. Indeed, the ILGWU had been on the brink of bankruptcy only a few years earlier. Yet both Dubinsky and Hillman had close ties to President Roosevelt and to the liberal wing of the Democratic Party. Herbert Lehman, a scion of one of the wealthiest families in New York and a liberal Democratic politician, had provided the ILG with a $50,000 loan when it had desperately needed it. Lehman had later relied on the ALP vote while being re-elected governor in 1936.[83] Whether Norman Thomas and his allies realized it or not, Valenti was clearing the way for wealthy Democrats to secretly fund a caucus within the SP that was pressing the Socialist Party to enter into a tacit alliance with the New Deal.

All of this is puzzling enough, but the mystery deepens when we consider the source of this revelation, and the impact it had on the internal debates of the Socialist Party. Robert Menaker had been one of those regularly attending the Militant Caucus meetings, but he withdrew in disgust after the August 3 meeting. Since Menaker was a staff member at the League for Industrial Democracy, where Laidler served as executive director, he was a likely person to be invited to these gatherings. Two weeks after the caucus meeting, Menaker informed the National Executive Committee of these shadowy developments, and yet there is no mention of Menaker's charges in Clarity's frequent and scathing criticisms of the Militant Caucus' maneuvers. Perhaps the initial letter never reached the members of the NEC, although this seems doubtful. After all, Menaker lived in New York City, and he could have easily contacted Clarity leaders such as Herbert Zam. More likely, Clarity declined to press the issue, fearful of triggering yet another damaging split.

Although it is still difficult to track the ramifications of Valenti's overture, the outcome of the referendum was clear. In the middle of August, the New York membership voted by a margin of 2 to 1 to authorize the local's leadership to negotiate Thomas' withdrawal as a mayoralty candidate. This victory gave a considerable boost to Party moderates, although several hurdles remained before a working relationship with the ALP could be concluded. Still, Altman issued an open letter lauding the referendum results as a "rejection of sectarianism."[84]

With the New York local having voted, the issues raised by the La Guardia campaign were brought to the Party's National Executive Committee meeting held the first days of September. All stops were pulled out to make sure that a majority assented to the New York plan. One NEC member replaced his alternate, a Clarity member, with a Militant supporter. Roy Burt, the SP national secretary, came under tremendous pressure, and finally accepted the proposal on the basis that the decision of the New York City local had to be respected. Norman Thomas stood at the center of these maneuvers. As the SP's three-time presidential candidate and its most respected public figure, Thomas staked his reputation on the La Guardia question. In private discussions, he reiterated a "constant implied threat" that his participation in the Party could be jeopardized by a rejection of the New York local's proposal.[85]

In spite of the devious maneuvers and the "irresponsible bullying" of Norman Thomas, the NEC vote was determined by the closest of margins. Maynard Krueger, a close personal friend of Thomas, held firm in his opposition to the New York local's overtures to the ALP. With the support of Clarity, Krueger proposed that the Socialist Party insist that cooperation with "labor political movements," such as the

ALP, be undertaken only "on the basis of STRICT INDEPENDENCE OF CAPITALIST PARTIES." This policy would have ruled out the endorsement of any candidate that accepted the nomination of either the Democratic or Republican parties. Krueger specifically rejected the New York local's decision on the La Guardia campaign by holding that no local could initiate the withdrawal of a socialist candidate "in the face of any candidate running for a capitalist party nomination." His motion was defeated by a vote of 8 to 7.[86]

With the NEC sharply divided, Devere Allen, the author of the 1934 Declaration of Principles and a Thomas supporter, sought to mollify the Clarity Caucus with a motion that endorsed the New York City decision, while tacking on certain restrictive conditions. The SP would not present its own candidate for mayor, but it would engage in "criticism of La Guardia from the socialist point of view." Furthermore, the ALP would "be urged vigorously" to endorse SP candidates for the city council. Finally, two Clarity members would be added to the delegation negotiating the final terms of the agreement with the ALP leadership. Allen's motion was approved by the identical vote of 8 to 7. The vote marked a major defeat for the Clarity Caucus. In protest, Tyler resigned as editor of the *Socialist Call*, the Party's official newspaper.[87]

Allen's restrictive conditions provided little more than window dressing. Negotiations had been going on for months with the ALP, so adding Clarity members for the last sessions was hardly likely to alter the outcome. Furthermore, the New York local had already made it very clear that it was reluctant to antagonize La Guardia, or his supporters, and, indeed, it moved very cautiously in its criticisms of the mayor throughout the campaign.

The NEC vote, narrow as it was, marked the definitive turning point in what had been a vitriolic and divisive controversy. Although the NEC resolution only authorized the New York local to engage in negotiations with the ALP on the basis for Thomas' withdrawal as a candidate for mayor, both sides understood that this was a mere formality, and that the Party had crossed a major divide.

In a confidential memorandum to the New York negotiators, Thomas recognized the difficulties caused by "the long drawn out strife" in the Party, and "even by the terms of the [NEC] resolution." Still, Thomas was convinced that the threat of his remaining a candidate would be sufficient to prod the ALP leaders into making concessions, since La Guardia was "going to need all the votes" he could get. Thomas continued to maintain his illusory hopes as to the future course of the American Labor Party. He urged the SP representatives to seek assurances "of the desire of the ALP, or important sections of it," to build "a party strong enough" to "stand on its own feet," so as "not to endorse old party candidates." This represented the politics of delusion. The union officials who controlled the ALP had not the slightest intention of breaking with President Roosevelt or the liberal wing of the Democratic Party. Thomas was so blinded by his desire to cooperate with the ALP that he steadfastly refused to recognize its fundamental underlying premise.[88]

For Clarity, the "NEC decision on the New York mayoralty campaign" represented "the first step toward party dissolution." By tacitly supporting La Guardia, the Militant Caucus was "committing the Party to a Popular Frontist line," and was thus "forcing clear cut socialists out of the Party in disgust." Through these maneuvers, the SP had "been delivered up to the tender mercies of the trade union bureaucrats for a piteously low price." Norman Thomas and his allies were pursuing the same strategic vision "which the Old Guard [had] advanced for years." They hoped that by "licking the boots of the trade union bureaucrats" they could gain their acceptance as trusted members of the ALP.

On September 20, 1937, the SP delegation met with Alex Rose to further consolidate the understanding that would permit Norman Thomas to withdraw as a candidate. In accordance with the NEC resolution, Thomas, Laidler and Altman spoke for the majority of the New York local, while Max Delson and Marion Severn attended as Clarity representatives. Rose "stressed the fact that he was meeting" with the SP delegation "as an individual," and not in his position as state secretary of the ALP. Furthermore, the ALP executive committee "had rejected any suggestion of cooperation" between the two organizations.[89]

Rose's comments would seem to have left very little for discussion, especially since he also made it clear that the American Labor Party had no interest in working with the SP in the formulation of a joint slate of candidates for the 1937 elections. In addition, the ALP had already decided that it would not nominate its own candidates in those state assembly districts where a "good man," in either the Democratic or Republican parties, was already standing for that seat.

In general, Rose did most of the talking during the hour-long meeting, devoting most of his comments to attacks on the Socialist Party for its supposed ideological rigidity. Still, Rose was interested in having the SP enter into the ALP orbit. He urged the Party to send its individual members into the ALP, where they could serve as an ideological counterweight to the Communist Party.

Delson and Severn left the meeting dismayed, convinced that the ALP leadership was committed to a "continuation of the policy of backing first one of the old parties, and then another." Not only was the ALP "not interested in cooperation" with the SP on an official basis, but also there was "no prospect of [SP] membership in the ALP on a federated basis." In conclusion, the SP had "nothing to gain and much to lose in withdrawing from the mayoralty contest."[90]

Needless to say, the moderate majority was not deterred by Rose's belligerent arrogance at the meeting. A few days later, the New York local's central committee issued a report concluding that the conditions set by the NEC had been met. The local insisted that it had issued a "sharp criticism of La Guardia's endorsement" of George Harvey, Queens borough president and a conservative Republican, and it pledged that it would "continue the line of constructive criticism." Of course, the NEC had mandated the New York local to present a socialist critique of La Guardia. Instead, Thomas and the New York local chastised the mayor for being an inconsistent liberal.[91]

In its statement, the New York local pointed to the one concession it had extracted from the ALP leadership. The 1937 municipal election was the first to be held on the basis of borough-wide preferential voting.[92] This system encouraged each political party to limit its slate to a few candidates in each borough, with the hope that its supporters would give their highest priority votes to these candidates. Although the ALP did not place any socialist candidates on its priority list, it did list two socialists, as well as several liberal Democrats, as friendly allies who should be supported, but with a lower-priority vote.[93]

In transmitting this report to the Party's National Executive Committee, the New York City local gave formal notice of its intention to withdraw Norman Thomas as a candidate for mayor. The local justified this decision on the basis of "the great progress of the ALP," and "the immense value to the Socialist Party of friendly relations with it." Indeed, the ALP was "a labor party controlled and financed by organized labor." In a direct challenge to the Clarity Caucus, the statement of the New York local argued that if, in fact, the ALP was "not a labor party," then there was "none in the United States," nor was "one likely to soon emerge."[94]

This last point presented the problem in a nutshell. Since the bureaucratized garment industry unions of New York City dominated the ALP, it was, in fact, a labor-based political formation. Indeed, it came as close to a labor party as the United States would ever see. Clarity therefore had to decide whether to abandon its repeated call for a labor party, or accept the American Labor Party, with its extensive ties to President Roosevelt and the liberal wing of the Democratic Party, as the best possible alternative.

For the majority of the New York City local, the choice was obvious. Although the ALP was not "the type of labor party" with which the SP could merge, it "was the type of party" with which the Party could "cooperate in a friendly fashion," while maintaining a "constructive criticism of its policy." The alternative was a Socialist Party "doomed to futility or empty sectarian isolation."[95]

By dispatching this statement to the National Executive Committee, the New York City local formally notified the Party leadership that it would proceed to withdraw Norman Thomas as a candidate for mayor, leaving the field open for La Guardia. Norman Thomas then dispatched an urgent letter to the NEC members who had voted with the majority on this issue urging them to hold firm and to give final approval to the New York decision. He informed them that even if the local's decision were to be reversed, he would not agree to continue as a candidate, since he was convinced that he "could not do a decent job." Furthermore, a negative vote by the NEC "would create such chaos in New York as to practically finish the Party."[96]

Thomas had decided several months earlier that he would not campaign for mayor of New York. Nevertheless, he had deliberately refrained from a public statement of his intentions, in part to preclude the possibility of another candidate emerging. With October 5, the final deadline for filing for the election, only a few days away, Thomas finally informed the Party's leadership of his decision. At this point, the question became moot. The Socialist Party would not be presenting a radical alternative to La Guardia.

Thomas' letter to his allies on the NEC also contained a provocative perspective on New York politics. Thomas reported that he had received "categorical assurances" from "high sources in the ALP" that the newly formed third party would quickly "establish itself as an independent party," and that it intended "to run its own candidates, and only its own candidates, as soon" as it felt "strong enough."[97] Thomas was either deliberately lying, or extremely gullible. Alex Rose had made it abundantly clear that the ALP would remain within the two party system. As the ALP's state secretary, Rose was in a position to know.

On September 26, 1937, Thomas formally withdrew as the SP candidate for mayor. Thomas publicly explained his decision to withdraw "as a token" of the Party's "desire to aid the cause of labor." The Socialist Party had opted not to officially endorse La Guardia, who had accepted the Republican nomination, as well as that of the ALP. Nevertheless, Thomas praised the La Guardia administration for its "undoubted progress," and he warned the voters that a victory for Tammany Hall "would set back immensely the growth of a real labor party." As Clarity had correctly predicted, in withdrawing as the socialist candidate for mayor, Thomas delivered an implicit endorsement of La Guardia.[98]

TROTSKY EXECUTES A SHARP TURN

The August 9 decision of the New York local's executive committee to expel 54 members of the Appeal Caucus marked the end of the entry experiment. Although further expulsions would follow over the next few weeks, the Trotskyists began to function as members of an independent organization with their own structure and politics. On August 14, *Socialist Appeal* resumed publication on a weekly basis, this time as the official organ of the Trotskyist movement.[99]

In its first issue, the *Appeal* cited the La Guardia campaign as a major reason for the recent split. La Guardia had relied on the American Labor Party to divert previously independent voters back into the two party system. As such, it represented "a movement for the liquidation of independent working class politics." The *Appeal* also reiterated the prevailing Trotskyist orthodoxy, arguing that it was not the "proper business" of revolutionary socialists "to 'advocate' or 'build'" a labor party, although "critical support" remained possible "under certain given conditions" for an already established labor party based directly on "the majority of the organized working class."[100]

As they departed the Socialist Party, the Trotskyists brought with them most of the Party's youth group, the Young People's Socialist League.[101] They did so in large part by stressing their total opposition to the creation of a working relationship with the ALP. Yet within weeks of the initial expulsions, Trotsky would once again shift his position on the labor party, this time bringing his position in close alignment with that of Norman Thomas and the Militant Caucus. The ironies implicit in this latest twist must have been maddening to all of those who had so recently been engulfed in the acrimonious debates concerning the La Guardia campaign.

Trotsky's sharp turn on the question of the labor party can only be understood in its historical context. Once again, his perspective on U.S. politics was heavily influenced by his changing views on more global issues, more specifically the role of the Communist parties in the advanced capitalist countries. The Spanish Civil War had a profound impact on Trotsky. Indeed, his earlier decision to instigate a split within the Socialist Party had been triggered by the Communist role in Spain, leading to the armed clash in Barcelona.

The issues that divided Stalinists and Trotskyists in Spain quickly descended from the level of a debate on strategic priorities to a defensive battle of life and death. Challenged by the radical anti-authoritarian politics of the Spanish revolution, Stalin opted to launch a campaign of assassinations aimed at those he viewed as Trotskyist troublemakers. In June 1937, agents of the Soviet secret police, the KGB, kidnapped and killed Andrés Nin, a prominent leader of the POUM, a small radical socialist party rooted in Catalonia. In addition, Trotskyist leaders who traveled to Spain to aid the revolution were murdered by the Soviets and their Spanish accomplices.[102]

This campaign of terror marked a new and ominous escalation in Stalin's assault on the Trotskyist opposition. Trotsky's supporters had been ruthlessly purged from the Communist Party of the Soviet Union, exiled and even killed. Nevertheless, Trotskyists had not been physically threatened outside of the Soviet Union. In the summer of 1937, this policy was reversed, as Stalin began employing the same lethal methods against Trotskyists residing in Western Europe. Stalin's paranoid fear of the Trotskyist opposition was further intensified in the wake of a defection from within the top ranks of the Soviet intelligence network.

As POUM leaders were jailed and killed in Spain, Ignace Poretsky, a Soviet intelligence officer operating undercover with the code name Reiss, defected from his post in Paris. Poretsky had been ordered to participate in a clandestine operation aimed at Trotsky's son, Leon Sedov, the coordinator of the Trotskyist movement in Western Europe. In spite of his two decades' service as a Soviet espionage agent, Poretsky remained a committed revolutionary. He contacted Trotskyist leaders and informed them that their organization had been penetrated by Soviet spies, and that Trotsky and his most prominent supporters had been targeted for elimination. As the Trotskyists tried to develop a coherent response to these chilling revelations, Stalin's agents assassinated Poretsky on September 4, 1937.[103]

Not surprisingly, Trotsky began to reassess his views of Stalin and the Communist parties of Europe and the United States. Although Trotsky could not bring himself to fully confront the dismal reality of the Soviet Union, insisting until his death that it remained some sort of workers' state, he was now convinced that Stalinism represented the most acute threat to the Left. Communist parties, under orders from Moscow, would betray the working class of the developed countries in the short-run interests of the Soviet rulers. Stalinism had become the "leprosy of the world labor movement." Indeed, Stalin had emerged as "the most sinister figure in the history of mankind."[104]

In the aftermath of the Stalinist attacks on the POUM, Trotsky reassessed his analysis of U.S. politics. He urged his supporters to harden their critique of the Socialist Party. Militant Caucus leaders such as Jack Altman were "agents of the Stalinist-reformist hangmen of the Russian revolution," and should be denounced as "traitors and rascals." Once having left the SP, the newly launched Trotskyist organization would have to "begin more systematic and persistent work within the CP."[105]

This was not a momentary impulse. From this point onward, Trotsky would consistently push his supporters in the United States to put a premium on actions aimed at dividing the Communist Party and undermining its influence within the Left. Needless to say, Trotsky proceeded to develop a strategic analysis to buttress this new perspective. The Communist Party would soon enter into a devastating dilemma, its Popular Front policies, under which the Communists worked closely with liberal Democrats, entirely discredited. Trotsky usually ascribed this disaster to a prolonged downturn in the economy, "a new terrible crisis, more terrible than the crisis of 1929." This would push the working class into a more militant stance, and thus the Communist Party's Popular Front would "crash."[106]

Trotsky expected that the CP would soon "pass through a period of inner conflict and splits." In the immediate aftermath of Nin's assassination, he emphasized the potential for drawing disaffected Communists into the Trotskyist movement. The coming disintegration of the Popular Front made it necessary to "prepare [for] an amalgamation" with disillusioned radicals leaving the CP.[107]

Poretsky's revelations, and assassination, led Trotsky to advance this argument to a further level. Shortly after Poretsky's death, Trotsky warned Cannon to be wary of his group's "complete isolation from the Stalinist party." In order to counter this, "systematic work should be begun immediately." Of necessity, such a project would have to start with only a few comrades, and yet it could still "prepare the groundwork for the larger penetration in[to] this milieu."[108]

Trotsky was not speaking in metaphors. On the contrary, he was instructing the Trotskyist organization in the United States to engage in a sensitive and dangerous covert operation. This was a recurrent theme in his letters to America during the months following Poretsky's murder. Trotsky's most detailed explanation came during informal talks in Mexico City with three Trotskyist leaders, Cannon, Shachtman and Vincent Dunne, held in March 1938. Trotsky insisted that it was "important to have a nucleus in the Stalinist party." This would involve two different kinds of operations. Secretaries to leading Communist Party officials with access to confidential files should be recruited as double agents. In addition, Trotskyist militants who were not well known on the Left should be sent into the CP as "direct agents."[109]

By the fall of 1937, Trotsky was obsessed with the need to counter Communist influence within the working-class movement. Trade unions were set as the highest priority, but labor-based political parties provided another critical venue. In this context, Trotsky proceeded to drop another bombshell. As the Appeal Caucus regrouped, Trotsky wrote Cannon a series of confidential letters outlining a radically different perspective on the question of the labor party. The first letter, dated October 2, 1937, reiterated the prediction of a "new crisis," that promised "to be more terrible than the last one." This drastic downturn in the economy would "deliver a terrible blow" to working-class illusions in the Popular Front and in the New Deal. In turn, there would be "a new political orientation" that would reinforce "all [of] the tendencies toward an independent labor party," one based directly on the newly formed industrial unions of the CIO. This shift in popular opinion would be accompanied by the "crash of the Stalinist party." In this context, the Trotskyist tendency could not "remain outside" of a labor party formation.[110]

Concerned that "the fragmentary character" of his previous letter might lead to a "misunderstanding," Trotsky wrote a further letter on October 10. The "new crisis" and "the inevitable disintegration of People's Front policies" made it "necessary" to prepare for "a sharp turn." This in turn required an orientation of "the whole organization toward the factories," and to the newly organized industrial unions. One aspect of this strategic priority would entail activity within the political expression of the trade unions, that is the American Labor Party and Labor's Nonpartisan League.[111]

Trotsky understood that his new perspective on the labor party question was bound to trigger a contentious debate among his supporters. Joseph Hansen, one of his secretaries, advised Cannon that the letters Trotsky had recently dispatched were "strictly confidential and personal," and "especially" should "*not* appear in the Internal Bulletin." Cannon also understood the need for cautious discretion, so he moved slowly before responding. By early November, Trotsky was admonishing Cannon of a "certain astonishment" that his letters had gone unanswered.[112]

Cannon quickly responded that he recognized the importance of the recent letters, and that he was "altogether in agreement with the political suggestions incorporated" in them. He hastened to reassure Trotsky that he would do everything he could "to orient the party along this path."[113]

Trotsky realized that his new perspective on the labor party question directly contradicted his previous position. The new formulation can only be understood in a historical setting in which the countering of Communist influence within the working-class movement had come to be seen as of paramount importance. This setting of priorities can be seen very clearly in an open letter from November 1937, only a month after Trotsky had instructed Cannon on the new line. Pointing to the lethal campaign of the Soviet secret police in Spain, and to the assassination of Poretsky in Switzerland, Trotsky vowed that Stalin had "overstepped" the outer limits. It was therefore "necessary" to "purge the horrible contagion of Stalinism from the ranks of the emancipatory movement." Accordingly, it was "necessary to institute in all labor organizations a regime of rigid mistrust of everyone directly or indirectly connected with the Stalinist apparatus."[114]

Although Trotsky had outlined his new position in his letters to Cannon, he provided the most complete explanation of the new turn in informal discussions with his supporters. Trotskyists operating within the framework of a labor party would enter into alliances "with the reformists, bureaucrats of trade unions, against the Stalinists." This was addressed particularly to Minneapolis, where Trotskyists controlled Teamsters Local 544, a vital force in the union movement of the Twin Cities.[115]

Yet Trotsky was certain that this would constitute only one aspect of the new turn. It was "essential to prepare ourselves for illegal work." The American Labor Party had barred both Communists and Trotskyists from joining. Nevertheless, the Communist Party had succeeded in using its base in New York City unions to gain a foothold in the new party. Cadre militants were also being sent into neighborhood ALP clubs, where they denied any organizational links to the CP. Trotsky argued that his supporters should do the same, insisting "that illegal work must be done in the New York Labor Party." This kind of covert operation was "genuine preparation for the new, more difficult illegal work" which could be expected once the United States entered the war against Nazi Germany.[116]

Trotsky made this point sharply and clearly. One reason to join the ALP was precisely because the union officials who controlled it had prohibited such an entry. Entering into the ALP would be "the first illegal work to be done." At the same time, it was necessary to counter Communist influence within the ALP, as well as within other labor-based political formations. Trotsky did not explicitly link these two arguments, but the conclusion seems clear. By entering the ALP, Trotskyist militants could not only gain experience in covert operations, but they could also make contact with Communist cadres, win over the disaffected, and perhaps even turn some of them into double agents. It might even be possible to utilize the ALP as an arena in which to introduce double agents into the Communist Party, with the aim of ultimately penetrating into the CP's higher ranks. Trotsky instructed his supporters that the "most important work" to be done was inside of "the CP, to penetrate even into the [Political] Bureau."[117]

Trotsky had made a dizzying series of shifts and zigzags in setting policy for his U.S. supporters. Given the resulting tensions, and the recent acrimonious debate within the Socialist Party, Cannon proceeded with caution in presenting the new turn on the labor party question. Although Trotsky's letters were circulated within the leadership, rank and file members were not informed of the new line.

Instead, as delegates to the founding convention met on December 31, 1937 in Chicago, they were presented with resolutions that reiterated the traditional position. Indeed, the declaration of principles for the Socialist Workers Party castigated the ALP for having been created "by the trade union bureaucrats to gather votes for Roosevelt." As revolutionary socialists, the Trotskyists could not "properly take the initiative in advocating the formation of labor or farmer-labor parties."[118]

Once the new party had been launched, Cannon, with Trotsky's personal support, began lining up support for the new perspective. This time the entire leadership rallied to the new turn, and yet Cannon still had a problem. Most of those who had been recruited out of the Socialist Party had been won over on the basis of the Appeal Caucus' adamant opposition to Thomas' desire to forge a working relationship with the ALP.

Shortly after the March 1938 discussions in Mexico, Trotsky prepared a written statement of his new position. He started with the "deepening crisis of capitalism," which would necessarily impart "to the question of the labor party a considerably greater sharpness than in all preceding periods." The SWP would therefore "doom itself to isolation and sectarian degeneration" if it remained aloof from the labor party movement. Instead, the SWP would enter labor-based political formations to promote independent politics, and to support "progressive tendencies against the reactionary."[119]

In spite of the revolutionary rhetoric in which Trotsky couched his thesis, this was very much the position that Norman Thomas had been defending within the Socialist Party. At the April plenum of the SWP, Trotsky's thesis was approved as the basis of a new perspective, and the Political Committee was instructed to submit an extended version of it to a membership referendum. Gregory Bardacke, who had been recruited out of the Clarity Caucus of the SP, opposed Trotsky's thesis and proposed that the SWP affirm its previous position. His motion was overwhelmingly defeated.[120]

The June meeting of the Political Committee approved the lengthier version of Trotsky's thesis, with only Hal Draper dissenting. Draper had joined YPSL, the Socialist Party's youth group, in 1934, adhering to a small left-wing faction. Once the Trotskyists entered the SP, he aligned himself with the Appeal Caucus and was expelled in the fall of 1937, along with most of the YPSL. In 1938, Draper represented the SWP youth group on the Political Committee.[121]

Draper accepted Trotsky's analysis of an impending economic collapse, which was, in fact, erroneous, but he arrived at a very different set of conclusions. The "deepening social crisis" would bring with it "convulsive upheavals" and thus "the possibility for the revolutionary party to advance in bold strides," with "great gains in influence and membership." Given this potential for upheaval, the CIO leadership might well decide to create a labor party that could "achieve an organizational, formal independence" from the two mainstream parties. At this point, Draper diverged from Trotsky. In such a period of mass radicalization, the formation of a labor party could only constitute "a positive obstacle on the road of development of the workers." The SWP should therefore continue to actively oppose calls for a nationwide labor party. Nevertheless, even Draper believed that if this movement should develop "much more far-reaching dimensions" it might "yet be necessary" to "throw a large portion" of the SWP's membership "into such activity."[122]

Draper stood alone within the SWP leadership, with the entire core of veteran leaders, including Burnham and Carter, falling behind Trotsky's new turn. In spite of this, 40 percent of the membership voted to reject the Political Committee's proposal in support of a labor party.[123]

By the fall of 1938, the Trotskyists were moving in the same direction as the Old Guard, their ideological polar opposite. Both groups sought to work within the American Labor Party, hoping to counter the influence of the Communist Party while advocating a more independent politics. Only the Socialist Party remained outside of the ALP, but its members would soon join as well.

ENTRY INTO THE AMERICAN LABOR PARTY

In the fall of 1937, with the Trotskyists expelled, and the Clarity Caucus in disarray, the moderates of the Militant Caucus moved to rapidly integrate the Party into the ALP. Norman Thomas spent election night at the Bronx headquarters of the ALP, where he celebrated La Guardia's convincing victory, and joined in a rousing chorus of the "Internationale."[124]

The 480,000 votes that La Guardia received on the ALP line proved to be the margin of victory. For Thomas, the election results further reinforced the argument for a cooperative arrangement with the ALP. In a memorandum written shortly after the election, he defended his decision to withdraw, insisting that a socialist campaign for mayor "would have meant a crushing loss with no gain for socialist education." It was essential for the SP to "seek cooperation" with the ALP. Furthermore, any criticisms of the ALP had to be undertaken in a "tone of friendly, not carping, criticism." In other words, the Socialist Party should submerge its political perspective into the liberal coalition being organized under the auspices of the American Labor Party. To implement this perspective, the Party would announce its "readiness for a complete merging" of "electoral functions" with a prospective independent labor party.[125]

Thomas still believed that the Party needed to retain its own ballot line, at least for the foreseeable future, while subordinating its electoral strategy to that of the ALP. Yet Thomas was prepared to go even further. He proposed that the state executive committee authorize certain "mature comrades" to join the ALP as individuals, but only if this could be done openly. Thomas was setting the stage for the organizational dissolution of the New York Socialist Party into the ALP. He did so although he understood that it was "scarcely more than a left-wing New Deal party," and that the Party could not "expect the ALP to become a federated party." For all the underlying problems, Thomas remained optimistic. The 1937 election had demonstrated "an encouraging drift to definite labor party action, ultimately even to independent labor party action."[126]

Thomas was placing his considerable influence behind a move to negotiate a permanent arrangement with the American Labor Party, one that would subordinate the SP to its New Deal politics. The New York state committee appointed a subcommittee, including Thomas, to negotiate with Rose and the ALP leadership. The talks dragged on for three months, but in early February the two sides reached a tentative accord. (The accord seems to have been strictly oral.) Although the specifics of the talks were kept secret, by request of the ALP, core activists in both the Clarity and Militant caucuses were informed of the general tenor of the discussions.[127]

Under the agreement, the SP pledged to abandon its historic role as an independent electoral party in the state of New York. Candidates on the ALP ticket would be endorsed by the Socialist Party. Under these conditions, the ALP would permit SP members to join as individuals, and to act openly as Party members. The SP state committee quickly approved the agreement, leaving it to the ALP state committee to make the final decision.

Norman Thomas endorsed the agreement, holding that the ALP was "a genuine labor party, even if" it remained "imperfect." Still, Thomas had to concede that the "problem of 1940" was "difficult," in part because of the lack of an "equivalent of the ALP on the national field." Yet the obstacles were more complex than that. For Thomas, there was no issue "more important" than the Party's "campaign to keep the United States out of war." Roosevelt was already steering the United States into a conflict with Germany and Japan, so Thomas was not prepared to relinquish the possibility of a presidential campaign in 1940. Indeed, he would become the SP candidate that year.[128]

Thomas lobbied hard for the tentative agreement. In a confidential letter to David Dubinsky, he confirmed that he was "extraordinarily anxious for the plan" to "go through." He guaranteed that the SP would undertake its "electoral or parliamentary work in New York State only through the ALP," so that, like the Social Democratic

Federation, the Party would become an educational current, "a Socialist League," in New York. Furthermore, Thomas assured Dubinsky that the proposed agreement would "go through the Party," although the membership had not yet been informed of its provisions, let alone been given an opportunity to approve it. In urging Dubinsky to use his considerable influence in favor of the tentative agreement, Thomas emphasized "the advantage of having socialists" in the ALP given "the general situation," specifically "Communist activities." Once inside of the ALP, the SP would align its members with Dubinsky and Rose in opposition to those who were linked to the Communist Party.[129]

As word of the tentative agreement reached the leaders of the Clarity Caucus, the cohesion of that group unraveled. The departure of the Trotskyist tendency had already demoralized the left-wing opposition within the Party. As a result, Clarity accepted in principle the strategic necessity of an accord with the ALP, while condemning the specific terms of the agreement. In analysing the tentative agreement, Gus Tyler conceded that the recent split had "weakened the general 'left.'" Tyler was prepared to accept an accord with the ALP, but only if the Party could nominate its own candidates whenever the ALP backed a politician from one of the two mainstream parties.[130] The ALP had already rejected this option.

Tyler's position represented a significant dilution of Clarity's critique of the ALP as formulated during the La Guardia campaign, but other leading members of the Clarity Caucus switched entirely to the Militant position. Lazare Becker had joined the SP in the fall of 1934, along with Zam and several other members of the Lovestone group. In February 1938, Becker wrote a lengthy memorandum calling upon the Party to accept the tentative agreement.

Becker chastised those who were "opposed to a labor party in principle," or those who objected to the ALP in specific because it was not "a genuine labor party," condemning them for their "sectarianism." Instead, Becker supported the tentative accord, although he did concede that entry was a policy "full of dangers." Still, only by "mobilizing the forces inside the ALP" could the Socialist Party "recover the influence" within the working class that it had once held. By acting as a "disciplined unit" within the ALP, the Party would avoid the dangers of becoming "lost in the sea of opportunism."[131]

While the SP debated and then endorsed the tentative accord, the ALP tabled it at its March 7 state committee meeting. Rose remained skeptical of a formal entry, although he understood the utility of bringing the SP in as a counterbalance to the Communist Party. Thus, the SP's continuing status as a ballot-certified party made it difficult for the ALP to absorb it. In spite of this setback, the Party's moderates still looked toward a cooperative relationship with the ALP.

When the Party's convention assembled in Kenosha, Wisconsin, on April 21, 1938, talks with the ALP remained on hold. Eager to avoid yet another divisive debate, the delegates passed a labor party resolution that straddled the remaining differences. The resolution started with the familiar claim that the "formation of a labor party would be a progressive move in America," but it also resolutely maintained that such a party "must be completely independent of the capitalist parties" for it to "serve this purpose." Needless to say, the ALP did not even begin to approach this standard.[132]

In any case, the resolution proposed that Party members be enlisted in those parties that were based on organized labor and under "its own control." Still, the resolution insisted "as an irreducible minimum" that in such an arrangement the Party reserved the right "to run Socialist Party candidates against capitalist candidates." Although the convention accepted this formulation with little dissent, Thomas would later comment that he "regretted the Kenosha resolution."[133]

Shortly after the Kenosha convention concluded, the stalled negotiations revived. David Dubinsky, the president of the ILGWU and a major financial backer of the ALP, "indicated his vigorous support for admission" of the Socialist Party, perhaps, in part, as a response to Thomas' confidential letter. Dubinsky had concluded that "the menace of Communist domination" had become "more acute and apparent," making it even more essential to bring SP members into the American Labor Party. At Rose's suggestion, the SP's state committee drew up "a formal proposition on entry."[134]

Intense negotiations were initiated to finalize the agreement and see it implemented. Altman and Laidler represented the Socialist Party, while Rose was joined by Luigi Antonini and Jacob Potofsky, two high-level garment union officials, in negotiating for the American Labor Party. The final terms called for SP members to join the ALP as individuals. Only ALP-endorsed candidates would be nominated on the SP line, and the Party pledged that it would not present its own candidates for any office where the ALP had endorsed a candidate that had also accepted the nomination of the Democratic or Republican parties. As the sole exception to this rule, the agreement permitted the SP to nominate a presidential candidate. In the state of New York, the Socialist Party would cease to exist as an electoral alternative and instead would function as an educational current within the ALP.[135]

With Dubinsky's emphatic support, the ALP state committee approved the tentative agreement. Over the Memorial Day weekend, the SP's National Executive Committee gave its approval to the agreement, although its provisions directly contradicted the labor party resolution recently approved at the Party's national convention in Kenosha. Up to this point, the talks had been held in secret, in accordance with the insistent requests of the ALP. In early June, Paul Tobenkian, a reporter from the *New York Herald Tribune*, visited Thomas and Laidler to warn them that his newspaper knew of the negotiations and was about to go public.[136]

Thomas agreed to answer Tobenkian's questions. He justified the Party's decision to abandon its own electoral activities, insisting that the ALP's decision in 1937 to nominate its own candidates to the New York city council, a line headed by La Guardia, had demonstrated that the ALP had become "a genuine labor party." Thomas also insisted that the SP reserved the right to present its own presidential candidate unless and until a farmer-labor party was formed at the national level.[137]

Rose was not pleased, both by the unwanted publicity and by the explicit assertion of the SP's right to go its own way in the presidential election in 1940. The ALP then demanded a "clarification" of the Socialist Party's position, and the New York state committee complied. Its response pointed out that the ALP could expel SP members if they supported socialist candidates rather than those endorsed by the ALP. Furthermore, the "clarification" virtually guaranteed that the SP would not put forward its own candidates in the 1938 election, no matter whom the ALP supported. As it turned out, the ALP endorsed the entire Democratic Party ticket at the state and federal level in 1938.[138]

In spite of the humiliating eagerness with which the SP pursued the ALP, the talks stalled. As long as the Socialist Party retained its own ballot line in New York, Rose and the ALP leadership were unwilling to enter into an explicit accord with the Party. The matter was resolved that fall when Norman Thomas accepted the nomination for governor, and proceeded to mount a token campaign. As a result, he received fewer than 25,000 votes statewide, far short of the 50,000 needed to retain ballot status. This cleared the way for a final resolution of the issue. With the Party no longer on the ballot, the ALP implemented the previously negotiated agreement, permitting SP members to join as individuals, as members of an educational organization with the same status as those in the Old Guard's Social Democratic Federation.[139]

The only remaining step was a referendum vote by the SP membership in New York ratifying the decision to enter the ALP. Militant Caucus leaders enthusiastically endorsed entry, without reservations. They insisted that the SP would find "many allies within the ALP, many Social Democrats, Lovestoneites and a large section of the trade union movement." Most Clarity leaders, including Herbert Zam, backed the agreement, while emphasizing that it did not preclude the possibility of a socialist campaign in 1940. Their statement also adopted Becker's argument, holding that the SP could prod the ALP into a more independent stance, but only if Party members acted "in an organized and disciplined manner." Despite the near unanimity within its leadership, 25 percent of the Party's New York members voted against entry.[140]

Once inside of the ALP, most Socialist Party members were quickly absorbed into the liberal mainstream. Among those in the Militant Caucus, Harry Laidler withdrew from active participation in the SP soon after joining the ALP. After being elected in 1939 to the city council on the ALP ticket, he left the SP to support the U.S. effort in World War II. Jack Altman became an ALP stalwart, and then worked as a union official and labor relations consultant. Within the ranks of Clarity, Gus Tyler accepted a position in the International Ladies Garment Workers Union in early 1939, left the socialist movement and remained loyal to David Dubinsky for the next three decades.[141]

This is not to argue that entry into the ALP can fully account for this pattern of cooptation. Certainly the popularity of the New Deal set the historical context, and, indeed, provided the initial impetus for the SP to merge into the ALP. Furthermore, U.S. participation in World War II led many Party members to reject a socialist vision and to become pro-war liberals. Nevertheless, the decision to withdraw Norman Thomas as a candidate for mayor, followed by the Party's entry into the ALP, accelerated this absorption into the mainstream. In effect, the Socialist Party abandoned its commitment to independent political action when it cozied up to the American Labor Party.

Ironically, Norman Thomas, who had been so instrumental in persuading the Party to enter the ALP, never actually joined. His application went to a New York City club dominated by the Communist Party, which shelved it. Thomas did campaign as the SP's presidential nominee in 1940, in opposition to Roosevelt, and he did oppose U.S. entry into World War II. Nevertheless, by 1949 he had adopted the strategy of working within the Democratic Party, a position he continued to uphold until his death in 1967.[142]

CONCLUSIONS

By January 1939, the entire range of tendencies that had debated the labor party question within the Socialist Party only a few years earlier were inside of the ALP, and in general strategic agreement. The Social Democratic Federation, the Socialist Party and the Socialist Workers Party had members within the ALP. Militants, Clarity supporters, the Old Guard and Trotskyists all worked together to counter the influence of the Communist Party. Yet none of these groups had any significant impact on the policies of the ALP.

The ALP remained as it had always been, a satellite of the Democratic Party. In 1944, the anti-Stalinist forces left the ALP and formed the Liberal Party. The ALP backed Henry Wallace in 1948 and then began fading away. With the backing of Dubinsky and most of the other trade union officials, the Liberal Party replaced the ALP as the organizational mechanism for union pressure on the Democratic Party. It survived until recently as a small ballot line engaging in an endless series of electoral maneuvers. Needless to say, none of this came anywhere near to a genuinely independent politics.[143]

For the Socialist Party, the volatile debates of the 1930s were the precursor to a later decision to enter the liberal wing of the Democratic Party. Norman Thomas became a mainstay of the progressive coalition, working with other liberals to cajole the Democratic Party into a more progressive direction, and failing to do so. During the 1960s, the SP became bitterly divided over the Vietnam War. Ultimately, the Party split into three different organizations, with the left-wing, the Debs Caucus, eventually reforming and reviving the Socialist Party on the basis of independent political action.[144]

The SWP tried hard to work within the ALP, with little success, and eventually moved on to other projects. Over the years, the Trotskyists have splintered into a myriad of small cadre organizations, and yet most of them continue to adhere to Trotsky's last position on the labor party. Sixty years later, many Trotskyists would join the latest incarnation of a labor party, and some would go on to support Ralph Nader as the Green Party's presidential candidate in 2000. Thus the debates of the 1930s remain highly relevant today.

7
Labor Party or Green Party: The Nader Campaign of 2000

As the Democratic Party shifts further to the Center, in a vain effort to keep up with the flow of corporate funds to Republican candidates, a growing number of working people have become so disaffected with the two party system that they have begun to seriously consider third party alternatives. Thus, the issues that have been so heatedly debated in the past have again moved to the forefront of debate.

Although the prospects for a labor party are still being debated, organized labor has come to represent a declining factor at the workplace. Thus, the impetus for independent politics has shifted to the Green Party, rather than to a labor party linked directly to the trade unions. The choices have therefore narrowed. Socialists can opt to join the Greens, a middle-class reform party committed to public oversight of a market economy, or to forge a party that rejects the capitalist market, an explicitly socialist party that carries on the tradition of Gene Debs and the left-wing of the SP during its heyday.

LABOR PARTY ADVOCATES

The last decade saw yet another attempt to form a viable labor party, an effort that originated directly from within the ranks of the union officialdom. Tony Mazzochi was born in 1926, and raised in a working-class family in Brooklyn. After serving in the military during World War II, Mazzochi took jobs at a steel mill and on an auto assembly line. In 1950, he began working in a cosmetics factory on Long Island. Two years later, he was elected president of the Oil, Chemical and Atomic Workers Union (OCAW) local representing that plant. Mazzochi soon became active in a variety of progressive causes, including protests against the testing of nuclear weapons. He also campaigned for Adlai Stevenson, the Democratic Party's presidential nominee in 1956.[1]

In 1965, Mazzochi moved up the union hierarchy to the national level, serving first as legislative director, and then as health and safety director. In 1970, he played a significant role in the passage of the

Occupational Safety and Health Act (OSHA). By this time, Mazzochi had become a leading figure within OCAW. He was elected vice-president in 1977, and in 1979 and 1981 he lost two closely contested elections for union president.[2]

Until this point, Mazzochi had followed the typical career path of a successful union official with progressive leanings. After 1981, he began moving outside of the norm. Spurning an offer of a staff position in Montana, Mazzochi decided to move back to his home local to work as a staff consultant. Seven years later, he returned to national office as secretary-treasurer. His years as his union's liaison with the Democratic Party had left him disenchanted with mainstream politics, so in 1989 he decided to poll the membership. To his surprise, when he sent out a survey to a random sample of OCAW members soliciting their views on electoral politics, he received an unusually high return of 20 percent. More than 55 percent of those who responded "rejected both parties as the parties of corporate interests," and called for the formation of "a new party, a labor party."[3]

Mazzochi began touring the country, meeting union activists who were interested in developing a labor party. In 1991, he helped to create an organizational network for his efforts, Labor Party Advocates (LPA). Mazzochi then gave up his position within the union hierarchy, in order to devote all of his energies to the building of a labor party. He remained on the union's payroll, with OCAW agreeing to fund his activities as chief organizer of LPA. (Nominally Mazzochi held the position of assistant to the union's president.)[4]

From the start, Mazzochi insisted that a labor party could only contest elections when it had already developed a large base of supporters. Indeed, to "run candidates and have them defeated would totally demoralize any group." Mazzochi insisted that it would take several years of organizing before a new labor party could be officially launched. In 1992, he set a goal of 100,000 members as a necessary prerequisite to calling a founding convention, with 1994 as the target date.[5] Needless to say, Labor Party Advocates never came anywhere near to fulfilling this membership goal.

Finally, in June 1996, 1,400 delegates assembled in Cleveland, Ohio to officially create a labor party. In addition to OCAW, the California Nurses' Association and the United Electrical Workers (UE) dispatched sizable delegations to the convention, while several other unions sent smaller contingents. In his keynote address, Bob Wages, the president of the Oil, Chemical and Atomic Workers Union, insisted that the delegates were about "to organize a political party" that would represent "the working class in this country."[6]

For the first time in several decades, it seemed that a significant section of organized labor was preparing to break with the two party system. Yet for all of the militant rhetoric, the Labor Party was a hollow shell from the start. The Cleveland convention defeated a proposal to begin nominating candidates at the local and state levels. Instead, at the behest of the OCAW leadership, the convention approved a policy blocking the consideration of any independent electoral campaigns until the next convention two years later.[7]

This policy constituted a feeble evasion. Political parties nominate candidates. Contrary to Mazzochi, new political parties in the United States virtually never succeed in electing their candidates when they first begin. They have to start by building a base of support over several election cycles as disaffected voters come to understand that there really is a meaningful choice. The Socialist Party constitutes the clearest case study of this process. Although it grew to become the only third party since the Civil War to build a solid presence at the national level, it took several years before it could elect any of its candidates to office. Furthermore, although Gene Debs became a popular hero, he never received more than 6 percent of the vote in a presidential election.

The truth is that the Labor Party was never more than an ineffectual bluff by a segment of the union leadership. Those officials who controlled it remained loyal Democrats, and, indeed, most of them publicly endorsed Democratic candidates. They envisioned the Labor Party as a means of putting pressure on the Democratic Party, and yet their threats to move outside of the two party system carried little conviction. For AFL-CIO unions, and OCAW was one of them, open support for an independent candidate could only lead to a direct confrontation with John Sweeney and the AFL leadership. This entailed risks that the Labor Party's leaders were never willing to hazard.

The organizational base of the Labor Party became even more tenuous after January 1999, when OCAW merged with the United Paperworkers Union to create PACE (Paperworkers, Allied Workers, Chemical and Energy Workers Union). Most of the new union's top leaders came from the Paperworkers, a union that had always been closely tied to the Democratic Party. Since its formation, PACE has shown little interest in either independent politics or the Labor Party.[8]

One provision of the merger agreement pledged the new union to continue its support for the Labor Party at its previous level.

Nevertheless, in March 2001 the PACE executive board decided to stop funding Mazzochi, and the Labor Party's Washington office manager as well, although it agreed to maintain a direct annual donation of $10,000. This decision resulted in a substantial cut in the core financial support for the Labor Party, leaving it even more adrift than before.[9]

During the presidential campaign of 2000, the Labor Party remained above the fray, although many of its activists, including Mazzochi, campaigned for Ralph Nader, the Green Party candidate. In addition, two affiliates, the UE and the California Nurses Association, officially endorsed Nader. Nevertheless, every AFL-CIO union that had previously participated in the Labor Party, including PACE, backed Al Gore, the Democratic presidential candidate.[10]

Over the last years, the Labor Party has approached the brink of dissolution. Mazzochi had been the single unifying factor holding those who remained together. His death of pancreatic cancer in October 2002 brought this episode in third party politics to a closure.[11] The remnant of the Labor Party has concentrated its energies on a grass-roots educational campaign for a single payer health plan. The Labor Party failed as an independent electoral party without ever having nominated a single candidate. Instead, the center of attention has shifted to the Greens.

THE GREENS AND NADER

The rise of the Green Party in the United States has generally tracked the creation of similar parties in Western Europe, and most especially in Germany. In turn, the German Greens emerged directly from the West German peace movement, and the mass demonstrations for disarmament of the 1970s. During this same period, the environmental movement gained strength as a reaction to the ecological devastation caused by West Germany's rapid growth model of economic development. In 1979, activists from both these movements came together to present a common slate of candidates for the European Parliament.[12]

Although the common slate received only 3 percent of the total vote, and thus fell below the threshold needed to elect candidates to parliament, its showing was promising enough to keep the coalition together. Then, in March 1983, the Greens broke through the 5 percent barrier, electing 27 of their candidates to the West German parliament, the Bundestag. These results were electrifying, demonstrating that a left-wing, grass-roots political party could be successful, and could make an impact on public policy.[13]

In the United States, a network of community activists viewed the meteoric emergence of the Greens as a model for independent politics. They hoped that the Greens could provide an organizational framework for breaking free from the narrow constraints that have limited the socialist movement since the 1930s. Within a year of the 1983 Bundestag elections, the Committees of Correspondence, later renamed the Green Committees of Correspondence, was formed as a loose network for those interested in politics. This network came together for its first national gathering in 1991, and promptly split. The Green Party USA, the more radical of the two splinters, stressed the necessity of combining electoral action with grass-roots activism. In contrast, the Green Politics Network, soon renamed the Association of State Green Parties, looked to the creation of a purely electoral formation, a coalition of ballot-certified state parties, with the activist segment entirely separate. Over the next few years, the Greens remained divided, seemingly at an impasse. All of this changed when Ralph Nader indicated his willingness to accept the Green presidential nomination in 1996.[14]

THE NADER IMAGE

Ralph Nader rose to celebrity status during the 1960s as the symbol of a new consumer-oriented activism. Nader's appeal has always been to middle-class progressives, the milieu from which he came. His parents were Lebanese immigrants who opened a successful restaurant in the small town of Winsted, Connecticut. Nader embodies the first-generation immigrants' drive to succeed, tempered by a commitment to public service.[15]

While a Harvard Law student, Nader became interested in the issue of auto safety. Until then, court judgments had focused on reckless drivers as the primary problem, but Nader came to believe that the auto manufacturers bore partial responsibility by producing cars with inherently dangerous design flaws. In 1965, Nader came to national prominence as the author of *Unsafe at Any Speed*, which censured the Chevrolet Corvair for treacherous handling. He went on to highlight the need for safety belts, and sparked the creation of the National Transportation Safety Board. Soon, he moved on to other issues, remaining in the public eye through the consumer advocacy investigations undertaken by a network of organizations, Nader's Raiders.[16]

By any standards, this represents an impressive record of achievements. Understandably, Nader has become an icon. Through the years, he has diligently honed a public persona as a dedicated, exacting and ascetic public advocate. Much is made of Nader's 100-hour workweeks, and his lack of a social life. Disdain for material objects makes up a major part of this image of asceticism. He resides in a small apartment while working in Washington, and rides the subway rather than owning a car. Although his efforts generate a considerable income, he lives on a modest $25,000 a year, while contributing generously to his network of public service organizations.[17]

Nader's carefully cultivated image would be of little importance except that his political campaigns rely so heavily on his personality. A closer look provides a more balanced picture. Nader personifies considerable virtues, but he also exhibits serious flaws, which have been generally shielded from public scrutiny.

Nader charges an average of $10,000 a speech, and he makes more than 40 paid appearances each year. This generates a sizable income, one that is supplemented by royalties from books he has written or co-authored. From 1967 to 2000, Nader earned $13 million in income, mostly from speakers' fees and book royalties. Although he claims to contribute 80 percent of his income, after taxes, to his network of non-profits, his total assets reached nearly $4 million in 2000, evenly divided between high-tech stocks and money market funds. Nader has done well for himself.[18]

In many ways, Nader's network of consumer advocacy organizations resembles the typical non-profit organization. As with many non-profits, the internal structure is rigidly hierarchical, with Nader and a few close associates making most of the policy decisions. Furthermore, those at the top receive far higher salaries than those at the bottom, who do much of the work. Indeed, this is an organizational model that corresponds, in a less extreme form, with the dominant corporate structure.

The distinctive feature of the Nader network of non-profits is the funding mechanism. Most non-profits depend on grants. Nader depends on speakers' fees, generated in part from his links to his network of consumer activist organizations. These fees, and book royalties, keep funds flowing in, while a substantial part of this income is returned to Nader's network of non-profit organizations, thereby keeping the pump primed.

In 1984, the contradictions inherent in this situation erupted into an open and public conflict. Nader fired the editor of the *Multinational*

Monitor, Tim Shorrock, for printing an article without getting Nader's prior approval. Since Nader funded the *Multinational Monitor*, both directly and through his fundraising efforts, he saw no problem in exercising total control over its publication.[19]

Under pressure, Nader agreed to keep Shorrock on for a three-month provisional extension. Shorrock and the two other staff members had been working 60–80 hours a week for a pittance. (Shorrock's salary came to $13,000 a year, or about $4 an hour.) Shorrock's dismissal inspired him and the other two *Monitor* staff members to begin organizing for a union contract, seeking a formal grievance procedure, higher wages, shorter hours and more staff. Nader responded by shifting ownership to an entity controlled by three of his closest associates, which then proceeded to dismiss all three staff members.[20]

More important than the specifics of this tawdry affair was Nader's justification. In his view, there was no more compelling need for a "union in [a] small, non-profit 'cause' organization" than within "a monastery or within a union."[21] In fact, union staff members confront the same problems of long hours and hierarchical power structures, although, in general, they are significantly better paid. In both situations, those on staff need the benefits of a collective bargaining agent. Unfortunately, the staff of Nader's network of non-profits remain overworked, underpaid and without the essential protections of a union contract.

For all of these problems, Nader and his network continue to do important work. Nevertheless, a closer examination of Nader suggests a considerably more complex, and flawed, reality than the carefully polished image he likes to present. Many of these problems – the celebrity focus, the top-down style of decision-making, and the pragmatic approach to fundamental social issues – have all carried over into Nader's presidential campaigns.

THE NADER CAMPAIGN OF 2000

In 1996, Nader accepted the nomination as the presidential candidate of the Greens. Over the years, Nader has succeeded in attracting a solid base of prosperous contributors. His credibility as a public advocate has been an important factor in raising funds for his network of consumer advocacy organizations. Thus, Nader's acceptance of the Green presidential nomination not only significantly increased the

Greens' legitimacy as a viable third party, but it also meant that they could tap into a far wider range of affluent middle-class progressives.

Both wings of the Greens eagerly backed the Nader campaign and yet the campaign remained a token effort. Nader insisted that he would limit his campaign to $5,000 in expenditures, thus sidestepping a provision in federal law requiring candidates to submit a list of contributors to the Federal Elections Commission. This would seem rather bizarre coming from a progressive candidate, but Nader insisted that some of his contributors would be frightened by the threat of reprisals should their names become known, and that he had to protect the funding sources for his non-profit network.[22]

Four years later, this argument was conveniently forgotten as Nader launched a full-scale campaign. He consistently attacked the large corporations for their greed and for the way they maintain their power by "tying the hands of both parties, funding both parties," thereby "controlling" the government. In addition, he frequently castigated the two party system, arguing that there are "few major differences" between the two mainstream parties. He even promised that "after November," there was "going to be a significant progressive party in this country."[23]

Yet Nader has preserved his close ties to influential political figures within the Democratic Party. In 1998, he campaigned throughout Massachusetts for Lois Pines, a state senator who was seeking the Democratic nomination for attorney general. Pines had sponsored environmental legislation such as a bottle bill, and she promised that she would use her authority as attorney general to oversee the health industry. Nevertheless, Pines was a 15-year veteran of the state legislature, and an integral member of the liberal establishment. At a press conference to promote her campaign, Nader extolled her "consistent, determined, successful record of protecting consumer rights and the environment."[24]

This was hardly the only case of Nader using his celebrity status to advance the electoral prospects of mainstream politicians. Indeed, these endorsements were consistent with his goals for his own campaign. Nader saw his ability to gain a hearing as a means of putting pressure on the Democratic leaders, thus forcing them to be more responsive to the concerns of the progressive forces he represented. On a campaign swing through Ohio, he met with several rank and file activists from the United Steelworkers Union, and advised them that they were being "taken for granted." Instead, organized labor should demonstrate that there was now "an alternative and the alternative is Nader." Once shown the dangers of their core voters defecting, the Democrats would have to respond. "They'll start calling."[25]

An even clearer exposition of this viewpoint surfaced during a televised dialogue between Jesse Jackson and Nader. Jackson had acted as the most visible liberal gadfly during the 1980s. Although his Rainbow Coalition had remained within the Democratic Party, it had frequently threatened to bolt. By the 2000 election campaign, having been thoroughly integrated into the Democratic Party structure, Jackson lavishly praised Gore, while chastising Nader for making it possible for Bush to become president. In an effort to deflect this argument, Nader retorted that the Democratic Party needed "to pull into the progressive wing." Indeed, Jackson had "been trying to do that" from within, while Nader was now "trying to do that with the Green Party [from] outside."[26]

The Nader campaign promoted the illusion that the Democratic Party can be induced into becoming a force for social change. This has always been a fantasy, but in a world of instantaneous, overnight international capital mobility and intertwined transnational corporations, efforts along these lines can only lead to cooptation and disillusionment.

Although Nader viewed his campaign as one element of a broader strategy to bring pressure to bear on the Democratic Party, he was also interested in assisting the Democrats as they were currently constituted. During the campaign, he frequently conceded that his vote might bring about Gore's defeat, but, at the same time, he insisted that his efforts could also aid Congressional Democrats by bringing disenchanted liberals, who might otherwise not vote, to the polls. Since the Greens contested fewer than 10 percent of the total seats in the House of Representatives, "the outpouring of votes" for his candidacy might well be enough to ensure a Democratic majority. That was "a nice prospect for the Democrats." Apparently for Nader as well, since he went on to categorize the House Republican leadership as "beyond the pale."[27]

As it turned out, the Democrats came closer to winning a majority in the Senate than in the House in the 2000 elections. With the Senate evenly divided, the decision of Senator James Jeffords of Vermont to leave the Republican Caucus in June 2001 shifted the majority alignment in that chamber. Nader was quick to take credit for this outcome. In Washington, the Democratic candidate for Senate, Marie Cantwell, had been elected by the narrowest of margins. This led

Nader to claim that his campaign had brought more progressives to the polls, thus providing Cantwell with her majority and making it possible for the Democrats to gain control of the Senate.[28]

Nader has never moved beyond the narrow constraints of the progressive liberal. Not only did his campaign foster the illusion that the Democratic Party could be reformed, but he also advocated the pragmatic virtues of the lesser evil, at least when it came to Congress. Yet the problems with the Nader campaign extended well beyond his links to the Democratic Party. Although issues related to the abuse of corporate power were at the forefront of his campaign, Nader remained an ardent defender of a capitalist market economy. His objections were those of the small business owner, squeezed by the enormous resources of the global corporation. While explicitly rejecting a democratic socialist vision, Nader looked back toward a mythological past of locally owned small businesses, perhaps like his father's small-town restaurant. The essential problem, from this perspective, was the lack of competition in markets dominated by a few huge firms which flagrantly disregard the interests of consumers while acting collusively to extract excessive profits. The remedy was straightforward, the strict enforcement of anti-trust laws.

During a televised interview, Nader was asked if he viewed himself as a Marxist. In completely rejecting such a label, he countered that it was "big corporations" that were "destroying capitalism." Small businesses were being "pressed and exploited and deprived by their big business predators." Thus, the progressive movement was saving capitalism from itself. In another interview, he insisted that it was "very important that the antitrust laws be viewed as the best friend of a capitalist, free-market system."[29]

These were not merely impromptu responses given to interviewers in the heat of the campaign. In 1968, Nader told a reporter that his efforts to highlight corporate abuses represented "an attempt to preserve the free-enterprise economy by making the market work better."[30]

One of the many ironies of the Nader campaign was its use of the Green Party as an organizational framework. Both of the competing national organizations, the Green Party USA and the Association of Green State Parties, fervently advocated the virtues of a decentralized, democratic decision-making process, and yet Nader insisted on organizing a campaign that was top-heavy and candidate-driven.

This could be clearly seen in Nader's total disdain for the program of the Green Party USA, the more radical of the two organizations.

Its platform called for an immediate 75 percent cut in military spending among other demands. When queried by the press, Nader dismissed the entire platform with the comment that he did not "really pay much attention" to it.[31]

Given the many drawbacks in the Nader campaign, some of which went to the core of its message, it remains difficult to understand the uncritical support extended to it by many of those on the Left. Of course, one can always fall back to the position that Nader's campaign, with all of its faults, represented a step forward. After all, for once the mass media covered a presidential candidate who attacked corporate greed and condemned the two party system.

In reality, these ideas have become a part of popular wisdom. Many working people understand that the corporations are ripping them off, and that both the Democrats and the Republicans carry out the wishes of these corporations. The question is, what can be done to stop this? Nader's proposed alternatives were woefully inadequate, and, in many cases, counterproductive. His faith in the workings of a competitive market economy, his continuing ties to the liberal wing of the Democratic Party and his insistence on a personality-based, candidate-driven campaign oriented the Left in the wrong direction. Nader remains a vocal defender of the small business owner, and a staunch believer in a regulated capitalist market economy.

NADER AND LA FOLLETTE

Nader's campaign in 2000 bore a striking resemblance to La Follete's campaign in 1924. Both Nader and La Follette were popular progressives who stood as independent presidential candidates. Both campaigns were personality-driven. La Follette made a point of running as an individual, although he also spoke of the importance of creating a third party. Nader campaigned as the nominee of the Greens, and yet he too determined his positions without paying heed to a party platform. Both retained ties to the two party system, and both saw themselves as saving capitalism from itself.

Nevertheless, in spite of the many similarities, there was one considerable difference between the two campaigns. La Follette looked to the trade unions as a primary source of funding. When these funds failed to be delivered, he was compelled to organize on a shoestring basis, with a minimal staff. Nader never looked toward unions as a significant source of contributions. Instead, he relied on the considerable pool of affluent liberals that had been supporting his network of non-profit organizations, while reaching out to the larger pool of those contributing substantial sums to progressive causes.

La Follette did far better in terms of electoral success than Nader. Although La Follette gained 16.6 percent of the total vote, and carried Wisconsin, Nader received only 2.7 percent of the vote, a slightly higher share than that tallied by Norman Thomas as the Socialist Party candidate in 1932. Yet La Follette raised only $237,000, while Nader collected $7.7 million, including $400,000 in matching federal funds. Thus, Nader spent about $3 per vote, while La Follette spent about 5 cents, a ratio of 60 to 1.[32]

Inflation accounts for part of this difference, but not all. Even taking rising prices into account, La Follette spent 49 cents per vote in current dollars, so that Nader outspent him in real terms by a ratio of 6 to 1.[33]

These calculations are not a purely academic exercise. La Follette depended on farmers being squeezed by the banks and the large corporations, while Nader relied on the affluent middle class. This gave Nader a more solid base of financial support, but it also further restricted the potential of his campaign.

THE AFTERMATH OF THE ELECTION

The 2000 elections marked a breakthrough in public visibility for the Green Party. Nader's campaign provided the Greens with a newfound legitimacy that has allowed them to become a significant electoral force in several communities where progressive movements have gained widespread popular support. In an effort to maintain their momentum, the Greens have sought to overcome their internal frag-mentation, and to create a more unified organization.

In July 2001, the Association of State Green Parties merged with a substantial section of the Green Party USA to form a new political party, the Green Party US. Recognized by the Federal Elections Commission as the sole Green electoral party, the merger has succeeded in bringing together most Greens into one broad umbrella organization. Although a left-wing tendency has been initiated within this new formation, it is clear that moderates dominate its political direction.

For Nader, the presidential campaign of 2000 led to few changes in political perspective. He remains aloof from the Greens as an organized political party, a move that has sparked considerable discontent among rank and file activists. Indeed, Nader has done little to promote alternative candidates at the Congressional, state or local levels. Instead, he has toured the country promoting a new consumer-advocacy initiative, Democracy Rising.[34]

Nader still looks to the liberal wing of the Democratic Party. In January 2003, he urged Representative Dennis Kucinich to seek the Democratic Party's presidential nomination. Nader was convinced that there needed "to be a clearly progressive candidate in the primaries." These comments constituted a tacit endorsement of Kucinich, who opted to enter the Democratic presidential primaries a month later.[35]

Nevertheless, Nader continues to position himself as a possible candidate for the Green Party presidential nomination. He has stated that although he is considering another presidential campaign, he has yet to reach a final decision. This posture has undermined the potential for a full-scale Green campaign in 2004, both because Nader should be assembling a campaign organization to ensure ballot access around the country, and because it makes it significantly more difficult to attract other potential presidential candidates should Nader decline the Green Party's nomination.

Yet the problem extends well beyond Nader. Greens from the local to the national level have shied away from nominating their own candidates in opposition to liberal Democratic Party incumbents. It has become increasingly evident that the Green Party views itself as a pressure group on the Democratic Party, and not as a genuinely independent political party. In addition, many Greens are eager to avoid a repetition of the 2000 presidential election, when the Nader vote allowed George W. Bush to maneuver his way into the White House. Thus, there will be a significant segment of Greens who will oppose the nomination of any presidential candidate in 2004, or who will opt for a token effort along the lines of Nader's candidacy in 1996.

The Green Party has already traveled a considerable distance along the same trajectory already set by previous third party efforts. Unwilling to sever relations with the Democratic Party, the Greens are being drawn back, over time, to an acceptance of the underlying assumptions of mainstream two party politics.

8
Conclusions:
The Socialist Alternative

A century ago, the future seemed bright for the socialist movement. Throughout Western Europe, democratic socialist political parties were winning the support of a solid majority of the working class. Socialists were confident, certain that capitalism would soon come to an end. The working-class movement was steadily growing in strength and cohesion, preparing for the coming conflict when the capitalist class would cede power and a new society would be created.

The transition to a socialist society, it was believed, would occur through a step-by-step process. Each country in the advanced capitalist world would follow along the same path toward the common final goal, a democratic socialist society. This was a vision of social change that seemed enormously persuasive for a period of several decades, most especially from the 1880s until the outbreak of World War I. Those who adhered to this perspective gained a sense of certitude. They were convinced that they understood the world, and its vast complexities, with a scientific precision.

This theoretical perspective also provided a sense of inevitability. Socialism was not only desirable; it was inexorable. The orthodox system started from a schematic analysis of the evolution of class society, but it also came with a set of guidelines outlining the steps required to advance beyond capitalism to a new socialist society. At its core was a belief in the smooth linear progression of social systems, moving from slavery to feudalism to capitalism, and then, in the near future, on to socialism. The economic laws of a capitalist market economy would create an industrial working class. It was this industrial working class that, when organized into a class-conscious proletariat, would set into motion the social movement that would topple capitalism and replace it with a new society without hierarchy or oppression.

Those who fully accepted the orthodox analysis came to view the rise of the working class as a clockwork mechanism. From this perspective, there was no reason to take risks, or to confront popular prejudices, or to criticize those who held on to the perspective of liberal reformism. After all, the inescapable workings of the capitalist system, the proletarianization of the middle class, the widening gap between the rich and poor, and the volatility of a market economy headed toward a cataclysmic crisis, all of this would push the working class, and its leaders, toward a socialist perspective. In each industrialized country, democratic socialist parties would be formed, and would rapidly gain the support of the majority of the working class. Workers would join trade unions to defend their interests at the workplace, unions that would act as an integral component of a unified socialist movement. As the movement gained momentum, the ruling class would either step aside, or provoke a direct confrontation, leading to a swift and painless transformation of society.

This was a compelling theoretical construct, a mixture of insightful analysis and dubious wishful thinking. Yet it soon became painfully clear that the United States did not fit the orthodox model. The first wave of industrialization failed to bring with it the formation of a mass-based socialist party. Furthermore, even after the Socialist Party USA was founded in 1901, and quickly grew, it was still unable to attract the support of a majority of the working class.

Throughout U.S. history, the majority of the working class has accepted the capitalist market economy as a given. Indeed, socialists have always represented a distinct minority, although at times an influential one. Most workers have spurned a radical critique of capitalism, and, instead, have focused on bettering their own individual position. Trade unions were organized as a practical means of gaining better wages and working conditions. In that same spirit, a majority of workers have remained within the two party system, casting their votes for the lesser evil.

In this context, one strand of the socialist movement has sought to adapt the orthodox perspective to the specific circumstances of the United States. Instead of building a mass-based socialist party, the strategic goal would be the formation of a labor party, a non-socialist electoral formation based directly on the mainstream unions. Such a labor party, so it was argued, would constitute an essential step in the development of a class-conscious working class. It would propel the U.S. working class toward the path leading to socialism as set in the orthodox theory, and as already put into practice in Europe. The sharpening edge of class conflict would compel a labor party to adopt a socialist program. Once this shift in political program occurred, it would occur quickly; the U.S. working class could readily link up with the global network of socialist parties working toward a total transformation of society.

Those socialists who advocated a labor party understood that their acceptance of this position brought them closer to the politics of liberal reformism. They sought to reconcile this inherent contradiction by emphasizing the unique characteristics of a labor party. Given its direct connections to industrial unions, a labor party was, by virtue of its structure, a working-class party. It was therefore merely a question of fully revealing the socialist implications of this class position. Thus, from this perspective, a labor party could enter into a simple, easy transition from a party dedicated to winning limited reforms within the capitalist system to one committed to the creation of a new society.

Friedrich Engels had already accepted the logic of this argument in 1886, when he enthusiastically endorsed the Henry George campaign for mayor of New York City. Nevertheless, at this point it was merely a conceptual possibility. Then in 1901 the Independent Labour Party joined with a coalition of trade unions to form the Labour Representation Committee, later renamed the British Labour Party. Originally formed on a platform that, by intention, was not socialist, the Labour Party adopted a nebulously socialistic statement of purpose in 1918. Shortly afterward, it became one of the two major parties in Britain.

Socialist advocates of a labor party in the United States pointed to the British Labour Party as a model, not only because of its electoral success, but, more significantly, because of its adoption of the 1918 program. From hindsight, it is clear that this position was wildly inaccurate. The Labour Party was never a genuinely socialist party, but recently, under Tony Blair, it has abandoned its commitment to social reform and, instead, has come to resemble the Democratic Party. A century of loyal support for a labor party has left the British working class back where it was then, searching to create a mass-based socialist party.

Nevertheless, at the time, a century ago, the rapid rise of the British Labour Party seemed to point the way forward for the United States as well. For three decades, the British success loomed as a tantalizing landmark. Still, nothing similar emerged in the United States to challenge the prevailing politics of the lesser evil. Instead, the business unions of the AFL continued to align themselves with the Democratic Party. Furthermore, each effort at launching a labor party was either quickly abandoned or speedily coopted.

It is this irreconcilable dilemma that lies at the core of the labor party question. Supporters of a labor party have insisted that only a political party based directly on the trade unions could attract the resources and project the credibility needed to appeal to the majority of the U.S. working class. Since the creation of such a party constituted the "true mission" of the socialist movement, electoral activity based on an explicitly socialist program would have to be jettisoned for the foreseeable future.

The labor party perspective has failed at every level. Mainstream business unions have consistently operated within the confines of the two party system for more than a century. In 1921, a coalition of railroad unions initiated the Conference for Progressive Political Action (CPPA), hoping to promote public support for their plan for quasi-governmental control of the railways. Although the CPPA spoke of an independent politics, it never severed its links to mainstream liberal politicians. The CPPA endorsed Robert La Follette's independent presidential campaign in 1924, and yet it resisted every initiative to form a permanent third party. Since the New Deal of the 1930s, most unions have cultivated even closer ties to the Democratic Party, ties that remain as tight as ever.

Labor parties in the United States have either been fleetingly transitory or stalking horses for the Democratic Party. This unbroken string of failures has persuaded many of those on the Left to work within broadly based third parties as the only realistic alternative to a labor party. Those socialists who have accepted this perspective have retreated even further from the essential principles of socialism. Certainly, third parties have proven to be more successful than labor parties within the U.S. context. Yet as liberal reform parties based on the middle class, these formations have never been truly independent of the Democratic and Republican parties. Instead, they have acted as a pressure group on the liberal mainstream, and, as such, they have been readily coopted back into the two party system.

Prior to World War I, even those socialists who advocated the formation of a labor party rejected any connection with a political party based on middle-class progressives. Engels held firm to this point, even as he endorsed the Henry George campaign. Two decades later, Morris Hillquit and the Socialist Party Center rejected any ties to the Progressive Party. Thus, the Socialist Party's decision to support the La Follette campaign in 1924 represented a major break from socialist principles. The SP had already backed the formation of a labor party, but this had been rationalized as support for a working-class party that could easily be transformed into an explicitly socialist party. La Follette's base of support rested with the small farmers of the Midwest. As an electoral expression of the progressive movement, the 1924 campaign, even it had been consolidated into a permanent party, could never have provided the basis for a socialist party.

The Socialist Party was sliding toward an acceptance of liberal reformist politics. To give this dubious shift a certain patina of credibility, the Party sought to link its electoral strategy to that undertaken by the more progressive trade unions. This process began in 1921, when the SP joined the CPPA, gathered further momentum during the La Follette campaign, and crystallized during the 1930s, when the SP tacitly backed the La Guardia campaign for mayor in 1937, and then joined the American Labor Party.

In the United States, the line between labor parties and third parties has never been clearly drawn. Trade union officials who are willing to test the boundaries of the two party system still insist on quick victories. Since organized labor has generally represented a minority of the workforce, successful electoral campaigns require candidates that can reach beyond this limited base. This was as true in 1886, when unions sought out Henry George, as it was in 1924, when unions rallied behind La Follette.

The last decade has seen the rise of the Green Party as a significant alternative party. Indeed, Ralph Nader's presidential campaign of 2000 gave the Greens national visibility. A celebrity-based campaign very much in the mold of the La Follette campaign, Nader presented an anti-corporate critique of the market economy, and yet his program never strayed beyond the limited reforms of a mainstream liberal.

Many socialists endorsed Nader, some even entered the Green Party hoping to act as a loyal left-wing. Most came from a Trotskyist tradition, citing Trotsky's decision in 1937 to move his supporters into the American Labor Party, where they could counteract the Popular Front politics of the Communist Party. By now, we have come a long way from the Socialist Party leaders of the early 1900s, who were eager to jettison the Party for a labor party tied directly to the trade unions; a party, they believed, that could quickly win the backing of a majority of the working class. During the 2000 presidential campaign, Nader's socialist supporters held out hopes for the development of a liberal reform party with a limited national visibility that might, in the future, become truly independent of the two party system. As we move toward 2004, with Nader lending his support to one of the many aspiring candidates for the Democratic presidential nomination, it would seem that yet another effort at third party politics has returned to the two party mainstream.

In spite of the intense pressure to back the lesser evil, the Democratic Party has less and less to offer. There is very little room for meaningful social reform in a globally integrated economy dominated by a few massive transnational corporations. It is therefore more necessary than ever to build a genuinely independent alternative party. The labor party perspective has failed to provide a viable strategy in moving toward that goal. Instead, socialists need to re-evaluate and reassess the entire labor party experience, and to begin again from a radically different starting point.

Contrary to the traditional orthodoxy, most workers in advanced capitalist countries do not see a socialist transformation of society as essential unless and until the system unravels. Thus, contrary to the unrealistically rosy views of Engels, as well as many others, there is no reason to believe that a radical socialist party will rapidly gain the support of a majority of the working class.

Historically, the German experience was set as the model to emulate, and yet World War I proved all too clearly the fragility of the Social Democratic Party's commitment to basic socialist principles. Over the last decade, most of the social democratic parties of Europe have collapsed into the corporate center, leaving a vacuum for more radical parties. Yet even the more successful of these new parties have been polling 5–10 percent of the total vote. Although the old social democratic parties have seen their base of support eroded from both the Right and the Left, they continue to retain the loyal support of a majority of working-class voters.

The true mission of a socialist party is not to rapidly achieve electoral success. Taking this as a goal can only point toward a morass of opportunistic compromises. Instead, socialists need to present a clearly defined radical perspective, to raise the demand for fundamental reforms that stretch the boundaries of the exist system, and to articulate a coherent vision of a new and egalitarian society.

This is as true in the United States as it is in Europe, and indeed around the world. A century ago the United States was viewed as an aberration, even when the Socialist Party developed a sizable, albeit minority, presence within the working class. Instead of seeking to build on this success, much of the Party's leadership looked to the formation of a labor party. As efforts to initiate a labor party foundered, many socialists shifted their support to progressive third parties, only to see those quickly coopted back into the two party system.

Yet the experience of the Socialist Party at the turn of the twentieth century demonstrates that it is possible to build a mass-based democratic socialist organization even in the United States. Only with World War I, when it became a target of intense government repression, did the Party falter. There can be no doubt that the U.S. working class has changed dramatically over the last century. Nevertheless, the opportunity remains. The struggle to counteract the globalization of capital, reinforced by the anti-war movement, has generated a new generation of activists. With this as a starting point, a coming together of the fragments of the Left, perhaps with the encouragement of European socialists, could create the basis for a new, revived mass-based socialist party. Only such a formation could present an attractive, and yet genuinely independent, alternative to the corporate dominated politics of the current two party system.

Notes

CHAPTER 1

1. Henry Wallace's presidential campaign as the candidate of the Progressive Party in 1948 followed the same general pattern set by La Follette, and later repeated by Nader. Wallace and Nader received a comparable share of the vote. Wallace received 2.4 percent in 1948, while Nader got 2.7 percent in 2000. La Follette reached a qualitatively different level with a 16.6 percent share. Wallace quit the Progressive Party in August 1950, leaving it adrift. In 1952, the Progressive Party presented its last slate of candidates at the national level, gaining far fewer votes than Wallace had four years previously. Two years later, the American Labor Party, the most significant affiliate of the Progressive Party, lost its ballot status. The official dissolution of the ALP two years later marked the end of the Progressive Party. Edward L. and Frederick H. Schapsmeier, *Prophet in Politics* (Ames: Iowa State University Press, 1970), p. 206; Joseph R. Starobin, *American Communism in Crisis, 1943–1957* (Cambridge, Mass.: Harvard University Press, 1977), pp. 11, 243.

CHAPTER 2

1. Friedrich Engels to August Bebel, August 18, 1886, Karl Marx and Friedrich Engels, *Collected Works* (New York: International Publishers, 1995), 47: 454.
2. Nathan Fine, *Labor and Farmer Parties in the United States, 1828–1928* (New York: Rand School of Social Sciences, 1928; Reprinted edition New York: Russell and Russell, 1961), pp. 12–18.
3. Charles Albro Barker, *Henry George* (New York: Oxford University Press, 1955), p. 458.
4. *John Swinton's Paper*, July 11, 1886; *New York Times*, June 24, 1886. The entire $1,000 was divided among the three trade unions. A sixth member of the boycott organizing committee, Michael O'Leary, was indicted with the five others. He agreed to testify for the prosecution, was bound over to a later trial before another judge, and thus avoided being victimized by Judge Barrett's harsh prison sentences.
5. Barker, *Henry George*, pp. 458–9; *New York Times*, July 1, 1886. Three of the five were convicted in two separate trials, while the other two pleaded no contest.
6. *New York Times*, July 3, 1886. The two defendants who had pleaded no contest were given lighter sentences by Judge Barrett, who made it clear that the trials had constituted a waste of time.
7. Louis F. Post and Fred C. Leubuscher, *Henry George's 1886 Campaign* (New York: John W. Lovell, 1887; reprinted edition New York: Henry George School, 1961), pp. 5–6; Barker, *Henry George*, p. 460.

8. Barker, *Henry George*, p. 460; *New York Times*, August 6, 1886; Post and Leubuscher, *1886 Campaign*, p. 6.

9. *New York Times*, August 27, 1886; Stuart Bruce Kaufman (ed.), *The Samuel Gompers Papers* (Urbana: University of Illinois Press, 1987), 2: 432.

10. Barker, *Henry George*, p. 461; *New York Times*, September 18, 1886.

11. Barker, *Henry George*, p. 461; Henry George, *Progress and Poverty: An Enquiry in the Causes of Industrial Depressions and of Increase of Want with Increase of Wealth: The Remedy* (New York: H. George, 1879).

12. Barker, *Henry George*, pp. 161, 227–9.

13. Karl Marx and Friedrich Engels, *Letters to Americans* (New York: International Publishers, 1953), p. 129.

14. Barker, *Henry George*, p. 458.

15. Post and Leubuscher, *1886 Campaign*, pp. 10–11.

16. Post and Leubuscher, *1886 Campaign*, p. 6; Barker, *Henry George*, p. 462.

17. Engels to Bebel, August 8, 1886, Marx and Engels, *Collected Works*, 47: 470. Manhattan had a population of 1.16 million in 1880 and 1.44 million in 1890. Brooklyn had grown to a city of 600,000 in 1880, but it would only be incorporated into New York City, along with the other outer boroughs, in 1898. *Statistical Abstract* (Washington, D.C.: GPO, 1916).

18. Howard H. Quint, *The Forging of American Socialism* (Columbia: University of South Carolina Press, 1953; reprinted edition Indianapolis, Ind.: Bobbs-Merrill, 1964), p. 41; Post and Leubuscher, *1886 Campaign*, p. 15.

19. Post and Leubuscher, *1886 Campaign*, p. 15.

20. *New York Times*, September 25, 1887.

21. Yvonne Kapp, *Eleanor Marx: The Crowded Years* (London: Lawrence & Wishart, 1976), pp. 148–9. Unfortunately, Eleanor Marx's letters to Engels from this period have not survived, but they appear to have been detailed and frequent. In three letters to Laura Lafargue from the fall of 1886, Engels mentions five different letters he has just received from Eleanor Marx during her travels in the United States. Marx and Engels, *Collected Works*, 47: 506, 524, 536.

22. Edward Aveling and Eleanor Marx Aveling, *The Working Class Movement in America* (London: 1887; reprinted edition New York: Arno and the New York Times, 1969), pp. 184–5.

23. *New York Times*, November 2, 1886; Louis F. Post, *The Prophet of San Francisco: Personal Memories and Interpretations* (New York: Vanguard Press, 1930), p. 78.

24. Kaufman, *Gompers Papers*, 1: 361.

25. Kaufman, *Gompers Papers*, 1: 439, 452; William H. Dick, *Labor and Socialism: the Gompers Era* (Port Washington, New York: Kennikat Press, 1972), p. 21.

26. Barker, *Henry George*, p. 462; Kaufman, *Gompers Papers*, 1: 431.

27. Kaufman, *Gompers Papers*, 1: 434. The quote is taken from the *New York Morning Journal*. The reporter is paraphrasing Gompers' speech.

28. Kaufman, *Gompers Papers*, 1: 446–7.

29. Bernard K. Johnpoll and Lillian Johnpoll, *The Impossible Dream: The Rise and Demise of the American Left* (Westport, Conn.: Greenwood Press, 1981), p. 171.

30. *New York Times*, October 13, 1886. Wilzig was a waiter himself, and had led the Waiters Union drive against Theiss' saloon.

31. Post and Leubuscher, *1886 Campaign*, pp. 109–10.

32. Post, *Prophet of San Francisco*, pp. 89–90; *New York Times*, December 12, 1886.

33. Fine, *Labor and Farmer Parties*, p. 49; Arthur Nichols Young, *The Single Tax Movement in the United States* (Princeton, N.J.: Princeton University Press, 1916), p. 112.

34. Lester Luntz, "Daniel DeLeon and the Movement for Social Reform," Typescript, Edward Bellamy Collection, Houghton Library, Harvard University, p. 5.

35. *New York Times*, October 28, 1886.

36. Post and Leubuscher, *1886 Campaign*, p. 133; Quint, *Forging of American Socialism*, p. 42.

37. Barker, *Henry George*, p. 472; Johnpoll and Johnpoll, *Impossible Dream*, p. 172; Quint, *Forging of American Socialism*, p. 41.

38. Barker, *Henry George*, p. 478; Post and Leubuscher, *1886 Campaign*, p. 139; *New York Times*, November 13, 1886.

39. Friedrich Engels to Laura Lafargue, November 24, 1886, Marx and Engels, *Collected Works*, 47: 525.

40. Barker, *Henry George*, p. 478; *New York Times*, November 7, 1886. The quotes are drawn from paraphrases of the speeches as formulated by the *Times* reporter.

41. *John Swinton's Paper*, November 14, 1886; Johnpoll and Johnpoll, *Impossible Dream*, p. 172.

42. Johnpoll and Johnpoll, *Impossible Dream*, p. 172.

43. Barker, *Henry George*, p. 485. Initially, Professor David Scott was chosen for the executive committee, but he was soon replaced by James Redpath. A journalist and social reformer, Redpath had been publicly identified with the single-tax movement some years prior to the 1886 election.

44. *New York Times*, December 3, 1886.

45. Kaufman, *Gompers Papers*, 2: 161.

46. Morris Hillquit, *History of Socialism in the United States* (Funk and Wagnalls, 1906), p. 277.

47. Friedrich Engels to Friedrich Sorge, November 29, 1886, Marx and Engels, *Collected Works*, 47: 531–2.

48. Engels to Sorge, November 29, 1886, Marx and Engels, *Collected Works*, 47: 531–2.

49. Friedrich Engels to Florence Kelley, December 28, 1886, Marx and Engels, *Collected Works*, 47: 541–2. As a student at the University of Zurich, Kelley had met the leaders of the German Social Democratic Party, then living in exile. She was attracted to the socialist movement, and agreed to translate Engels' *Condition of the English Working Class* into English. After her return to the United States in the fall of 1886, Engels maintained a steady correspondence with her. Briefly a member of the Socialist Labor Party, she rejected socialism for the perspective of a

progressive social reformer, becoming a leading activist around the issue of child labor.

50. Friedrich Engels to Florence Kelley, January 27, 1887, Karl Marx and Friedrich Engels, *Letters to Americans, 1848–1895, A Selection* (New York: International Publishers, 1953), pp. 168–9.
51. Friedrich Engels. "Preface to the American Edition of the *Condition of the English Working Class*," in Karl Marx and Friedrich Engels, *Collected Works* (New York: International Publishers, 1975), 26: 435–6.
52. *New York Times*, September 2, 1886.
53. Friedrich Engels, "Preface," in Marx and Engels, *Collected Works*, 26: 440–1.
54. Engels, "Preface," in Marx and Engels, *Collected Works*, 26: 437–8.
55. Post and Leubuscher, *1886 Campaign*, p. 136.
56. Post and Leubuscher, *1886 Campaign*, p. 139; Pope Leo XIII [Vincenzo Gracchino Pecci], "Socialism, Communism, Nihilism," in *The Great Encyclical Letters of Pope Leo XIII* (New York: Benziger Brothers, 1903), p. 31. Pecci held the papacy as Leo XIII for 25 years, from 1878 to 1903.
57. *New York Times*, December 12, 1886; Young, *Single Tax Movement*, pp. 112, 114; Fine, *Labor and Farmer Parties*, p. 50.
58. Barker, *Henry George*, p. 491.
59. Barber, *Henry George*, p. 486.
60. Johnpoll and Johnpoll, *Impossible Dreams*, p. 172.
61. *Dictionary of American Biography* (New York: Charles Scribner's Sons, 1932), 8:14–15; *National Cyclopedia of American Biography* (New York: James T. White, 1909), 11: 199.
62. Laurence Grönlund, *The Insufficiency of Henry George's Theory* (New York: New York Labor News, 1887), pp. 7, 19.
63. Grönlund, *Insufficiency of Henry George's Theory*, p. 1.
64. Johnpoll and Johnpoll, *Impossible Dream*, p. 174.
65. Friedrich Engels to Friedrich Sorge, April 23, 1887, Marx and Engels, *Letters*, p. 184; Friedrich Engels to Friedrich Sorge, June 30, 1887, Marx and Engels, *Letters*, p. 189.
66. Fine, *Labor and Farmer Parties*, p. 46; *New York Times*, May 22, 1887.
67. Fine, *Labor and Farmer Parties*, p. 46.
68. *New York Times*, June 26, 1887.
69. Quint, *Forging of American Socialism*, p. 44.
70. Barker, *Henry George*, p. 498; Johnpoll and Johnpoll, *Impossible Dream*, p. 174. The first signs of a coming split came on July 13, when the chair of one of the district assembly conventions convened to nominate delegates to the statewide convention ruled that members of the SLP could not serve as delegates. Without the active and public support of Henry George, this initial effort to exclude the SLP was quickly shelved. Fine, *Labor and Farmer Parties*, p. 46.
71. Barker, *Henry George*, p. 496; *New York Times*, August 5, 1887.
72. Barker, *Henry George*, pp. 498–9.
73. Friedrich Engels to Friedrich Sorge, August 8, 1887, Marx and Engels, *Letters*, p. 190.
74. Friedrich Engels to Friedrich Sorge, August 8, 1887, Marx and Engels, *Letters*, p. 190.

75. Friedrich Engels to Friedrich Sorge, September 16, 1887, Marx and Engels, *Letters*, p. 192. In spite of Engels' determined optimism, his interest in U.S. political developments waned after the expulsion of the socialists from the United Labor Party.

76. Barker, *Henry George*, pp. 498, 502.

77. Barker, *Henry George*, pp. 164–7.

78. Arthur Schlesinger (ed.), *History of Presidential Elections, 1789–1968* (New York: Chelsea House, 1971), "President Cleveland's Third Annual Message to Congress," 2: 1670; Robert F. Wesser, "The Election of 1888," in Schlesinger, *Presidential Elections*, 2: 1621.

79. Post, *Memoirs*, p. 119; Barker, *Henry George*, pp. 513–14.

80. Post, *Memoirs*, pp. 120–1; Barker, *Henry George*, pp. 513–14. The Union Labor Party, which had emerged from the Cincinnati convention and the Greenback Party, was somewhat more successful, garnering 147,000 votes nationwide. Its base of support was concentrated in the farm states of the Midwest and the Southwest, regions that would soon give rise to the grassroots radicalism of the Populist movement. Wesser, "Election of 1888," in Schlesinger, *Presidential Elections*, 2: 1649.

81. Barker, *Henry George*, p. 576.

82. Kaufman, *Gompers Papers*, 1: 496; Dick, *Labor and Socialism*, pp. 33–4. Although Gompers worked almost invariably within the constraints of the two party system after 1886, he did support independent candidates as individuals in certain exceptional circumstances. For Gompers' role in Robert La Follette's 1924 presidential campaign, see Chapter 5.

83. Barker, *Henry George*, pp. 603, 607–8.

84. Friedrich Engels to Florence Kelley, February 22, 1888, Marx and Engels, *Letters*, p. 197.

CHAPTER 3

1. Eugene V. Debs, *The Socialist Party and the Working Class* (Chicago: Socialist Party, 1904). This pamphlet is a transcript of Debs' acceptance speech marking the start of his 1904 presidential campaign.

2. Eugene V. Debs, *Unionism and Socialism: A Plea for Both* (Terre Haute, Indiana: Standard Publishing, 1904).

3. Sally M. Miller, "Milwaukee: Of Ethnicity and Labor," in Bruce M. Stave (ed.), *Urban Socialism* (Port Washington, New York: Kennikat Press, 1975), p. 50. The Socialist Party not only elected Seidel mayor of Milwaukee, but it also elected 21 out of 35 members of that city's board of aldermen.

4. Norma Fain Pratt, *Morris Hillquit: A Political History of an American Jewish Socialist* (Westport, Conn.: Greenwood Press, 1979), p. 38; Sally M. Miller, *Victor Berger and the Promise of Constructive Socialism, 1910–1920* (Westport, Conn.: Greenwood Press, 1973), pp. 17–32.

5. Miller, *Victor Berger*, pp. 23–4.

6. Benjamin Stolberg, *Tailor's Progress* (New York: Doubleday, Doran, 1944), pp. 66–7.

7. Pratt, *Morris Hillquit*, pp. 6, 20–1, 26–31. Daniel DeLeon dubbed the SLP opposition the Kangaroos, presumably referring to its members' belief in a step by step transition toward a socialist society.

8. Pratt, *Morris Hillquit*, p. 147. Four years later, in 1914, Hillquit was appointed chief counsel of the ILGWU. He remained a trusted advisor to the union's leadership until his death in 1933. Pratt, *Morris Hillquit*, pp. 197–203.

9. Allen F. Davis, *Spearheads for Reform: The Social Settlements and the Progressive Movement, 1890–1914* (New York: Oxford University Press, 1967), pp. 10, 12, 18.

10. *Dictionary of American Biography, Supplement 3* (New York: Charles Scribner's Sons, 1973), pp. 372–4; Robert Hunter, *Poverty* (New York: Macmillan, 1904); Robert Hunter, Memoir, *Marion Gray Papers*, Indiana Historical Society, Indianapolis, Indiana. University Settlement was the oldest settlement house in the United States, having opened in 1887. James Boylan, *Revolutionary Lives: Anna Strunsky and William English Walling* (Amherst: University of Massachusetts, 1998), p. 55.

11. *Dictionary of American Biography, Supplement 3*, p. 373.

12. Peter d'A. Jones, "Introduction to the Torch Book Edition," in Robert Hunter, *Poverty*, reprint edition (New York: Harper & Row, 1965), pp. x–xii; Ira Kipnis, *The American Socialist Movement, 1897–1912* (New York: Columbia University Press, 1952), pp. 376–8.

13. Gerald Friedberg, "Marxism in the United States: John Spargo and the Socialist Party of America," Ph.D. Thesis, 1964, Harvard University Archives, Harvard University, Cambridge, Mass., pp. 3–11, 15, 22, 29.

14. Friedberg, "Marxism in the United States," pp. 95–8; John Spargo, "Reminiscences," October 1950, interview by Wendell Link and Dean Albertson, Bennington, Vermont, Oral History Project, Columbia University, pp. 142–6. Ironically, the primary target of the New York Child Labor Committee was John McMackin, the state's labor commissioner, who had functioned as one of the most prominent union officials in the Henry George campaign of 1886.

15. Friedberg, "Marxism in the United States," pp. 96–8; John Spargo, *Bitter Cry* (New York: Macmillan, 1906); Kipnis, *American Socialist Movement*, p. 376; *New York Times*, June 2, 1917.

16. *Dictionary of American Biography, Supplement 4*; Kent Kreuter and Gretchen Kreuter, *An American Dissenter: The Life of Algie Martin Simons, 1870–1950* (Lexington: University of Kentucky Press, 1969) pp. 41–58.

17. Kreuter, *An American Disaster*, pp. 41, 94; Kipnis, *American Socialist Movement*, pp. 186, 200, 376; Miller, *Victor Berger*, p. 120.

18. Boylan, *Revolutionary Lives*, pp. 48–55; *New York Times*, May 24, 1903. Walling came from a socially prominent Kentucky family, his father having been an affluent doctor, and the proprietor of a wholesale drug firm. His maternal grandfather had enjoyed a successful career as a banker, before going on to become an unsuccessful vice-presidential candidate on the Democratic ticket in the 1880 election.

19. *National Cyclopedia of American Biography* (New York: James T. White, 1968), 50: 25–6.

20. Kipnis, *American Socialist Movement*, p. 200.

21. Robert Dwight Reynolds Jr., "The Millionaire Socialists: J.G. Phelps Stokes and His Circle of Friends," Ph.D. Thesis, University of South Carolina, Columbia, South Carolina, 1974, pp. 97–101, 105, 126.

22. William M. Dick, *Labor and Socialism in America: The Gompers Era* (Post Washington, New York: Kennikat Press, 1972), pp. 34–6.

23. Carl F. Brand, *The British Labour Party: A Short History*, revised edition (Stanford, Ca.: Hoover Institution Press, 1974), pp. 15, 19.

24. Stuart B. Kaufman, Peter J. Albert and Grace Palladino, "Introduction," *The Samuel Gompers Papers* (Urbana: University of Illinois Press, 1999), 7: xv. The AFL had abandoned its consumer boycott list in February 1908, after the Supreme Court upheld a judgment against the hatters' union for its boycott of a hat maker. The AFL paid most of this $250,000 fine.

25. Brand, *British Labour Party*, p. 19.

26. Kenneth O. Morgan, Keir Hardie: Radical and Socialist (London: Weidenfeld & Nicolson, 1975), p. 155.

27. Samuel Gompers to the AFL Executive Council, February 9, 1906, *Gompers Papers*, 6: 526; "Labor's Bill of Grievances," March 21, 1906, *Gompers Papers*, 7: 3–5; "AF of L Campaign Programme," July 22, 1906, *Gompers Papers*, 7: 61–3.

28. Samuel Gompers, "Debs, The Apostle of Failure," reprinted in Kaufman, Albert and Palladino, *Gompers Papers*, 7: 405, 402. The piece originally appeared as an editorial in the September 1908 issue of the *American Federationist*.

29. "Excerpts from the Proceedings of the 1906 Convention of the AFL in Minneapolis," November 20, 1906, *Gompers Papers*, 7: 130.

30. "Excerpts," November 20, 1906, *Gompers Papers*, 7: 134.

31. Morgan, *Keir Hardie*, p. 10.

32. Morgan, *Keir Hardie*, pp. 15–17, 25–30, 51–2.

33. Morgan, *Keir Hardie*, pp. 80–1, 109.

34. Phillip P. Poirier, *The Advent of the British Labour Party* (New York: Columbia University Press, 1958), pp. 186–90.

35. Morgan, *Keir Hardie*, p. 188; *Labour Leader*, September 18, 1908.

36. Morgan, *Keir Hardie*, p. 184. Hardie had made a brief trip to the United States during the presidential elections of 1896, but this was well before the formation of both the Industrial Workers of the World and the Socialist Party (Morgan, *Keir Hardie*, p. 85).

37. *Labour Leader*, September 25, 1908; Robert Hunter, *Socialists at Work* (New York: Macmillan, 1908), p. 101.

38. Hunter, *Socialists at Work*, p. 106.

39. *Labour Leader*, October 9, 1908.

40. *Labour Leader*, January 15, 1908; *New York Times*, January 17, 1909.

41. *New York Times*, January 17, 1909. In fact, Senator Robert La Follette, with the support of the union structure and the backing of the Socialist Party, would garner 5 million votes in the 1924 presidential election.

42. Walton Bean, *Boss Ruef's San Francisco: The Story of the Union Labor Party, Big Business and Graft Prosecution* (Berkeley, University of California Press, 1952).

43. Bean, *Boss Ruef's San Francisco*, pp. 37, 78, 145–51. Schmitz, the mayor of San Francisco from 1901 to 1907, when he was forced to resign after being convicted of taking bribes, unsuccessfully sought the Republican nomination for governor in 1906.

44. Grace Heilman Stimson, *Rise of the Labor Movement in Los Angeles* (Berkeley: University of California Press, 1955), pp. 229–35; Socialist Party, *National Convention of the Socialist Party* (Chicago, 1904), pp. 153, 316.

45. Job Harriman to Morris Hillquit, November 10, 1908, Hillquit Papers, State Historical Society of Wisconsin in Microfilm, Reel 1, *The Morris Hillquit Papers* (Frederick, Md.: University Publications of America, 1969). Hillquit and Harriman had a political history that went back to 1899, when both had been leading members of the Kangaroo split with the Socialist Labor Party. The two were such close personal friends that Hillquit advanced Harriman money when the latter became sick in the early 1900s. (Both Hillquit and Harriman suffered from tuberculosis, and died from its complications.) Pratt, *Morris Hillquit*, p. 39.

46. Harriman to Hillquit, November 10, 1908, Reel 1, *Hillquit Papers*.

47. Harriman to Hillquit, November 10, 1908, Reel 1, *Hillquit Papers*.

48. Harriman to Hillquit, November 10, 1908, Reel 1, *Hillquit Papers*.

49. John Spargo, Circular Letter, May 31, 1917, Box 2, *Spargo Papers*, University of Vermont, Burlington, Vermont.

50. William English Walling, "Laborism versus Socialism," *International Socialist Review* (March 1909) 9: 685–9.

51. Robert Hunter, "The British Labor Party: A Reply," *International Socialist Review* (April 1909) 9: 755. Lenin's argument was formulated most clearly in his speech to the Third Congress of the Communist International in August 1920. ("Speech on Affiliation to the British Labour Party," in *Collected Works*, 31: 257–63, Moscow, Foreign Languages Publishing House, 1966.) Lenin's decision, as implemented by the Communist International, to enter the British Labour Party, and its implications for the United States are thoroughly discussed in the following two chapters.

52. Hunter, *International Socialist Review*, 9: 761, 763.

53. J.G. Stokes to Morris Hillquit, December 2, 1909, *Hillquit Papers*, Reel 1.

54. Interview with John Spargo, Gerald Friedberg, November 16, 1963, Old Bennington, Vermont, *Friedberg Material for a Dissertation*, Special Collections, University of Vermont, Burlington, Vermont.

55. Morris Hillquit and John Spargo, Draft Manifesto, "To Socialist Party Comrades," *Friedberg Material for a Dissertation*, Special Collections, University of Vermont, Burlington, Vermont.

56. Hillquit and Spargo, Manifesto, University of Vermont, Burlington, Vermont.

57. Max Hayes to Dora Hayes, November 13, 1909, Ohio Historical Society, Reel 1, Microfilm, *Max S. Hayes Papers* (Columbus Ohio: Ohio Historical Society, 1968).

58. John Spargo to J.G. Phelps Stokes, December 3, 1909, Reel 4, *Socialist Party Papers*.

59. *New York Call*, December 11, 1909. The original letter was written on November 19, 1909. The next three paragraphs are drawn from this letter.

60. Rose Pastor Stokes to Stephen Reynolds, November 26, 1909, Box 1, *Reynolds Papers*, Indiana Historical Society, Indianapolis, Indiana.

61. Stokes to Reynolds, November 26, 1909, Box 1, *Reynolds Papers*, Indiana Historical Society.

62. William English Walling, Circular Letter, November 26, 1909, *Socialist Party Papers*, William R. Perkins Library, Duke University, Microfilm, Reel 4, *Socialist Party of America Papers* (Glen Rock, N.J.: Microfilming Corporation of America, 1975). The next paragraphs are drawn from this circular.

63. Algie Simons to William English Walling, December 1, 1909, Microfilm, Reel 4, *Socialist Party Papers*.

64. Interview with John Spargo, Gerald Friedberg, April 3, 1963, *Friedberg Material for a Dissertation*, Special Collections, University of Vermont, Burlington, Vermont; John Spargo to Algie Simons, November 29, 1909, Microfilm, Reel 4, *Socialist Party Papers*.

65. John Spargo to J.G. Stokes, December 3, 1909, Microfilm, Reel 4, *Socialist Party Papers*. Walling did suffer from severe emotional problems. He was also under enormous personal stress. In July 1909, a former girlfriend had sued him for breach of promise, a court battle that greatly delighted the tabloid press. Boylan, *Revolutionary Lives*, pp. 165–7. All of this, of course, had nothing to do with the question of the labor party, but the willingness of Spargo and other moderate leaders to use Walling's personal problems to discredit and silence him is indicative of the importance they ascribed to the issue, and their readiness to use any means available to reach their goal.

66. *New York Call*, January 4, 1910.

67. *New York Call*, January 4, 1910.

68. *New York Call*, January 6, 1910.

69. *New York Call*, January 18, 1910.

70. *New York Call*, January 18, 1910.

71. V. I. Lenin, *Collected Works* (Moscow: Foreign Languages Publishing House, 1963) 15: 233–4.

72. *New York Call*, March 6, 1910.

73. Eugene Debs to William English Walling, December 7, 1909, *The Letters of Eugene Victor Debs*, ed. by J. Robert Constantine (Urbana: University of Illinois Press, 1990) 1: 309.

74. Eugene Debs to William English Walling, December 13, 1909, *Letters of Debs*, 1: 310; *International Socialist Review*; Robert Hunter to Eugene Debs, January 27, 1910, *Letters of Debs*, 1: 331.

75. *New York Call*, December 11, 1909.

76. Victor Berger to Morris Hillquit, February 13, 1910, Reel 1, Microfilm, *Hillquit Papers*.

77. Berger to Hillquit, February 13, 1910, Microfilm, Reel 1, *Hillquit Papers*; Eugene Debs to William English Walling, February 2, 1910, *Letters of Debs*, 1: 342–3.

78. Robert Hunter to Adolph Germer, March 18, 1910, State Historical Society of Wisconsin, in Microfilm, Reel 1, *Adolph Germer Papers* (Frederick, Md.: University Publications of America, 1987).

79. Adolph Germer to Robert Hunter, March 28, 1910, Microfilm, Reel 1, *Germer Papers*.

80. Germer to Hunter, March 28, 1910, Microfilm, Reel 1, *Germer Papers*.

81. Max Hayes, "The World of Labor," *International Socialist Review* (October 1910) 11: 246.

82. Max Hayes, "The World of Labor," *International Socialist Review* (December 1910) 11: 372.

83. Allen Ruff, *"We Called Each Other Comrade": Charles H. Kerr Company, Radical Publishers* (Urbana: University of Illinois Press, 1997), pp. 118–19.

84. Bernard K. Johnpoll and Harvey Klehr (eds), *Biographical Dictionary of the American Left* (Westport, Conn: Greenwood Press, 1986), p. 38.

85. Ruff, *"We Called Each Other Comrade,"* p. 141.

86. Frank Bohn, "The Socialist Party and the California Labor Party," *International Socialist Review* (June 1911) 11: 766.

87. Bohn, "The Socialist Party and the California Labor Party," p. 767.

88. Frank Bohn to Theodore Debs, September 25, 1911, *Letters of Debs*, 1: 429.

89. Bohn to Theodore Debs, September 25, 1911, *Letters of Debs*, 1: 430. James Maurer of Pennsylvania and Henry Slobodin of New York were considered for inclusion in the left-wing slate. Both were prominent members of the SP, but neither was elected to the National Executive Committee in the 1912 election.

90. Bohn to Theodore Debs, *Letters of Debs*, 1: 430; Theodore Debs to Frank Bohn, October 5, 1911, *Letters of Debs*, 1: 431.

91. William Haywood, "News and Views," *International Socialist Review* (December 1911) 12: 375.

92. Frank Bohn, "News and Views," *International Socialist Review* (December 1911) 12: 375.

93. *Socialist Party Monthly Bulletin*, January 1912.

94. *Socialist Party Monthly Bulletin*, January 1912.

95. Clyde A. Berry and Stephen M. Reynolds, "Verdict – Not Guilty: Report of [the] National Investigating Committee," *International Socialist Review* (June 1912) 12: 864. Hunter's resolution, as approved by the national executive committee, had called upon the national committee of the Party to establish a three-person committee. This committee totally cleared the ISR, reporting that Kerr received a salary of $1,500 as editor and publisher, while Mary Marcy received $1,000 as managing editor. The committee also pointed out that Hunter was a stockholder, and as such all of this information would have been readily available to him.

96. "The National Convention of 1912," *International Socialist Review* (June 1912) 12: 827. Seidel had just completed a two-year term as mayor of Milwaukee, and was one of the most prominent leaders of the Wisconsin Socialist Party. He would be chosen as Debs' running mate for the 1912 campaign. Russell was a renowned journalist and muckraker. He would campaign as the Party's candidate for governor of New York in 1912.

97. Eugene Debs to George Goebel, August 3, 1912, *Letters of Debs*, 1: 545.

98. "Shall Bossism Prevail in the Socialist Party," *International Socialist Review* (July 1912) 13: 77.

99. Kipnis, *American Socialist Movement*, pp. 164, 379–80.

100. Eugene Debs to Walter Lanfersiek, August 11, 1912, *Letters of Debs*, 1: 540.
101. "Shall Bossism Prevail in the Socialist Party," pp. 77–8.
102. "Shall Bossism Prevail in the Socialist Party," pp. 77–8. Kerr indicated to Barnes that this editorial represented a collaborative effort by the *ISR* editorial staff. Obviously, Kerr, as publisher, and Mary Marcy, as managing editor, bore the ultimate responsibility for the editorial.
103. J. Mahlon Barnes to Morris Hillquit, June 27, 1912, Microfilm, Reel 2, *Hillquit Papers*.
104. Peter Carlson, *The Life and Times of Big Bill Haywood* (New York: Norton, 1983), pp. 26–41.
105. Carlson, *Haywood,* pp. 52–4.
106. Carlson, *Haywood*, p. 58.
107. Carlson, *Haywood*, pp. 78, 86, 93–9, 134.
108. Carlson, *Haywood*, pp. 105–6, 149.
109. William D. Haywood and Frank Bohn, *Industrial Socialism* (Chicago: Charles H. Kerr, 1911), p. 54.
110. Haywood and Bohn, *Industrial Socialism*, p. 57.
111. *New York Call*, November 20, 1911.
112. *New York Call*, December 9, 1911.
113. Stolberg, *Tailor's Progress*, pp. 66–7.
114. Haywood and Bohn, *Industrial Socialism*, sixth edition (Chicago: Charles H. Kerr, 1914), p. 1. It is highly likely that neither of the authors was responsible for this foreword. Haywood would not have written such a passage, and by 1914 Bohn was working in Germany as a foreign correspondent for the *New York Post*. The foreword was probably written by Kerr.
115. *New York Call*, November 29, 1910.
116. Kipnis, *American Socialist Movement*, p. 386.
117. Eugene V. Debs, "Sound Socialist Tactics," *International Socialist Review* (February 1912) 12: 482–5. The next paragraphs are taken from this same source.
118. Eugene V. Debs, "This Is Our Year," *International Socialist Review* (July 1912) 12: 13–17. This article was written in the immediate aftermath of the SP national convention, which adopted a constitutional amendment providing for the expulsion of those advocating sabotage.
119. Joseph R. Conlin, *Big Bill Haywood and the Radical Union Movement* (Syracuse, New York: Syracuse University Press, 1969), p. 164; *Socialist Party Monthly Bulletin*, April 1912.
120. Conlin, *Haywood*, p. 164; Adolph Germer to Robert Hunter, December 23, 1912, Microfilm, Reel 1, *Germer Papers*; *Socialist Party Monthly Bulletin*, May 1912.
121. Kipnis, *American Socialist Movement*, p. 396; "The National Convention of 1912," *International Socialist Review* (June 1912) 12: 811.
122. "The National Convention of 1912," *ISR* (June 1912) 12: 822; "What Haywood Says on Political Action," *International Socialist Review* (February 1913) 13: 622.
123. Kipnis, *American Socialist Movement*, pp. 403–8; "The National Convention of 1912," *ISR* (June 1912) 12: 825–7.

124. *Socialist Party Monthly Bulletin,* July 1912.
125. William D. Haywood, "No Labor Party Representatives," *International Socialist Review* (August 1912) 13: 145.
126. *Labour Leader,* September 5, 1912. Hardie visited North America for six weeks in the fall of 1912. He made a few stops in Canada, but the great majority of his itinerary was located within the United States. Hardie spoke to 42 public meetings during his tour. *Labour Leader,* November 21, 1912.
127. *Labour Leader,* December 19, 1912.
128. *Labour Leader,* September 5, 1912.
129. *Socialist Party Monthly Bulletin,* January 1913.
130. Kipnis, *American Socialist Movement,* pp. 413, 417.
131. Keir Hardie to Adolph Germer, February 4, 1913, Microfilm, Reel 1, *Germer Papers.*
132. Adolph Germer to Keir Hardie, February 18, 1913, Microfilm, Reel 1, *Germer Papers.*
133. Conlin, *Haywood,* p. 165; Eugene Debs, "A Plea for Solidarity," *International Socialist Review* (March 1914) 14: 537–8.
134. Conlin, *Haywood,* p. 165.
135. *Party Builder,* November 15, 1913; *Party Builder,* December 13, 1913.
136. Reino Nikolai Hannula, *Blueberry God: The Education of a Finnish-American* (San Luis Obispo, Calif.: Quality Hill Books, 1979), pp. 202–3.

CHAPTER 4

1. James Weinstein, *The Decline of Socialism in America, 1912–25* (New York: Monthly Review Press, 1967), pp. 129–31.
2. Socialist Party, "War Proclamation and War," April 17, 1917, *Revolutionary Radicalism* (Albany, New York: J.B. Lyon, 1920), Part I, Volume I, pp. 617–18.
3. Socialist Party, "Proceedings of the National Emergency Convention," in Microfilm, Reel 1, *Papers of Darlington Hoopes* (State College: Pennsylvania State University).
4. Louis Fraina, "Syndicalism and Industrial Unionism," *International Socialist Review* (July 1913), 14: 25.
5. Theodore Draper, *The Roots of American Communism* (New York: Viking Press, 1957), p. 84.
6. Draper, *Roots,* p. 155.
7. Draper, *Roots,* pp. 155–8; *New York Call,* May 21, 1919.
8. Draper, *Roots,* p. 168.
9. John Howard Keiser, "John Fitzpatrick and Progressive Unionism, 1915–25," (Ph.D. Thesis, 1965, Northwestern University, Evanston, Illinois), p. 117.
10. Elizabeth McKillen, *Chicago Labor and the Quest for a Democratic Diplomacy, 1914–24* (Ithaca, New York: Cornell University Press, 1995), pp. 46–7, Keiser, "John Fitzpatrick," p. 117.
11. McKillen, *Chicago Labor,* pp. 79, 82–4.

12. Keiser, "John Fitzpatrick," p. 118; Carl F. Brand, *The British Labour Party: A Short History*, revised edition (Stanford, Ca.: Hoover Institution Press, 1974), pp. 46–53.

13. Brand, *Bristish Labour Party*, p. 54.

14. G.D.H. Cole, *A History of the Labour Party from 1914* (London: Routledge & Kegan Paul, 1948), p. 72.

15. Brand, *British Labour Party*, p. 58.

16. Andrew Strouthous, *U.S. Labor and Political Action, 1918–24: A Comparison of Independent Political Action in New York, Chicago, and Seattle* (New York: St. Martin's Press, 2000), p. 23; *Dictionary of American Biography, Supplement 4* (New York: Charles Scribner's Sons, 1974), p. 543.

17. Strouthous, *U.S. Labor and Political Action*, p. 178.

18. McKillen, *Chicago Labor*, p. 130.

19. McKillen, *Chicago Labor*, pp. 130, 142–3.

20. Robert Loren Morlan, *Political Prairie Fire: The Nonpartisan League, 1915–1922* (Minneapolis: University of Minnesota Press, 1955), p. 296; McKillen, *Chicago Labor*, p. 153.

21. McKillen, *Chicago Labor*, p. 154.

22. McKillen, *Chicago Labor*, p. 154; Stanley Shapiro, "'Hand and Brain': The Farmer-Labor Party of 1920," *Labor History* 26 (Summer 1985): 418.

23. Socialist Party, *Campaign Book* (Chicago, 1920), p. 76.

24. Socialist Party, *Campaign Book*, p. 76.

25. Otto Branstetter to Eugene Debs, July 17, 1920, *Socialist World*, August 15, 1920.

26. Theodore Debs to Otto Branstetter, July 29, 1920, *Socialist World*, August 15, 1920.

27. McKillen, *Chicago Labor*, p. 154.

28. Morris Hillquit, "Radicalism in America," *American Appeal*, October 15, 1920, p. 18.

29. Hillquit, "Radicalism in America," *American Appeal*, October 15, 1920, p. 19.

30. Eugene V. Debs, "After the Battle," *American Appeal*, January 5, 1921, p. 11.

31. Congressional Quarterly, *Guide to U.S. Elections* (Washington, D.C., 1975), p. 286. Debs received 75,000 votes in Illinois, most of them from the Chicago area, while Christiansen polled 50,000 in Illinois.

32. Philip Taft, *The A.F. of L. in the Time of Gompers* (New York: Harper & Brothers, 1957), p. 462; Leo Troy, "Labor Representation on American Railways," *Labor History* (Fall 1961) 2: 296–8.

33. Walker D. Hines, *War History of American Railroads* (New Haven: Yale University Press, 1928), pp. 153–5; William G. McAdoo, *The Crowded Years: Reminiscences* (Boston: Houghton Mifflin, 1931), pp. 460–1, 471, 488–90.

34. *New York Times*, December 3, 1918; *New York Times*, May 21, 1919; *New York Times*, February 8, 1919. McAdoo floated the idea of a five year extension of government control, but without the president's public support, the proposal was quickly shelved. *New York Times*, January 5, 1919.

35. *New York Times*, February 7, 1919; *New York Times*, February 8, 1919; Edward Keating, *The Story of "Labor": Thirty-Three Years on the Rail Workers' Fighting Front* (Washington, D.C.: Rufus Darby, 1953), p. 26.
36. Keating, *Story of "Labor"*, pp. 21–3.
37. Selig Perlman and Philip Taft, *History of Labor in the United States, 1896–1932* (New York: Macmillan, 1935), 4: 515; Troy, "Labor Representation," p. 300.
38. *Labor*, January 20, 1920.
39. *New York Call*, June 28, 1921.
40. *New York Call*, June 28, 1921; *New York Call*, May 30, 1921.
41. Socialist Party National Executive Committee, "Report," *Socialist World*, May 1922, p. 2.
42. Otto Branstetter to Eugene V. Debs, November 25, 1921, *Debs Papers*, Indiana State Library; Morris Hillquit, *Loose Leaves of a Busy Life* (New York: Macmillan, 1934), p. 306. The quote is from Hillquit's distillation of Johnston's letter.
43. *Labor*, February 11, 1922. Officially the invitation was issued by the Associated of Recognized Standard Railway Organizations, the loose federation of 15 unions and the AFL Railway Employees Department that had been created to promote the Plumb Plan.
44. *New York Times*, February 22, 1922; Morris Hillquit to Vera Hillquit, February 20, 1922, *Hillquit Papers*, State Historical Society of Wisconsin, Microfilm, Reel 2, *The Morris Hillquit Papers* (Frederick, Md.: University Publications of America, 1969).
45. *New York Times*, February 22, 1922; Hillquit, *Loose Leaves*, pp. 310–11.
46. Conference for Progressive Political Action, "A Call to Action," March 15, 1922, Reel 2, *Hillquit Papers*.
47. "Statement of the Socialist Party Group," *Socialist World* (March 1922), pp. 14–15. Otto Branstetter, Morris Hillquit, Daniel Hoan, James Oneal and Bertha Hale White signed the statement. Victor Berger was invited but did not attend.
48. John H.M. Laslett, *Labor and the Left: A Study of Socialist and Radical Influences in the American Labor Movement, 1881–1924* (New York: Basic Books, 1970), p. 174.
49. Morris Hillquit to Fred C. Howe, April 8, 1922, Microfilm, Reel 2, *Hillquit Papers*.
50. "Convention Minutes," *Socialist World*, May 1922, p. 12.
51. "Convention Minutes," *Socialist World*, May 1922, p. 12.
52. Troy, "Labor Representation," pp. 301–3. Wages for shop workers were lowered by seven cents an hour. The pay cut meant that shop workers would be paid less than they had been two years previously, not allowing for the impact of inflation.
   The slash in wages was only the last in a series of corporate assaults on the wages and working conditions of the railroad workers. Some lines subcontracted much of their repair work to non-union shops. Many of the lines also insisted that their own employees agree to become independent contractors, working for piece rates rather than an hourly wage, without benefits or the protections of a union contract. When the Railway Labor Board ruled that these unilateral changes in labor

relations constituted a violation of the law, the railway lines blocked
the implementation of the Board's orders by appealing the ruling
through every level of the judicial system.

The Pennsylvania Railroad went even further by refusing to recognize
the legitimate unions representing their workforce, and instead creating
their own company unions. Once again the Railway Labor Board ruled
for the AFL unions, and once again the Pennsylvania Railroad
indefinitely delayed compliance by appealing the decision. The inability
of the Railway Labor Board to implement crucial decisions that went
against the railway lines incensed the railroad unions, and set the
groundwork for the bitter strike that followed.

53. Perlman and Taft, *History of Labor*, 4: 519; Troy, "Labor Representation,"
p. 304; *Labor*, June 10, 1922.
54. Eugene Nelson, *Break Their Haughty Power: Joe Murphy in the Heyday of
the Wobblies* (San Francisco: Ism Press, 1993), pp. 95, 101–8.
55. *New York Times*, July 18, 1922.
56. Editorial, *Socialist World*, July 1922, p. 2. *Socialist World* did carry an
article by Joseph E. Cohen that discussed the strike in general terms,
arguing that "no unions should lift a finger to assist in breaking a strike."
Still, Cohen's article did not specifically mention that the railroad
brotherhoods had ordered their members to remain on the job, despite
the strike. "On Strike Again," *Socialist World,* August 1922, p. 6.
57. Mark Perlman, *The Machinists: A New Study in American Trade Unionism*
(Cambridge, Mass.: Harvard University Press, 1961), p. 59; *New York
Times,* July 20, 1922; Robert H. Zieger, *Republicans and Labor, 1919–1929*
(Lexington: University of Kentucky Press, 1969), p. 130; Perlman and
Taft, *History of Labor*, 4: 520.
58. Perlman and Taft, *History of Labor*, 4: 520.
59. Perlman and Taft, *History of Labor*, 4: 521–2.
60. *Labor*, September 16, 1922; Zieger, *Republicans and Labor*, p. 138; Perlman
and Taft, *History of Labor*, 4: 523; Troy, "Labor Representation," p. 304.
61. *Labor*, September 16, 1922; Zieger, *Republicans and Labor*, p. 138; Perlman
and Taft, *History of Labor*, 4: 523; Troy, "Labor Representation," p. 304.
62. Eugene V. Debs, "The End of Craft Unionism," *Debs Magazine*, October
1922, p. 4.
63. Kenneth Campbell MacKay, *The Progressive Movement of 1924* (New
York: Columbia University Press, 1947), p. 67; *Labor*, October 21, 1922.
64. *Labor*, November 25, 1922.
65. *Labor*, December 23, 1922.
66. "Platform Adopted by the Cleveland Conference," December 1922, Box
B98, *La Follette Papers*, Library of Congress; MacKay, *The Progressive
Movement*, pp. 69–70.
67. *Communist*, October 18, 1919.
68. Vladimir Lenin, "Left Wing Communism: An Infantile Disorder," in
Lenin, *Collected Works* (Moscow, 1966), 31: 89.
69. Lenin, *Collected Works*, 31: 202, 260.
70. Lenin, *Collected Works*, 31: 260.
71. Lewis Corey (Louis Fraina), interview with the Federal Bureau of
Investigation, 1949–50, Box 2, *Corey Papers*, Columbia University.

72. Draper, *Roots of American Communism*, pp. 277, 279–80, 295–6; Theodore Draper, *American Communism and Soviet Russia* (New York: Viking Press, 1960), p. 32.
73. Draper, *Roots of American Communism*, p. 379.
74. Draper, *Roots of American Communism*, p. 58.
75. J.B. Salutsky to H. Rosenfeld, February 17, 1923, Box 38, *J.B.S. Hardman Papers*, Tamiment Institute, New York University.
76. Draper, *Roots of American Communism*, pp. 330–1; Salutsky to Rosenfeld, February 17, 1923, Box 38, *Hardman Papers*, Tamiment Institute, New York University. Salutsky was the editor of the Amalgamated journal, *Advance*, and thus a delegate to the CPPA conference.
77. Salutsky to Rosenfeld, February 17, 1923, Box 38, *Hardman Papers*.
78. MacKay, *The Progressive Movement*, pp. 69–70; Laslett, *Labor and the Left*, p. 174; *Labor*, December 23, 1922.
79. Strouthous, *U.S. Labor and Political Action*, p. 127; Draper, *Roots of American Communism*, p. 39.
80. John Pepper (Josef Pogány), "A Revolt of Framers and Workers in the United States," *International Press Correspondence* (August 23, 1923) 53: 553.
81. W.R. Snow, "Why an Independent Labor Party," *Socialist World*, January 1923, p. 11.
82. "Agenda," *Socialist World*, May 1923, p. 6; "Minutes of the National Convention," *Socialist World*, June 1923, p. 11.
83. "Agenda," *Socialist World*, May 1923, p. 6; "Minutes of the National Convention," *Socialist World*, June 1923, p. 12.
84. "Reply to the Farmer-Labor Party," *Socialist World*, June 1923, p. 9. William H. Henry, Algernon Lee and James Oneal signed the open letter.
85. Draper, *Roots of American Communism*, pp. 42–3.
86. Draper, *Roots of American Communism*, pp. 42–3.
87. Strouthous, *U.S. Labor and Political Action*, p. 131.
88. Draper, *Roots of American Communism*, pp. 42–3, 79.
89. Morris Hillquit, "Moscow and London," *Socialist World*, July 1923, p. 6; Morris Hillquit, "The Story of the British Labor Party," *Socialist World*, September 1923, p. 4.
90. Hillquit, "Moscow and London," p. 6; Hillquit, "The Story of the British Labor Party," p. 4.
91. Hillquit, "The Story of the British Labor Party," p. 4.

CHAPTER 5

1. Margaret Leslie Davis, *The Dark Side of Fortune: Triumph and Scandal in the Life of Oil Tycoon Edward L. Doheny* (Berkeley: University of California Press, 1989), p. 62.
2. Robert Loren Morlan, *Political Prairie Fire: The Nonpartisan League, 1915–22* (Minneapolis: University of Minnesota Press, 1955), pp. 23–5, 33–4.
3. Millard L. Gieske, *Minnesota Farmer-Laborism: The Third Party Alternative* (Minneapolis: University of Minnesota Press, 1979), pp. 39, 45, 61, 64.

4. Gieske, *Minnesota Farmer-Laborism*, pp. 81–4, 93.
5. Gieske, *Minnesota Farmer-Laborism*, pp. 17, 75–6. In the 1922 elections, the Minnesota FLP elected one of its nominees to the U.S. Senate and two to the U.S. House of Representatives.
6. Morlan, *Political Prairie Fire*, pp. 31, 85; Gieske, *Minnesota Farmer-Laborism*, p. 66.
7. *Minnesota Star*, August 16, 1952.
8. Eugene V. Debs to Otto Branstetter, March 25, 1922, in Eugene V. Debs, *Letters of Eugene Victor Debs*, edited by J. Robert Constantine (Urbana: University of Illinois Press, 1990), 3: 300.
9. Eugene V. Debs to William Mahoney, November 8, 1923, in Debs, *Letters of Debs*, 3: 413–14.
10. Gieske, *Minnesota Farmer-Laborism*, p. 83.
11. Kenneth Campbell MacKay, *The Progressive Movement of 1924* (New York: Columbia University Press, 1947), p. 75.
12. Davis, *The Dark Side of Fortune*, pp. 160–3.
13. Edward Keating, *The Story of "Labor": Thirty-Three Years on the Rail Workers' Fighting Front* (Washington, D.C.: Rufus Darby, 1953), p. 156; Morris Hillquit, *Loose Leaves of a Busy Life* (New York: Macmillan, 1934), p. 318.
14. *Labor*, February 23, 1924.
15. *Labor*, May 10, 1924.
16. *Labor*, May 10, 1924.
17. Oswald Garrison Villard, *Fighting Years: Memoirs of a Liberal Editor* (New York: Harcourt Brace, 1939), p. 503.
18. *New York Times,* March 2, 1924.
19. Eugene V. Debs, "July 4th Convention," *St. Louis Labor*, April 28, 1924 in Microfilm, Reel 8, *The Papers of Eugene V. Debs* (Glen Rock, N.J.: Microfilming Corporation of America, 1983).
20. Eugene V. Debs, "Our Party – Its Past and Its Future," *Socialist World*, June 1924, p. 3.
21. Debs, "Our Party", p. 3.
22. Gieske, *Minnesota Farmer-Laborism*, p. 83.
23. William Mahoney to Morris Hillquit, January 4, 1924, Hillquit Papers, State Historical Society of Wisconsin, Microfilm, Reel 3, *The Morris Hillquit Papers* (Frederick, Md.: University Publications of America, 1987); William Mahoney to William Johnston, April 16, 1924, Microfilm, Reel 3, *Hillquit Papers*.
24. Samuel Gompers, "Statement to the AFL Executive Committee," August 2, 1924, American Federation of Labor Papers, State Historical Society of Wisconsin, Microfilm, Reel 7, *American Federation of Labor Records, The Samuel Gompers Era* (Sanford, N.C.: Microfilming Corporation of America, 1979). La Follette did not attend this gathering of prominent progressives, probably because it was held while he was still recovering from pneumonia.
25. Gompers, "Statement to the AFL Executive Committee," August 2, 1924, Microfilm, Reel 7, *AFL Records*.
26. Basil Manly to Robert La Follette, May 15, 1924, Box B99, *La Follette Papers*, Library of Congress; Gilbert Roe to Robert La Follette Jr., May 23, 1924, *La Follette Papers*, Library of Congress.

27. *Daily Worker*, April 24, 1924.
28. Edward Hallett Carr, *Socialism in One Country 1924–1926* (New York: Macmillan, 1964), 3: 243–4; Theodore Draper, *American Communism and Soviet Russia* (New York: Viking Press, 1960), p. 105; *Daily Worker*, May 16, 1924.
29. Isaac Deutscher, *The Prophet Unarmed: Trotsky, 1921–1929* (New York: Oxford University Press, 1959), pp. 74–160.
30. Charles Ruthenberg to Israel Amter, February 18, 1924, Harvey Klehr, John Earl Haynes, and Kyrill Anderson, *The Soviet World of American Communism* (New Haven, Conn.: Yale University Press, 1998), pp. 26–7; Max Shachtman, "A Visit to the Island of Prinkipo," *Militant*, May 10, 1930, reprinted in *Writings of Leon Trotsky, Supplement 1929–33*, edited by George Breitman (New York: Pathfinder Press, 1979), p. 28.
31. Leon Trotsky, *The First Five Years of the Communist International*, translated by Joseph Vanzler [John G. Wright] (New York: Monad Press, 1975), 1: 12–13.
32. Shachtman, "A Visit to the Island of Prinkipo"; Vasil Kolerov to Communist Party USA, Telegram, [May 1924], Klehr, Haynes and Anderson, *Soviet World*, pp. 27–9; Kolerov was a Comintern official. The telegram was not dated, but the Politburo meeting that set the new policy was held soon after Trotsky's telegram of May 20.
33. *New York Times*, May 29, 1924. Earl Browder, a high official in 1924 who would later become the Communist Party's general secretary, was certain that La Follette had heard of the reversal of policy and was splitting with the Communists before they split with him. Browder was wrong. La Follette's advisors had started urging La Follette to publicly attack the Communists well before the Comintern's decision to reverse its orientation toward the La Follette campaign. La Follette was ill at the time, and clearly dependent on his key advisors for strategic advice. Earl Browder, Oral History, interview with Joseph R. Starobin, 1964, Columbia University Oral History Project, p. 163.
34. *New York Times*, May 29, 1924; Robert Marion La Follette, *La Follette–Wheeler Campaign Book* (Chicago, 1924), p. 126; Samuel Gompers, Frank Morrison and James O'Connell, "To All Organized Labor," May 28, 1924, Microfilm, Reel 18, *AFL Records*. Gompers, Morrison and O'Connell constituted the executive committee of the AFL's National Nonpartisan Political Campaign Committee, reporting directly to the AFL executive committee.
35. *New York Times*, May 29, 1924; *Daily Worker*, May 29, 1924.
36. Draper, *American Communism*, p. 116.
37. Draper, *American Communism*, pp. 116–17.
38. Gieske, *Minnesota Farmer-Laborism*, p. 91.
39. Gilbert Roe to Robert La Follette, June 17, 1924, Box B101, *La Follette Papers*, Library of Congress.
40. Hillquit, *Loose Leaves*, p. 318.
41. Hillquit, *Loose Leaves*, p. 317.
42. La Follette, *Campaign Book*, pp. 31–2.
43. La Follette, *Campaign Book*, p. 37.
44. La Follette, *Campaign Book*, p. 37.

45. La Follette, *Campaign Book*, pp. 31, 37.

46. *New York Times*, July 3, 1924.

47. Jacob Panken, "What We Got," *Socialist World* (January 1925): p. 10.

48. *New York Times*, July 6, 1924. The quotes are drawn from the *Times'* report of Hillquit's speech.

49. Memorandum, William Johnston to Labor, Farmers and Other Progressive Groups, December 30, 1924, Microfilm, Reel 3, *Hillquit Papers*; *New York Times*, July 6, 1924.

50. Hillquit, *Loose Leaves*, p. 320.

51. Minutes of the 1924 Convention, *Socialist World* (July 1924): 1.

52. 1924 Convention, *Socialist World* (July 1924): 12.

53. 1924 Convention, *Socialist World* (July 1924): 12.

54. "Minutes of the N.E.C.," *Socialist World* (September 1924): 15. Debs did not attend this NEC meeting.

55. "1924 Convention," *Socialist World* (July 1924): 13; Nick Salvatore, *Eugene V. Debs: Citizen and Socialist* (Urbana: University of Illinois, 1982), p. 339.

56. Eugene V. Debs, "Debs Accepts Party Chairmanship," *Socialist World* (August 1924): 12–13. The next paragraphs are drawn from the same source.

57. Nancy C. Unger, *Fighting Bob La Follette* (Chapel Hill: University of North Carolina Press, 2000), pp. 294–5.

58. "Progressive Platform," in Arthur Schlesinger Jr. (ed.), *History of American Presidential Elections, 1797–1968* (New York, Chelsea House, 1971), 3: 2517–23.

59. Morris Hillquit to William Johnston and Robert La Follette, July 8, 1924, Box B98, *La Follette Papers*, Library of Congress. Sidney Hillman, the president of the Amalgamated Clothing Workers Union and a prominent supporter of the La Follette campaign, directed Ervin to aid the campaign's efforts in media relations and fundraising. Charles W. Ervin, *Homegrown Liberal: The Autobiography of Charles W. Ervin* (New York: Dodd Mead, 1954), p. 106.

60. When the Iowa Republican Party spurned Brookhart and rallied behind the Democratic candidate, the election deadlocked in a virtual tie, with the Senate finally ruling against Brookhart.

61. Florence Thorne, "His Last Years," in Samuel Gompers, *Seventy Years of Life and Labor* (New York: E.P. Dutton, 1925), 2: 537.

62. "Labor's Political Demands," *American Federationist* 31 (July 1924): 554; "American Labor in the Campaign," *American Federationist* 31 (June 1924): 465.

63. Thorne, "His Last Years," 2: 537.

64. Benjamin Mandel, *Samuel Gompers: A Biography* (Yellow Springs, Ohio: Antioch Press, 1963), pp. 432, 518; Thorne, "His Last Years," p. 537. Throughout the months from July through October, Gompers convalesced at resort hotels on Long Island and in Atlantic City.

65. Frank Morrison, Matthew Woll, Edgar Wallace, and Chester Wright, July 12, 1924, Microfilm, Reel 108, *AFL Records*. Wright was a journalist and the managing editor of the *American Federationist*. Edgar Wallace

worked as a lobbyist for the AFL. In addition, Arthur Nolder, an AFL staff member, attended the meeting.

66. Morrison, Woll, Wallace, and Wright, July 12, 1924, Reel 108, *AFL Records*.

67. Matthew Woll and Chester Wright to Samuel Gompers, July 25, 1924, Reel 108, *AFL Records*.

68. Samuel Gompers, "We Are In to Win," *American Federationist* 31 (September 1924): 741.

69. Samuel Gompers to Frank Morrison, August 19, 1924, Reel 108, *AFL Records*.

70. Samuel Gompers, "Why Labor Should Support La Follette and Wheeler," *American Federationist* 31 (October 1924): 808; MacKay, *The Progressive Movement*, p. 200.

71. MacKay, *The Progressive Movement*, p. 188; Unger, *Fighting Bob La Follette*, p. 299.

72. J. Mahlon Barnes, "Confidential Letter," August 15, 1924, Socialist Party Papers, William R. Perkins Papers, Microfilm, Reel 10, *Socialist Party of America Papers* (Glen Rock, N.J.: Microfilming Corporation of America, 1975).

73. National Executive Committee, "Rules of Political Conduct for All Socialist Party Organizations" [1924], Microfilm, Reel 10, *Socialist Party Papers*.

74. "Rules of Political Conduct," Reel 10, *Socialist Party Papers*.

75. Bertha Hale White to the Socialist Party National Executive Committee, August 18, 1924, Microfilm, Reel 3, *Hillquit Papers*.

76. William Coffey, "Matthew S. Holt," *West Virginia History* (January 1978) 39: 200–9.

77. *Who Was Who in America* (Chicago: A.N. Marquis, 1942), Volume 1.

78. White to the Socialist Party NEC, August 18, 1924, Microfilm, Reel 3, *Hillquit Papers*.

79. Bertha Hale White to William Johnston, October 21, 1924, Microfilm, Reel 3, *Hillquit Papers*.

80. White to Johnston, October 21, 1924, Microfilm, Reel 3, *Hillquit Papers*.

81. *Wheeling Register*, November 5, 1924; *Congressional Quarterly, Guide to U.S. Elections*, third edition (Washington, D.C., 1994), pp. 451, 844. The *Register* for November 5 provided results for the Senate race with only half the precincts reporting. Unfortunately, later issues did not supply complete results. There is no reason to believe that the final tally would have substantially diverged from the earlier result.

   Goff received 50.9 percent of the total vote. La Follette gained 6.3 percent of the vote in West Virginia, far below his results nationwide, and yet far ahead of Holt's vote.

82. Morris Hillquit to Friedrich Adler, September 13, 1924, Microfilm, Reel 3, *Hillquit Papers*.

83. Eugene V. Debs, "Labor Day, 1924," *Socialist World* (September 1924): 2. This article was also published in the *New Leader* issue of August 30, 1924.

84. Debs, "Labor Day," *Socialist World* (September 1924): 2.

85. Shannon, *Socialist Party*, p. 179; *New York Times*, November 6, 1924; W.A. Swanberg, *Norman Thomas: The Last Idealist* (New York: Charles Scribner's Sons, 1976), p. 94.

86. Unger, *Fighting Bob La Follette*, p. 297.

87. Samuel Gompers, "Reaction has Rose – and Thorns," *American Federationist* (December 1924) 31: 989–90.

88. Mark Perlman, *The Machinists: A New Study in American Trade Unionism* (Cambridge: Harvard University Press, 1961), pp. 68–73; Laslett, *Labor and the Left*, p. 175.

89. *New York Times*, November 6, 1924.

90. Morris Hillquit to Friedrich Adler, December 5, 1924, Microfilm, Reel 3, *Hillquit Papers*.

91. *New York Times*, December 13, 1924.

92. Eugene V. Debs, "The American Labor Party," *Socialist World* (January 1925): 1.

93. Debs, "The American Labor Party," *Socialist World* (January 1925): 1.

94. Debs, "The American Labor Party," *Socialist World* (January 1925): 1.

95. John H.M. Laslett, *Labor and the Left: A Study of Socialist and Radical Influences in the American Labor Movement, 1881–1924* (New York: Basic Books, 1970), p. 177; *New York Times*, February 21, 1925.

96. Eugene V. Debs, "Speech to the CPPA Conference," February 21, 1925, Microfilm, Reel 8, *Debs Papers*. Quotes from the next two paragraphs are drawn from the same source.

97. *New York Times*, February 22, 1925; *New York Times*, February 23, 1925. The National Progressive Headquarters failed to generate any momentum, and was dissolved in November 1927. Most of its leaders would become avid supporters of the New Deal a few years later. Mercer Johnston to the Executive Committee, January 3, 1928, Box 70, Mercer Johnston Papers, Library of Congress.

98. Socialist Party, "Statement of Party Policy," *Socialist World* (March 1925): 5.

99. "Statement of Party Policy," *Socialist World* (March 1925): 5.

100. "Minutes of the National Convention," *Socialist World* (March 1925) p. 14.

101. "Minutes of the National Convention," *Socialist World* (March 1925) p. 14.

102. Cohen was an official in the Typographers Union (ITU) in Philadelphia and a long-time member of the Socialist Party. He had attended Party conventions from 1908 to 1920 as a delegate, and was thus a close acquaintance of both of the Debs brothers. Debs, *Letters*, 1: 422.

103. Nick Salvatore, *Eugene V. Debs: Citizen and Socialist* (Urbana: University of Illinois Press, 1982), pp. 140–1, 218.

104. Theodore Debs to Joseph E. Cohen, March 4, 1925, Debs, *Letters*, 3: 470.

105. Unger, *Fighting Bob La Follette*, p. 303.

106. Norman Thomas, *America's Way Out* (New York: Macmillan, 1931), p. 285; Norman Thomas, Oral History, July 1950, interviewed by Wendell Link, Columbia University Oral History Project.

107. Eugene Victor Debs to Mrs. Edward H. Weber, February 3, 1926, Debs, *Letters*, 3: 542–3.

108. Henry had succeeded Bertha Hale White as national secretary in May 1926. He had previously served as state secretary of Indiana. He was also one of the most prominent activists to have opposed the Party's participation in the CPPA. Debs, *Letters*, 3: 598.

109. Eugene V. Debs to William H. Henry, June 10, 1926, Microfilm, Reel 4, *Debs Papers*.

110. Debs to Henry, June 10, 1926, Microfilm, Reel 4, *Debs Papers*.

111. Debs to Henry, June 10, 1926, Microfilm, Reel 4, *Debs Papers*.

CHAPTER 6

1. Eric Leif Davin, "The Very Last Hurrah," in *"We are All Leaders": The Alternative Unionism of the Early 1930s*, edited by Staughton Lynd (Urbana: University of Illinois Press, 1996), pp. 132–55.

2. Murray Benjamin Seidler, *Norman Thomas, Respectable Rebel* (Syracuse, New York: Syracuse University Press, 1961), p. 105; *New York Times*, November 6, 1929.

3. Norma Fain Pratt, *Morris Hillquit: A Political History of an American Jewish Socialist* (Westport, Conn.: Greenwood Press, 1979), p. 197. Hillquit provided legal counsel to the International Ladies Garment Workers Union. Louis Waldman, who would succeed Hillquit as the leading member of the Old Guard, was also a labor attorney. He served as counsel to the Amalgamated Clothing Workers Union and the Hatters Union. Accession Sheet, *Louis Waldman Papers*, New York Public Library.

4. Bernard K. Johnpoll, *Pacifist's Progress: Norman Thomas and the Decline of American Socialism* (Chicago: Quadrangle, 1970), pp. 79–81.

5. Johnpoll, *Pacifist's Progress*, p. 80.

6. Johnpoll, *Pacifist's Progress*, p. 93; Seidler, *Respectable Rebel*, p. 110.

7. *New York Times*, November 9, 1932; Johnpoll, *Pacifist's Progress*, p. 97. Hillquit had received fewer votes when campaigning for mayor in 1917, but, with women excluded from the vote and a smaller population, his share of the total vote was higher, 26 percent. *New York Times*, November 8, 1917.

8. *New York Times*, November 8, 1933; Seidler, *Respectable Rebel*, p. 115.

9. Thomas Kessner, *Fiorello H. La Guardia* (New York: McGraw-Hill, 1989), p. 269.

10. Seidler, *Respectable Rebel*, p. 127; Frank A. Warren, *An Alternative Vision: The Socialist Party in the 1930s* (Bloomington: University of Indiana Press, 1974), pp. 193–4.

11. Seidler, *Respectable Rebel*, p. 190.

12. Seidler, *Respectable Rebel*, pp. 161–2; Johnpoll, *Pacifist's Progress*, pp. 170–1.

13. Johnpoll, *Pacifist's Progress*, pp. 157–8.

14. Constance Ashton Myers, *The Prophet's Army: Trotskyists in America, 1928–41* (Westport, Conn.: Greenwood Press, 1977), pp. 112–13; Albert Glotzer, "Albert Goldman," *Biographical Dictionary of the American Left* (Westport, Conn: Greenwood Press, 1986), p. 160.

15. Myers, *The Prophet's Army*, pp. 87–9, 93–5.

16. Isaac Deutscher, *The Prophet Outcast, 1929–40* (London: Oxford University Press, 1963), pp. 271–2; Leon Trotsky, "The Way Out," *Writings*

of Leon Trotsky, 1934–35, edited by George Breitman and Bev Scott (New York: Pathfinder, 1971), pp. 81–8; Leon Trotsky, *The Crisis of the French Section, 1935–36*, edited by Naomi Allen and George Breitman (New York: Pathfinder, 1977), p. 21.

17. Trotsky, *Crisis of the French Section*, pp. 27–8. Trotsky had warned his followers at the time of the Mulhouse convention that they "must know how to effect a new turn." Trotsky, *Crisis of the French Section*, p. 179.

18. Myers, *The Prophet's Army*, pp. 113–20.

19. Leon Trotsky, *The Communist International after Lenin*, translated by Joseph Vanzler [John G. Wright] (New York: Pioneer Publishers, 1936), p. 120. Trotsky, who had already been sent into internal exile in Alma-Ata, wrote a lengthy critique of Comintern policy. It was circulated among the delegates attending the Sixth Congress of the Communist Party of the Soviet Union in 1928. James Cannon read a censored version, and was deeply impressed. He then smuggled a copy out when he returned to the United States and began showing it to a few trusted comrades. Within weeks, the entire group had been expelled from the Communist Party for Trotskyist deviations. Theodore Draper, *American Communism and Soviet Russia* (New York: Viking Press, 1960), p. 365.

20. Martin Abern, James P. Cannon, Max Shachtman, Arne Swabeck, "The Platform of the Communist Opposition," in James P. Cannon, *The Left Opposition in the U.S., 1928–31* (New York: Monad Press, 1981), pp. 106–7. The platform was presented by the national leadership in February 1929, and approved by the delegates to the first CLA convention in Chicago in May 1929. The section on the labor party met with significant opposition, given the widespread "skepticism about the labor party," within the ranks of the CLA and the radical Left as a whole. James P. Cannon, *Militant*, June 1, 1929.

21. Max Shachtman, "A Visit to the Island of Prinkipo," *Militant*, May 10, 1930, reprinted in *Writings of Leon Trotsky, Supplement 1929–33*, edited by George Breitman (New York: Pathfinder Press, 1979), p. 29.

22. Leon Trotsky to Max Shachtman, June 20, 1930, *Writings, Supplement 1929–33*, p. 43.

23. *Militant*, July 25, 1931; *Militant*, October 10, 1931. The national leadership presented its proposed platform in July 1931 for approval by the delegates to the second conference that September. This time the labor party section was adopted without dissent.

24. *New York Times*, March 3, 1932; Leon Trotsky to Albert Glotzer, May 1, 1932, *Writings, Supplement 1929–33*, p. 111.

25. Leon Trotsky, "The Labor Party Question in the United States," May 19, 1932, *Writings of Leon Trotsky, 1932*, edited by George Breitman and Sarah Lovell (New York: Pathfinder Press, 1973), p. 95.

26. Trotsky, "The Labor Party Question in the United States," May 19, 1932, *Writings, 1932*, pp. 96–7.

27. "Declaration of Principle of the Workers Party of the U.S." [1934], Microfilm, Reel 2, *Papers of the Socialist Workers Party*, Tamiment Library, New York University, New York, New York. The draft of this statement of principles had been hammered out in negotiations involving Cannon

and Shachtman representing the CLA and A.J. Muste representing the American Workers Party. James P. Cannon, *The Communist League of America, 1932–34* (New York: Monad Press, 1985), p. 430.

28. *New York Times*, April 2, 1936; Warren Moscow, *Politics in the Empire State* (New York: Knopf, 1948), p. 104.

29. *New York Times*, April 2, 1936; Kenneth Alan Waltzer, "The American Labor Party: Third Party Politics in New Deal–Cold War New York, 1936–54," Ph.D. Thesis, 1977, Harvard University, Cambridge, Massachusetts, p. 79. Berry was a conservative trade union official who avoided strikes and worked for industrial conciliation. He would be appointed to the Senate as a Democrat, filling a vacancy from Tennessee, and serving from May 1937 through 1939. Gary M. Fink, *Biographical Dictionary of American Labor* (Westport, Conn: Greenwood Press, 1984), p. 111.

30. *New York Times*, May 12, 1936.

31. Moscow, *Politics in the Empire State*, p. 105; Waltzer, "The American Labor Party," pp. 78, 502; Edward Flynn, interview with Owen Bombard, March 1950, pp. 20–1, Oral History Project, Columbia University.

32. Moscow, *Politics in the Empire State*, p. 65; Waltzer, "The American Labor Party," p. 78.

33. *New York Times*, July 17, 1936; *New York Times*, August 3, 1936; Waltzer, "The American Labor Party," pp. 80–1. In addition to Roosevelt and Lehman, the ALP endorsed five candidates to the U.S. House of Representatives who were already on the Democratic ticket. Two of the five were elected. Congressional Quarterly, *Guide to U.S. Elections*, Fourth Edition (Washington, D.C., 2000), 2: 1065.

34. *New York Times*, July 15, 1970; *Contemporary Authors, New Revision Series* (Detroit: Gale Research, 1982), 5: 319.

35. *New York Times*, January 30, 1959.

36. James P. Cannon to Albert Glotzer, August 20, 1936, Box 2, *Albert Glotzer Papers*, Hoover Institute for War and Peace, Stanford University, Palo Alto, California.

37. "The Socialist Party and the Labor Non-Partisan League" [1936], Microfilm, Reel 35, *Norman Thomas Papers*. This public statement was cosigned by Harry Laidler as chair of the New York SP, a leading moderate, and Frank Trager, state secretary, who would soon emerge as a leading member of the Clarity Caucus.

38. Norman Thomas to Maynard Krueger, November 1, 1936, Microfilm, Reel 6, *Norman Thomas Papers*.

39. Norman Thomas, interview with Allen Nevins and Dean Robertson, February–May, 1949, Columbia University Oral History Project, p. 74; Thomas to Krueger, November 1, 1936, Microfilm, Reel 6, *Norman Thomas Papers*; *New York Times*, September 9, 1936.

40. Thomas to Krueger, November 1, 1936, Reel 6, *Norman Thomas Papers*.

41. Norman Thomas to Clarence Senior, Jack Altman and Harry Laidler, November 6, 1936, Reel 6, *Norman Thomas Papers*.

42. It was conceivable that La Guardia would campaign exclusively on the ALP and SP tickets in 1937 since he had been elected to Congress in 1924 while slated exclusively on the Socialist Party ticket, a nomination

he had accepted after having been rebuffed by the Republicans for his open support of La Follette. Kessner, *Fiorello H. La Guardia*, pp. 102–3.

43. *New York Times*, November 30, 1936; Harvey Klehr, *The Heyday of American Communism: The Depression Decade* (New York: Basic Books, 1984), p. 266.

44. *New York Times*, March 30, 1937; Klehr, *Heyday of American Communism*, pp. 267–9.

45. Norman Thomas to Roy Burt, February 2, 1937, Microfilm, Reel 7, *Norman Thomas Papers*.

46. *Contemporary Authors*, 130: 450.

47. Draper, *American Communism*, pp. 429–30.

48. Arne Swabeck to Vincent Dunne, January 9, 1937, *Leon Trotsky Papers*, Houghton Library, Harvard University.

49. "Minutes of the Socialist Appeal Institute," February 20 to 22, 1937, Box 5, *Glotzer Papers*, Hoover Institute, Stanford University. Cannon had moved to California soon after the Trotskyist entry into the SP. There he edited *Labor Action*, nominally the newspaper of the California SP, but in fact a factional organ for the Trotskyists within the Party. He returned to New York in the spring of 1937, nearly a year after his move. Myers, *The Prophet's Army*, p. 124.

50. Thomas opposed the mass expulsion of Trotskyists well into 1937. Norman Thomas, "The Party Structure" [June 1937], Microfilm, Reel 54, *Norman Thomas Papers*.

51. Johnpoll, *Pacifist's Progress*, p. 182.

52. *Labor Action*, April 17, 1937.

53. Norman Thomas to Harry Laidler, March 31, 1937, Reel 6, *Norman Thomas Papers*.

54. Thomas to Laidler, March 31, 1937, Reel 6, *Norman Thomas Papers*.

55. Max Shachtman to Leon Trotsky, April 15, 1937, *Trotsky Papers*. Trotsky had moved to Mexico in January 1937, after having been forced to leave Norway, his previous place of exile.

56. Albert Glotzer, *Trotsky* (Buffalo, New York: Prometheus Books, 1989), pp. 257–8; Pierre Broué and Emile Témime, *The Revolution and the Civil War in Spain* (Cambridge, Mass.: MIT Press, 1972), pp. 282–6.

57. Leon Trotsky, *Writings of Leon Trotsky, 1936–37*, edited by George Breitman and Naomi Allen (New York: Pathfinder Press, 1970), pp. 306–7.

58. Shachtman, interview, Columbia University Oral History Project, pp. 296–9.

59. Norman Thomas, "The New York Municipal Campaign" [June 1937], Microfilm, Reel 54, *Norman Thomas Papers*.

60. Norman Thomas, "Memorandum on the New York Municipal Election," Microfilm [June 1937], Reel 54, *Norman Thomas Papers*.

61. Norman Thomas to Jack Altman, June 26, 1937, Microfilm, Reel 7, *Norman Thomas Papers*.

62. Max Delson and Herbert Zam, "For a Clean Election Campaign," *Socialist Review* (September 1937): 18.

63. Delson and Zam, *Socialist Review* (September 1937): 19.

64. Delson and Zam, *Socialist Review* (September 1937): 18, 20.

65. Hal Draper et al., "Statement to the National Executive Committee," June 18, 1937, Microfilm, Reel 55, *Norman Thomas Papers*; Gus Tyler, "Save the Socialist Party from the Wreckers" [July 1937], Box 28, *Daniel Bell Papers*, Tamiment Archives, New York University.
66. Tyler, "Save the Socialist Party," Box 28, *Bell Papers*.
67. Tyler, "Save the Socialist Party," *Bell Papers*.
68. Tyler, "Save the Socialist Party," *Bell Papers*.
69. Max Delson and Herbert Zam, "ALP–Communist Alliance for La Guardia: For a Full Socialist Ticket and a Vigorous Socialist Campaign" [July 1937], Box 45, *James P. Cannon Papers*, State Historical Society of Wisconsin, Madison, Wisconsin.
70. *New York Times*, July 8, 1937; *New York Times*, September 27, 1937.
71. Delson and Zam, "ALP–Communist Alliance for La Guardia," Box 45, *Cannon Papers*.
72. Delson and Zam, "ALP–Communist Alliance for La Guardia," Box 45, *Cannon Papers*.
73. *New York Times*, July 14, 1937.
74. Grievance Committee, Report [1937], Box 28, Bell Papers; Martin Abern to John [?], July 20, 1937, Box 28, *Bell Papers*. Since Abern had opposed the initial entry into the SP, he may have deliberately sent the letter to the New York local's headquarters to speed the coming split.
75. Grievance Committee, Report [1937], Box 28, *Bell Papers*; Myers, *The Prophet's Army*, p. 139. Burnham and Carter were joined by Hal Draper in voting against the motion to split from the Socialist Party. They represented a small minority of the July 1937 plenum. Ernest E. Haberkern and Arthur Lipow (eds.) *Neither Capitalism nor Socialism: Theories of Bureaucratic Collectivism* (Atlantic Highlands, N.J.: Humanities Press, 1996), p. 191.
76. Herbert Zam, "Open Letter" [June 1937], Box 28, *Bell Papers*. Norman Thomas and Harry Laidler addressed the 150 members who attended the Militant Caucus meeting, staunchly defending the decision to withdraw a socialist candidate from the mayoralty campaign.
77. Herbert Zam to Arthur McDowell, July 28, 1937, Box 38, *Bell Papers*.
78. Zam to McDowell, July 28, 1937, Box 38, *Bell Papers*. Negotiations between the moderate wing of the SP and the SDF would continue over the next few years, with the talks eventually reaching an impasse on the issues arising out of World War II. Ultimately, a merger would come to fruition in 1957, under a very different set of circumstances. Harry Fleischman, *Norman Thomas: A Biography* (New York: W.W. Norton, 1964), p. 239.
79. Moscow, *Politics in the Empire State*, p. 107; *New York Times*, July 30, 1937.
80. Robert Menaker to the National Executive Committee, August 16, 1937, Box 28, *Bell Papers*; Robert Delson, "The Altman Group Tramples on the Party Constitution" [August 1937], Microfilm, Reel 54, *Norman Thomas Papers*; *New York Times*, August 12, 1937.
81. Menaker to the National Executive Committee, August 16, 1937, Box 28, *Bell Papers*.

82. Using the Consumer Price Index as the measuring rod, prices increased by a factor of 12 over the period from 1937 to 2000. U.S. Census Bureau, *Statistical Abstract of the United States* (Washington: GPO, 2001); *U.S. Bureau of the Census, Historical Statistics of the United States: Colonial Times to 1970* (Washington: GPO, 1975) 1: 210–11.

83. Allen Nevins, *Herbert H. Lehman and His Era* (New York: Scribner's 1963), p. 91; David Dubinsky and A.H. Raskin, *A Life with Labor* (New York: Simon & Schuster, 1977), p. 75. Dubinsky reported that the ILGWU leadership had sought loans from Lehman, and from other wealthy Jewish businesspeople as well, soon after Benjamin Schlesinger's election as union president in October 1928.

84. Jack Altman, Open Letter, August 26, 1937, Microfilm, Reel 54, *Norman Thomas Papers.*

85. National Executive Committee, Minutes, September 2, 1937, Microfilm, Reel 55, *Norman Thomas Papers*; Clarity, "The Struggle for Revolutionary Socialism Must Go On" [September 1937], Microfilm, Reel 55, *Norman Thomas Papers*. The meeting was held in New York City. Albert Sprague Coolidge replaced Arthur McDowell with Alfred Baker Lewis as his alternate. This provided the Militant Caucus its slim majority on the NEC.

86. NEC Minutes, September 2, 1937, Reel 55, *Norman Thomas Papers.*

87. NEC Minutes, September 2, 1937, Reel 55, *Norman Thomas Papers.*

88. Norman Thomas, Memorandum to Laidler, Altman and Lipsig, September 3, 1937, Microfilm, Reel 7, *Norman Thomas Papers*. James Lipsig was a leader of the Militant caucus and state secretary of the New York Socialist Party.

89. Marion Severn and Max Delson, Box 24, *Harry Laidler Papers*, Tamiment Institute, New York University.

90. Severn and Delson, Box 24, *Laidler Papers.*

91. Central Committee of the New York City Local to the National Executive Committee, "Statement on the New York Municipal Campaign" [September 1937], Microfilm, Reel 54, *Norman Thomas Papers*. Harvey had been antagonistic to the ALP, which refused to endorse him. Charles Garrett, *The La Guardia Years: Machine and Reform Politics in New York City* (New Brunswick, N.J.: Rutgers University Press, 1961), p. 263.

92. A city council with 26 members was elected at the November 1937 elections. Each borough was treated as a single district, with the number to be elected from each borough calculated on the basis of its share of the total citywide vote in the previous election. Candidates qualified for the ballot by collecting 2,000 signatures in their borough. The election was on a partisan basis, with each candidate carrying a party designation. Voters ranked as many of the candidates in their borough as they wished by order of preference. In general, this system led to a city council with political parties gaining representation proportionate to their vote. In the 1937 elections, ALP candidates received 21 percent of the vote, enabling it to elect five of its candidates to the council. The voting system acted to exclude smaller parties from representation. As a result, the SP failed to elect any of its candidates to the city council. Garrett, *The La Guardia Years*, pp. 232–3.

93. Central Committee, "Statement," Microfilm, Reel 54, *Norman Thomas Papers*. Aaron Levenstein and Harry Laidler were the two SP candidates given a low priority endorsement by the ALP. Neither was elected to the city council.
94. Central Committee, "Statement," Microfilm, Reel 54, *Norman Thomas Papers*.
95. Central Committee, "Statement," Microfilm, Reel 54, *Norman Thomas Papers*.
96. Norman Thomas to Devere Allen et al. [September 1937], Microfilm, Reel 54, *Norman Thomas Papers*.
97. Thomas to Allen [September 1937], Reel 54, *Norman Thomas Papers*.
98. *New York Times*, September 27, 1937.
99. Myers, *The Prophet's Army*, p. 140.
100. *Socialist Appeal*, August 14, 1937.
101. Myers, *The Prophet's Army*, p. 145. As the Trotskyists were being expelled, 90 percent of the YPSL membership, and most of its leadership, left the Socialist Party.
102. Bernard Bolloten, *The Spanish Civil War: Revolution and Counterrevolution* (Chapel Hill: University of North Carolina, 1991), pp. 503–13; Broué and Témime, *The Revolution and the Civil War in Spain*, p. 305.
103. Leon Trotsky, "A Tragic Lesson," September 21, 1937, *Writings, 1936–37*, p. 450. Poretsky was a senior Soviet intelligence officer. His warnings were not idle rumor. Sedov was killed on February 16, 1938. Trotsky died on August 21, 1940, assassinated by a Soviet agent.
104. Leon Trotsky, "The Beginning of the End," *Writings, 1936–37*, pp. 328, 332. This article appeared in the *Socialist Appeal* of October 16, 1937. It was first drafted that June, and revised throughout the summer.
105. Leon Trotsky, "The Situation in the SP and Our Next Tasks," June 15, 1937, *Writings, 1936–37*, p. 335.
106. Leon Trotsky, "Answers to Questions," October 1, 1937, *Writings, 1936–37*, p. 469.
107. Leon Trotsky, "The Situation in the SP and Our Next Tasks," October 1, 1937, *Writings, 1936–37*, p. 335; Leon Trotsky, "Perspectives for the Future," October 19, 1937, *Writings, 1936–37*, p. 501.
108. Leon Trotsky, "More Pedagogical Patience Toward New Elements," September 11, 1937, *Writings, 1936–37*, p. 439.
109. Leon Trotsky, "Discussions with Trotsky," March 25, 1938, *Writings of Leon Trotsky, 1937–38*, edited by Naomi Allen and George Breitman (New York: Pathfinder Press, 1979), pp. 306–7.
110. Leon Trotsky to James P. Cannon, October 2, 1937, *Writings of Leon Trotsky, Supplement, 1934–40*, edited by George Breitman (New York: Pathfinder Press, 1979), pp. 743–4.
111. Leon Trotsky to James P. Cannon, October 10, 1937, *Writings, 1936–37*, p. 489.
112. Joseph Hansen to James P. Cannon, October 28, 1937, *Trotsky Papers*; Leon Trotsky to James P. Cannon, November 14, 1937, *Writings, 1937–38*, p. 49.
113. James P. Cannon to Leon Trotsky, November 15, 1937, Box 12, *Cannon Papers*.

114. Leon Trotsky, "It is High Time to Launch a World Offensive Against Stalinism," November 2, 1937, *Writings, 1936–37*, p. 32.

115. Leon Trotsky, "Three Possibilities with a Labor Party", July 23, 1938, in *The Transitional Program for Socialist Revolution,* edited by George Breitman and Fred Stanton, third edition (New York: Pathfinder Press, 1977), p. 193. This provides a transcript of a discussion that Trotsky had with Americans who had come to Mexico to serve on Trotsky's staff.

116. Trotsky, July 23, 1938, *Transitional Program*, pp. 192–3.

117. Trotsky, July 23, 1938, *Transitional Program*, p. 192; "A Summary of Transitional Demands," March 23, 1938, *Transitional Program*, p. 105. The latter provides a transcript of one of the six discussions Trotsky held with Cannon, Shachtman, Dunne and Rose Karsner, Cannon's partner, in Mexico City.

118. "Declaration of Principles," in *The Founding of the Socialist Workers Party*, edited by George Breitman (New York: Monad Press, 1982), p. 197. The declaration was drafted by Burnham and revised by Shachtman and Maurice Spector.

119. Leon Trotsky, "The Problem of the Labor Party" [April 1938], *Transitional Program*, pp. 107–8.

120. "Minutes of the April 1938 Plenum," in Breitman, *Founding of the Socialist Workers Party*, pp. 222–4, 370. Bardacke quit the SWP a year later.

121. Haberkern and Lipow, *Neither Capitalism nor Socialism*, pp. 192–3.

122. Hal Draper, "Minority Resolution on the Labor Party," in Breitman, *Founding of the Socialist Workers Party*, pp. 243–5, 248.

123. Breitman, *Founding of the Socialist Workers Party*, p. 250. The results of the membership referendum were announced in September 1938 and the vote was given as 304 to 198 with 10 abstentions. The total vote of 512 represented about half of the SWP's membership.

124. Johnpoll, *Pacifist's Progress*, p. 193.

125. Thomas, "Reflections," Reel 55, *Norman Thomas Papers*.

126. Thomas, "Reflections," Reel 55, *Norman Thomas Papers*.

127. Norman Thomas to Harry Laidler, February 9, 1938, Microfilm, Reel 35, *Socialist Party Papers*.

128. Thomas to Laidler, February 9, 1938, Reel 35, *Socialist Party Papers*.

129. Norman Thomas to David Dubinsky, February 9, 1938, Box 150, Dubinsky Papers, Catherwood Library, Cornell University.

130. Gus Tyler to Ben Fischer, January 13, 1938, Box 29, *Bell Papers*.

131. Lazare Becker, Memorandum, February 7, 1938, Microfilm, Reel 55, *Norman Thomas Papers*.

132. "Labor Party Resolution" [April 1938], Microfilm, Reel 55, *Norman Thomas Papers*.

133. "Labor Party Resolution," Reel 55, *Norman Thomas Papers;* Norman Thomas to Paul Porter, June 17, 1938, Reel 7, *Norman Thomas Papers*.

134. Arthur G. McDowell, "Report," July 21, 1938, Microfilm, Reel 35, *Socialist Party Papers*.

135. *New York Herald Tribune*, June 3, 1938.

136. Norman Thomas to Paul Porter, June 17, 1938, Reel 7, *Norman Thomas Papers; New York Herald Tribune*, June 3, 1938.

137. *New York Herald Tribune*, June 3, 1938. Rose, Antonini and Potofsky were all former socialists who had risen to become influential figures in garment trade unions. Rose was vice-president of the United Hatters and state secretary of the ALP. Antonini was vice-president of the Ladies Garment Workers Union and state chair of the ALP. Potofsky was vice-president of the Amalgamated Clothing Workers. Fink, *Biographical Dictionary of American Labor*, pp. 90, 469, 492–3.
138. Dave Felix to Socialist Party National Office, July 20, 1938, Microfilm, Reel 35, *Socialist Party Papers*.
139. Harry Laidler, Aaron Levenstein, Jack Altman and Brendan Sexton, "Vote 'Yes' in the Referendum" [December 1938], Microfilm, Reel 55, *Norman Thomas Papers*. The ALP was correct in viewing the SP's loss of ballot status as a significant factor. When Thomas campaigned as the Party's presidential nominee in 1940, he could only tally 19,000 write-in votes in New York, 0.3 percent of the total vote, as compared to 87,000 votes in 1936. Congressional Quarterly, *Guide to U.S. Elections*, pp. 454–5.
140. Laidler, Levenstein, Altman and Sexton, "Vote 'Yes,'" Reel 55, *Norman Thomas Papers*; Robert Delson, Herbert Zam, Frank Trager and Ben Horowitz, "Vote 'Yes' in the Referendum," December 24, 1938, Microfilm, Reel 55, *Norman Thomas Papers*; *New York Times*, December 25, 1938. Marion Severn was one of the few Clarity leaders to oppose entry. She pointed out that the ALP was still "trading posts" with mainstream politicians. Instead of working within the ALP, Severn argued that the focus of activities should be "devoted to the strengthening and recreating" of the SP itself. Marion Severn, "Vote 'No' in the Referendum" [December] 1938, Microfilm, Reel 55, *Norman Thomas Papers*.
141. *Contemporary Authors*, 5: 319; *New York Times*, January 30, 1959; Johnpoll, *Pacifist's Progress*, pp. 190, 195; *Contemporary Authors*, 130: 450.
142. Norman Thomas, Open Letter, December 20, 1939, Microfilm, Reel 54, *Norman Thomas Papers*; Norman Thomas, interview with Allen Nevins and Dean Robertson.
143. Steven Fraser, *Labor Will Rule: Sidney Hillman and the Rise of American Labor* (New York: Free Press, 1991), p. 522; *Newsday*, February 26, 2003.
144. Maurice Isserman, *The Other American: The Life of Michael Harrington* (New York: Public Affairs Press, 2000), pp. 290–311.

CHAPTER 7

1. *New York Times*, October 9, 2002.
2. Dave Campbell, "Tony Mazzochi," *Labor Notes* (November 2002): 6, 15; *New York Times*, October 9, 2002.
3. Campbell, "Mazzochi," pp. 6, 15; Tony Mazzochi, "Beyond 1992: For a Labor Party," *Against the Current* (July–August 1992): 25.
4. Barbara Koeppel, "An Interview with Tony Mazzochi," *Progressive* (September 1992): 33.

5. Laura McClure, "A Labor Party," *Z* (January 1992): 90; Mazzochi, "Beyond 1992: For a Labor Party," *Against the Current* (July–August 1992): 25.
6. Dan La Botz, "An Historic Beginning," *Against the Current* (July–August 1996): 3.
7. La Botz, "An Historic Beginning," p. 4.
8. *Wall Street Journal*, January 6, 1999.
9. Leah Samuel, "PACE to Continue Contributions to Labor Party but Axes Staff Salaries," *Labor Notes*, May 2001.
10. *Los Angeles Times*, August 31, 2000; Jane Slaughter, "Nader's Labor Supporters," *Labor Notes*, October 2000.
11. Campbell, "Mazzochi," pp. 6, 15.
12. Charlene Spretnak and Fritjof Capra, *Green Politics: The Global Promise*, second edition (Santa Fe, N.M.: Bear and Co., 1986), pp. 17–18.
13. Spretnak and Capra, *Green Politics*, pp. 20–1; *New York Times*, March 7, 1983.
14. Howie Hawkins, "Independent Progressive Politics," *Z* (March 1996): 17.
15. Patrick Anderson, "Ralph Nader, Crusader; or, the Rise of a Self-Appointed Lobbyist," *New York Times Magazine* (October 29, 1967): 111.
16. Ralph Nader, *Unsafe at Any Speed* (New York: Grossman, 1965); Anderson, "Nader," p. 112.
17. Anderson, "Nader," p. 25; *Washington Post*, June 18, 2000.
18. *Baltimore Sun*, June 17, 2000; *Washington Post*, June 18, 2000; *Village Voice*, July 26, 2000.
19. Pat Aufderheide, "Nader's Unhappy Raiders," *Columbia Journalism Review* (September–October 1984) 23: 10; *Washington Post*, June 28, 1984.
20. Aufderheide, "Nader's Unhappy Raiders," p. 12; *Washington Post*, June 28, 1984; *Washington Post*, July 3, 1984.
21. *Washington Post*, June 28, 1984.
22. Howie Hawkins, "Independent Progressive Politics," p. 19.
23. Interview with Jesse Jackson, Cable Network News, August 20, 2000; *New York Times*, August 12, 2000; *Columbus Dispatch*, July 22, 2000.
24. *Boston Globe*, August 15, 1998.
25. *New York Times*, July 23, 2000.
26. Cable Network News, August 20, 2000.
27. *One on One with John McLaughlin*, Public Broadcasting System, August 11, 2000; *Washington Post*, August 17, 2000; *New York Times*, July 1, 2000.
28. *New York Times*, August 6, 2001; *New York Times*, June 7, 2001; *Los Angeles Times*, November 23, 2000.
29. *Talkback Live*, Cable Network News, July 5, 2000; Cable Network News, August 9, 2000.
30. *Newsweek*, January 22, 1968, p. 67.
31. Green Party, USA Website, August 2000; *Washington Post*, August 17, 2000.
32. Congressional Quarterly, *Guide to U.S. Elections*, third edition (Washington, D.C., 1994), p. 451; Lyn Ragsdale, *Vital Statistics on the Presidency* (Washington, D.C., 1996), p. 143; *New York Times*, November 9, 2000.

33. Using the Consumer Price Index, prices increased by a factor of ten from 1924 to 2000.
34. *New York Times*, August 6, 2001.
35. Cleveland Plain Dealer, January 12, 2003; Cleveland Plain Dealer, February 20, 2003.

Glossary

Altman, Jack (1906?–1959)   Joined the Socialist Party during the first years of the Great Depression. A founder and leading member of the Militant Caucus. During 1936–37, the secretary of the New York City local. Became a close ally of Norman Thomas. Went into the American Labor Party in 1939, and became a leading activist. Supported U.S. entry into World War II and dropped out of the SP. Organizer for the Retail, Wholesale and Department Store Workers Union. Spent last years as a labor relations consultant.

Bohn, Frank A. (1878–1975)   Joined the Socialist Labor Party while a graduate student at the University of Michigan in 1900. Quit the SLP in 1904. A founding member of the Industrial Workers of the World in 1905, he served as an IWW organizer in the West. Joined the staff of the *International Socialist Review* in 1909. Wrote *Industrial Socialism* with William Haywood. Central figure in the left-wing of the Socialist Party during the labor party debate from 1909 to 1912. Worked as a correspondent for the *New York Post* in Germany from 1913 to 1917. Quit the Socialist Party to become an avid supporter of U.S. participation in World War I. After the war, worked as a journalist and university lecturer.

Burnham, James (1905–87)   While a lecturer in philosophy at New York University he was attracted to socialism. Joined the American Workers Party in 1933 and went into the Workers Party as one of its foremost leaders in 1934. When the Trotskyists merged into the Socialist Party in 1936, he accepted this turn, but became disillusioned when Trotsky ordered a split only a year later. Shortly afterward, initiated the debate on the class nature of the Soviet Union. Quit the Socialist Workers Party in May 1940. Became a conservative ideologue and a staunch Cold Warrior.

Cannon, James Patrick (1890–1974)   Radicalized in high school, he became a traveling organizer for the IWW. Opposed U.S. entry into World War I and joined the left-wing of the Socialist Party. A national leader of the Communist Party during the 1920s, he was expelled in 1928 for Trotskyism. He remained the most influential figure in the Trotskyist movement for its first 25 years. Moved from New York to San Francisco in 1936 to edit *Labor Action*, returning a year later. Served as the general secretary of the Socialist Workers Party from 1938 to 1942. Jailed for 16 months for sedition during World War II. Moved to Los Angeles in 1952 to live in semi-retirement.

Debs, Eugene Victor (1855–1926)   Raised in Terre Haute, Indiana. Active local officer in the Brotherhood of Locomotive Firemen, he was elected its secretary-treasurer in 1885. Elected as a Democrat to the Indiana state legislature in 1884 for one term. Founded the American Railway Union as an industrial union in 1893, but it was destroyed during the Pullman strike the following year. A member of the Socialist Party from the beginning, he was its presidential nominee five different times. Briefly a member of the IWW. Opposed U.S. entry into World War I, and was jailed for two and a half years for sedition. Released from prison at Christmas, 1921, his health shattered.

Engels, Friedrich (1820–1895)   The son of a German textile manufacturer, he became a socialist in 1842. Beginning in 1844, he and Karl Marx were friends and collaborators. Worked as an executive in his father's mill in Manchester England. In 1870, he retired and moved to London. After Marx's death in 1883, he became the final authority on Marxism. Author of *The Condition of the English Working Class* (1845) and the editor of volumes two and three of Marx's *Das Kapital*.

Fitzpatrick, John (1871–1946)   Born in Ireland and came to the United States at age of eleven. Worked as a journeyman blacksmith. Active in his craft union. President of the Chicago Federation of Labor from 1906 to his death. Leader of the 1919 steel strike. Instrumental in forming Chicago Labor Party in 1919. Soon after, campaigned for mayor. Advocated formation of a nationwide labor party. Worked with Communist Party in early 1920s, but split after Farmer-Labor Party convention in 1923. Dropped support for independent politics and began endorsing Democrats. Became an enthusiastic adherent of New Deal. Opposed formation of the CIO in the 1930s.

George, Henry (1839–1897)   As a teenager, he moved to San Francisco. Worked as a journalist and then editor. Active in Democratic Party politics. Published *Progress and Poverty* in 1879, to great acclaim. Campaigned as an independent candidate for mayor of New York in 1886, and was barely defeated. Returned to the Democratic Party in 1888, and retained this political allegiance until his death.

Gompers, Samuel (1850–1924)   Born in London. Came to New York City at the age of 13. Worked as a cigar maker for 15 years. Became a union activist and craft union official. Remained president of the American Federation of Labor from its founding in 1886 until his death, with the exception of one year. Supported Henry George campaign for mayor. Actively promoted the U.S. military effort during World War I. A staunch proponent of lesser evil politics, he adamantly opposed an independent labor party.

Hardie, James Keir (1856–1915)   Started working in the coalmines of Scotland at the age of seven. Became active in the miners union and was blacklisted from work. Edited local paper and stood as an independent for parliament in 1888. Elected to parliament in 1892 and helped found the Independent Labour Party. Defeated for re-election in 1895. Became a staunch supporter of a labor party and instrumental in the formation of the Labour Representation Committee. Elected to parliament in 1900 and held seat until his death. Visited the United States in 1908 and 1912.

Haywood, William Dudley (1869–1928)   Hard rock miner. Served as president of a Western Federation of Miners local. In 1901, elected secretary-treasurer. Founding member of Industrial Workers of the World. Charged with murder of ex-governor Frank Steunenberg in 1906, but acquitted in 1907. Pushed out of union leadership. Elected to Socialist Party National Executive

Committee in January 1912, but recalled in February 1913 for his advocacy of sabotage. Became secretary-treasurer of IWW in 1915. Under Haywood, IWW did not oppose U.S. entry into World War I. Nevertheless, arrested for sedition in September 1917 and given 20-year jail term. Jumped bail in 1921 and went to Soviet Union. Disillusioned and ill, died in Moscow.

Hillquit, Morris (1869–1933)   Born in Latvia, but immigrated to the United States in 1885. Attended law school and became a lawyer in 1893. Joined the Socialist Labor Party as a teenager. Led the Kangaroo split from the SLP in 1899. A founding member of the Socialist Party in 1901. The leader of the moderate Center of the SP. His campaign for mayor of New York in 1917 on an anti-war platform gained substantial support. A staunch supporter of a labor party, he played an influential role in the Conference for Progressive Political Action.

Holt, Matthew Samuel (1850–1939)   Physician and newspaper publisher in West Virginia. Socialist Party activist, candidate for governor and Senate. Opposed World War I and remained active in SP after war. Chosen by Progressive Party as its candidate for Senate in 1924, but cajoled into a token effort. Remained a prominent member of the West Virginia SP into the 1930s.

Hunter, Robert (1874–1942)   Raised in Terre Haute, Indiana, the son of an affluent carriage manufacturer. A social worker in Chicago and New York, he joined the Socialist Party in 1905. A key figure in the behind the scenes effort to create a labor party from 1908 to 1912, he became discouraged and politically inactive, quitting the SP in 1914. He supported the U.S. entry into World War I, but moved to Berkeley, California, in ill health. Became increasingly conservative and hostile to the New Deal in the 1930s.

Johnston, William Hugh (1874–1937)   Born in Nova Scotia, his family moved to Rhode Island. As a youngster, he started working as a machinist. Starting in 1895, he became an activist in the International Association of Machinists (IAM). Briefly joined the Socialist Party. Elected IAM president in 1911. A spokesperson for industrial unionism within the AFL. Supported World War I. Chair of the CPPA and a key figure in promoting the La Follette campaign within organized labor. After suffering a stroke in September 1925, resigned as IAM president in July 1926. Went to work as an officer of a bank that the IAM had created.

Keating, Edward (1875–1965)   Born in Kansas City, his family moved to Colorado in 1889. Starting as a newsboy, he became a journalist and editor. In 1912, elected to Congress as a Democrat and served three terms. Editor of *Labor*, the newspaper of the railroad union alliance, from 1919 to 1953. Instrumental in the formation of the CPPA, and a vocal supporter of La Follette, he remained committed to working within the two party system.

La Follette, Robert Marion (1855–1925)   Raised in rural Wisconsin. Became a lawyer and a Republican state legislator. Organized a caucus of progressive dissenters. Elected governor from 1900 to 1906 and U.S. Senator from 1906 until his death. After initially opposing U.S. entry into World War I, he supported the war effort, but opposed government repression of radical dissidents. Campaigned as independent candidate for president in 1924, but was already in poor health.

Laidler, Harry Wellington (1884–1970)   Founding member of the Intercollegiate Socialist Society in 1905. Became its secretary in 1910 and its executive director in 1921, when it was renamed the League for Industrial Democracy. Prolific author of books written from a social democratic perspective. A close ally of Norman Thomas and a leading member of the Militant Caucus. Chair of the New York state Socialist Party in the 1930s. Elected to New York's city council in 1939 on the American Labor Party ticket. Withdrew from the SP to support U.S. participation in World War II. Failed to be re-elected in 1941. Retired as executive director of LID in 1957.

Mazzochi, Anthony (1924–2002)   Born in Brooklyn, New York. Worked on the assembly line at Ford from 1946 to 1950. President of a local of the Oil, Chemical and Atomic Workers Union (OCAW) from 1952 to 1965. Became a member of its executive board from 1965, legislative liaison, vice-president with special responsibility for health and safety and assistant to the president. Founding member of the Labor Party Advocates in 1991, he continues to act as the Labor Party's chief spokesperson.

Nader, Ralph (1934–)   Born and raised in Connecticut. Attended Harvard Law School, where he became interested in auto safety. Returned to Hartford, Connecticut, to open a private law practice. After handling several automobile accident cases, he decided the issue had to be handled as one of public policy. Went to Washington as advisor to the Department of Labor. Wrote *Unsafe at Any Speed* in 1965, which made him a public figure. Initiated an array of consumer advocacy non-profit organizations. Nominated as the Green Party candidate for president in 1996, but restricted himself to a token campaign. Actively campaigned in 2000 and received 2.7 million votes.

Shachtman, Max (1904–1972)   Born in Poland. Came to the United States as a young child. Dropped out of City College and joined the Communist Party. Expelled in 1928 as a Trotskyist. A leading figure in Trotskyist organizations during the 1930s. After the Soviet invasion of Poland in 1939, he adopted the position that the Soviet Union was controlled by a new class. Led a split from the Socialist Workers Party in April 1940. In 1958 his group merged into the Socialist Party. In his last years, he became an avid Cold Warrior and a firm believer in working within the Democratic Party.

Simons, Algie Martin (1870–1950)   Born in a small town in Wisconsin. Worked as a social worker in Cincinnati and Chicago. Founding member of the Socialist Party. Editor of the *International Socialist Review* from 1901 to 1908. Proponent of a labor party. Ardent advocate of U.S. entry into World War I. Expelled from SP in 1917 for urging its suppression by the federal government. Became an efficiency expert. Increasingly conservative, he attacked the New Deal for being too radical.

Spargo, John (1876–1966)   Born in England. Worked as a stonecutter. Immigrated to the United States in 1900. Soon became active in the Socialist Party. A leader of the Party's moderate wing, he was elected to the National Executive Committee in 1909. A strong proponent of a labor party. Staunch supporter of U.S. entry into World War I. Quit the Socialist Party in 1917. By the mid-1920s, his political perspective was that of a conservative Republican. Withdrew from active politics to become the director of the Bennington, Vermont, museum and an expert in the history of the colonial United States.

Thomas, Norman Mattoon (1884–1968)   Graduated from Princeton University and became a Presbyterian minister. Opposed conscription during World War I. Joined the Socialist Party in 1918. Stood for president six times from 1928 through to 1948. In 1937, he withdrew as the SP candidate for mayor of New York City to allow La Guardia to be elected. Argued for socialist entry into the American Labor Party. During the last two decades of his life, he sought to work within the Democratic Party to move it in a more progressive direction.

Trotsky, Leon (1879–1940)   Born in Russian countryside, he was raised in Odessa. Became a socialist activist as a teenager and spent several years in Siberia as an exile. A leader of the St. Petersburg soviet in 1905. Spent three months in New York in early 1917. Returned to Russia in May 1917 and joined the Bolshevik Party that August. After the revolution, chosen foreign minister and then war minister. After Lenin's death, he was moved to the margins of power and then expelled to Turkey in 1928. Wound up in Mexico. Kept close watch on the Trotskyist movement in the United States.

Tyler, Gus (1911–)   Became an active member of the Socialist Party youth group during the first years of the Great Depression. A radical activist, he gravitated to the left-wing of the Militant Caucus. Leading member of the Clarity Caucus. Editor of the *Socialist Call*, the Party's weekly newspaper, in 1936 and 1937. In early 1939, joined the staff of the International Ladies Garment Workers Union. Left the SP. Supported U.S. entry into World War II and served in the Air Force. Held a series of posts in the ILGWU until being named assistant to the president in 1963, a post he retained until retirement.

Walling, William English (1877–1936)   Came from a wealthy family. Worked as a social worker in Chicago and New York. Opposed the formation of a labor party. Joined the Socialist Party in 1910. Wrote several books popularizing socialist ideas. Proponent of U.S. entry into World War I and quit SP. Became close ally of Gompers. Nominated for Congress as a Democrat in 1924 but lost.

ORGANIZATIONAL GLOSSARY

American Labor Party (ALP)   Formed in July 1936 to create an electoral vehicle for socialists and progressives to vote for President Franklin Roosevelt without voting Democratic. Endorsed liberal Democrats for national and statewide offices, but nominated its own candidates for New York city council and state assembly. Nominated La Guardia for mayor in 1937. Dominated by the garment industry unions. Split in 1944 with the anti-Communist faction forming the Liberal Party. Dissolved in 1956, although the Liberals remain as a small patronage machine.

Conference for Progressive Political Action (CPPA)   Founded in 1921 on the initiative of an alliance of railroad unions. Initially created to act as a pressure group for progressive politics within the two party system. The Socialist Party functioned as an active participant. In 1924, it acted as the organizational base for La Follette's independent campaign for president. Dissolved in 1925 when the railroad unions decided they were no longer interested in independent politics.

Industrial Workers of the World (IWW)   Founded in 1905 by trade union militants interested in creating a unified, radical industrial union. Led several militant strikes. Gained a base primarily among agricultural workers and lumberjacks in the West. Persecuted by federal and state governments during World War I, although it did not oppose U.S. entry into the war. Already demoralized, it suffered a devastating split in 1924. Continues today but on a smaller scale. The IWW can be contacted at P.O. Box 13476, Philadelphia, PA. 13476.

International Socialist Review (*ISR*)   Founded by Charles Kerr as an adjunct to his book publishing venture. Edited by Algie Simons from 1900 to 1908. Kerr then fired Simons and turned it into a more popular magazine. With Mary Marcy as managing editor and Frank Bohn on its staff, it became the focal point for the left-wing of the Socialist Party. Achieved a circulation of 40,000 in 1911. Suppressed by the federal government in 1918 for its militant opposition to World War I.

Labour Party, British   Created in 1900 as a federation composed of unions and the Independent Labour Party under the name of the Labour Representation Committee. Renamed the Labour Party in 1906, after it elected a significant number of its candidates to parliament. A moderate social democratic party, it supported World War I and entered the war cabinet as a junior partner. After the war, it became the second largest party, supplanting the Liberals. The current governing party of Britain.

Minnesota Farmer-Labor Party   Initially came together in 1918 as a loose coalition of progressive farmers and trade union activists. More permanent party created in 1922. Very successful, electing governor, senators and legislators. Although primarily based on membership clubs in rural areas, it also had the direct representation of unions in the Minneapolis area. Never entirely independent, it became closely aligned with the Democratic Party during the New Deal. Merged with the Democrats in 1943.

Socialist Labor Party (SLP)   Founded in 187 with its base in recent German immigrants. Supported Henry George in 1886, but later opposed the creation of a labor party. Dominated by Daniel DeLeon from 1891 until his death in 1914. Remained a small group in early 1900s when Socialist Party grew to be mass party. Still active today as a small educational organization.

Socialist Party (SP)   Founded in 1901. Grew to be a mass party, electing candidates to state assemblies and the U.S. House of Representatives. Split from the start between moderate and radical tendencies. At its height in 1912, enrolled more than 120,000 members. The target of intense federal repression during World War I for its opposition to the war. Further demoralized when its left-wing split in 1919 to form the Communist Party. Continues today on a smaller scale. The Socialist Party can be contacted at 339 Lafayette Street, #303, New York, N.Y. 10012.

Socialist Workers Party (SWP)   Founded as the official Trotskyist party in January 1938 by those recently expelled from the Socialist Party. The first Trotskyist organization was formed in 1929, then after merger, became Workers Party US in 1934 and entered the SP in 1936. Experienced a major split in April 1940 concerning the nature of the Soviet Union. Leadership jailed during World War II. In recent years, rejected Trotskyism for a variant of Castroism.

United Labor Party (ULP)   Formed in New York City in November 1886 in the wake of Henry's George's campaign for mayor. Not actually a labor party, but a middle-class reform party dominated by supporters of George and the single-tax theory. Pushed out socialist supporters in August 1887. Ran token campaign for president in 1888 and then dissolved.

Bibliography

ARCHIVES

Hoover Institute for War and Peace, Stanford University, Palo Alto, California
  Burnham, James
State Historical Society of Wisconsin, Madison, Wisconsin
  Berger, Victor Louis
  Cannon, James Patrick
  Gompers, Samuel
  Hillquit, Morris
  Simons, Algie
  Socialist Workers Party
  Walling, William English
Rare Books, Manuscripts and Special Collections Library, Duke University, Durham, North Carolina
  Socialist Party
Ohio Historical Society, Columbus, Ohio
  Germer, Adolph
  Hayes, Max
Rare Books and Manuscripts, Butler Library, Columbia University, New York
  Corey, Lewis
  Phelps Stokes, James Graham
Special Collections, Bailey/Howe Library, University of Vermont, Burlington, Vermont
  Spargo, John
  Friedberg, Gerald
Indiana Historical Society, Indianapolis, Indiana
  Reynolds, Stephen Marion
Indiana State Library, Indianapolis, Indiana
  Debs, Eugene Victor
Houghton Library, Harvard University, Cambridge, Massachusetts
  Trotsky, Leon
Tamiment Library, Bobst Library, New York University, New York
  Bell, Daniel
  Breitman, George
  Laidler, Harry W.
  Shachtman, Max
  Vladeck, Baruch Charney
Catherwood Library, Cornell University, Ithaca, New York
  Potofsky, Jacob
Special Collections, New York Public Library, New York
  Waldman, Louis
Minnesota Historical Society, Minneapolis, Minnesota
  Teigen, Henry George

Library of Congress, Washington, D.C.
La Follette, Robert
Roe, Gilbert

UNPUBLISHED MANUSCRIPTS

Friedberg, Gerald. "Marxism in the United States: John Spargo and the Socialist Party of America." Ph.D. Thesis, 1964. Harvard University, Cambridge, Massachusetts.
Keiser, John Howard. "John Fitzpatrick and Progressive Unionism, 1915–25." Ph.D. Thesis. 1965. Northwestern University, Evanston, Illinois.
Reynolds Jr., Robert Dwight. "The Millionaire Socialists: J.G. Phelps Stokes and His Circle of Friends." Ph.D. Thesis, 1974. University of South Carolina, Columbia, South Carolina.
Waltzer, Kenneth Alan. "The American Labor Party: Third Party Politics in New Deal–Cold War New York, 1936–54." Ph.D. Thesis. 1977. Harvard University, Cambridge, Massachusetts.

BOOKS

Aveling, Edward and Aveling Marx, Eleanor. *The Working Class Movement in America.* London: 1887. Reprinted edition. New York: Arno and the New York Times, 1969.
Barker, Charles Albro. *Henry George.* New York: Oxford University Press, 1955.
Barrett, James R. *William Z. Foster and the Tragedy of American Radicalism.* Urbana: University of Illinois Press, 1999.
Bean, Walton. *Boss Ruef's San Francisco: The Story of the Union Labor Party, Big Business and Graft Prosecution.* Berkeley: University of California Press, 1952.
Boylan, James. *Revolutionary Lives: Anna Strunsky and William English Walling.* Amherst: University of Massachusetts, 1998.
Brand, Carl F. *The British Labour Party: A Short History.* Revised edition. Stanford, Ca.: Hoover Institution Press, 1974.
Breitman, George (ed.). *The Founding of the Socialist Workers Party: Minutes and Resolutions, 1938–39.* New York: Monad Press, 1982.
Cannon, James Patrick. *The Communist League of America, 1932–34.* New York: Monad Press, 1985.
——. *The Left Opposition in the U.S., 1928–31.* New York: Monad Press, 1981.
Carlson, Peter. *The Life and Times of Big Bill Haywood.* New York: Norton, 1983.
Cole, G.D.H. *A History of the Labour Party from 1914.* London: Routledge & Kegan Paul, 1948.
Conlin, Joseph R. *Big Bill Haywood and the Radical Union Movement,* Syracuse: Syracuse University Press, 1969.
Debs, Eugene V. *Letters of Eugene Victor Debs.* Edited by J. Robert Constantine. Three Volumes. Urbana: University of Illinois Press, 1990.
Dick, William M. *Labor and Socialism in America: The Gompers Era.* Post Washington, New York: Kennikat Press, 1972.
Draper, Theodore. *American Communism and Soviet Russia.* New York: Viking Press, 1960.

———. *The Roots of American Communism*. New York: Viking Press, 1957.

Dubinsky, David and Raskin, A. H. *A Life with Labor*. New York: Simon & Schuster, 1977.

Dubofsky, Melvin. *We Shall be All: A History of the Industrial Workers of the World*. Chicago: Quadrangle Books, 1969.

Fine, Nathan. *Labor and Farmer Parties in the United States, 1828–1928*. New York: Rand School of Social Sciences, 1928. Reprinted edition. New York: Russell & Russell, 1961.

Fleischman, Harry. *Norman Thomas: A Biography*. New York: W.W. Norton, 1964.

Fraser, Steven. *Labor Will Rule: Sidney Hillman and the Rise of American Labor*. New York: Free Press, 1991.

Garrett, Charles. *The La Guardia Years: Machine and Reform Politics in New York City*. New Brunswick, N.J.: Rutgers University Press, 1961.

Gieske, Millard L. *Minnesota Farmer-Laborism: The Third Party Alternative*. Minneapolis: University of Minnesota Press, 1979.

Glotzer, Albert. *Trotsky*. Buffalo, New York: Prometheus Books, 1989.

Gompers, Samuel. *The Samuel Gompers Papers*. Edited by Stuart Bruce Kaufman, Peter J. Albert, and Grace Palladino. Urbana: University of Illinois Press, 1986–.

———. *Seventy Years of Life and Labor*. New York: E.P. Dutton, 1925.

Haberkern, Ernest E. and Lipow, Arthur (eds.) *Neither Capitalism nor Socialism: Theories of Bureaucratic Collectivism*. Atlantic Highlands, N.J.: Humanities Press, 1996.

Hansen, Joseph (ed.). *The Transitional Program for Socialist Revolution*. Third Edition. New York: Pathfinder Press, 1977.

Haywood, William D. and Bohn, Frank. *Industrial Socialism*. Chicago: Charles H. Kerr, 1911. Sixth edition, 1914.

Henderson, W.O. *The Life of Frederick Engels*. Two Volumes. London: Frank Cass, 1976.

Hillquit, Morris. *Loose Leaves of a Busy Life*. New York: Macmillan, 1934.

Hines, Walker D. *The War History of American Railroads*. New Haven: Yale University Press, 1928.

Hulse, James W. *The Forming of the Communist International*. Stanford, Ca.: Stanford University Press, 1964.

Hunter, Robert. *Socialists at Work*. New York: Macmillan, 1908.

Johnpoll, Bernard K. *Pacifist's Progress: Norman Thomas and the Decline of American Socialism*. Chicago: Quadrangle, 1970.

Johnpoll, Bernard K. and Johnpoll, Lillian. *The Impossible Dream: The Rise and Demise of the American Left*. Westport: Conn.: Greenwood Press, 1981.

Kapp, Yvonne. *Eleanor Marx: The Crowded Years*. London: Lawrence & Wishart, 1976.

Kaufman, Stuart Bruce. *Samuel Gompers and the Origins of the American Federation of Labor*. Westport, Conn.: Greenwood Press, 1973.

Keating, Edward. *The Gentleman from Colorado: A Memoir*. Denver: Sage Books, 1964.

———. *The Story of "Labor": Thirty-Three Years on the Rail Workers' Fighting Front*, Washington, D.C.: Rufus Darby, 1953.

Kessner, Thomas. *Fiorello H. La Guardia and the Making of Modern New York*. New York: McGraw-Hill, 1989.

Kipnis, Ira. *The American Socialist Movement, 1897–1912*. New York: Columbia University Press, 1952.

Klehr, Harvey, Haynes, John Earl and Anderson, Kyrill. *The Soviet World of American Communism*. New Haven, Conn.: Yale University Press, 1998.

Kreuter, Kent and Kreuter, Gretchen. *An American Dissenter: The Life of Algie Martin Simons, 1870–1950*. Lexington: University of Kentucky Press, 1969.

La Follette, Belle Case and La Follette, Fola. *Robert M. La Follette*. New York: Macmillan, 1953. Two volumes.

La Follette, Robert Marion. *La Follette–Wheeler Campaign Book*. Chicago, 1924.

Laslett, John H.M. *Labor and the Left: A Study of Socialist and Radical Influences in the American Labor Movement, 1881–1924*. New York: Basic Books, 1970.

Lenin, Nikolai. *Collected Works*. Moscow: Foreign Languages Publishing House, 1960–63.

Lukas, J. Anthony. *Big Trouble: A Murder in a Small Western Town Sets Off a Struggle for the Soul of America*. New York: Simon & Schuster, 1997.

McAdoo, William G. *The Crowded Years: Reminiscences*. Boston: Houghton Mifflin, 1931.

MacKay, Kenneth Campbell. *The Progressive Movement of 1924*. New York: Columbia University Press, 1947.

McKillen, Elizabeth. *Chicago Labor and the Quest for a Democratic Diplomacy, 1914–24*. Ithaca, New York: Cornell University Press, 1995.

Mandel, Bernard. *Samuel Gompers: A Biography*. Yellow Springs, Ohio: Antioch Press, 1963.

Marx, Karl and Engels, Friedrich. *Collected Works*, Vol. 47. New York: International Publishers, 1995.

——. *Letters to Americans, 1848–95, A Selection*. New York: International Publishers, 1953.

Miller, Sally M. *Victor Berger and the Promise of Constructive Socialism, 1910–1920*. Westport, Conn.: Greenwood Press, 1973.

Morgan, Kenneth O. *Keir Hardie: Radical and Socialist*. London: Weidenfeld & Nicolson, 1975.

Morlan, Robert Loren. *Political Prairie Fire: The Nonpartisan League, 1915–1922*. Minneapolis: University of Minnesota Press, 1955.

Moscow, Warren. *Politics in the Empire State*. New York: Knopf, 1948.

Myers, Constance Ashton. *The Prophet's Army: Trotskyists in America, 1928–41*. Westport, Conn.: Greenwood Press, 1977.

Nelson, Eugene. *Break Their Haughty Power: Joe Murphy in the Heyday of the Wobblies*. San Francisco: Ism Press, 1993.

Nevins, Allen. *Herbert H. Lehman: His Era*. New York: Charles Scribner's Sons, 1963.

Perlman, Mark. *The Machinists: A New Study in American Trade Unionism*. Cambridge, Mass.: Harvard University Press, 1961.

Perlman, Selig and Taft, Philip. *History of Labor in the United States, 1896–1932*. New York: Macmillan, 1935.

Poirier, Phillip P. *The Advent of the British Labour Party*. New York: Columbia University Press, 1958.

Post, Louis F. *The Prophet of San Francisco: Personal Memories and Interpretations.* New York: Vanguard Press, 1930.

Post, Louis Freeland and Leubuscher, Fred C. *Henry George's 1886 Campaign.* New York: John W. Lovell, 1887. Reprinted edition. New York: Henry George School, 1961.

Pratt, Norma Fain. *Morris Hillquit: A Political History of an American Jewish Socialist.* Westport, Conn.: Greenwood Press, 1979.

Quint, Howard H. *The Forging of American Socialism.* Columbia: University of South Carolina Press, 1953. Reprinted edition. Indianapolis, Ind.: Bobbs-Merrill, 1964.

Ruff, Allen. *"We Called Each Other Comrade": Charles H. Kerr Company, Radical Publishers.* Urbana: University of Illinois Press, 1997.

Salvatore, Nick. *Eugene V. Debs: Citizen and Socialist.* Urbana: University of Illinois, 1982.

Seidler, Murray Benjamin. *Norman Thomas, Respectable Rebel.* Syracuse, New York: Syracuse University Press, 1961.

Shannon, David. A. *The Socialist Party of America.* New York: Macmillan, 1955.

Stimson, Grace Heilman. *Rise of the Labor Movement in Los Angeles.* Berkeley: University of California Press, 1955.

Strouthous, Andrew. *U.S. Labor and Political Action, 1918–24: A Comparison of Independent Political Action in New York, Chicago, and Seattle.* New York: St. Martin's Press, 2000.

Swanberg W.A. *Norman Thomas: The Last Idealist.* New York: Charles Scribner's Sons, 1976.

Taft, Philip. *The A.F. of L. in the Time of Gompers.* New York: Harper & Brothers, 1957.

Trotsky, Leon. *Writings of Leon Trotsky.* Edited by George Breitman, Naomi Allen, Sarah Lovell and Reed, Evelyn. 14 Volumes. New York: Pathfinder Press, 1969–79.

——. *The First Five Years of the Communist International.* Translated by Joseph Vanzler [John G. Wright]. New York: Pioneer Press, 1945.

Tsuzuki, Chushichi. *The Life of Eleanor Marx, 1855–1898: A Socialist Tragedy.* Oxford: Clarendon Press, 1967.

Unger, Nancy C. *Fighting Bob La Follette.* Chapel Hill: University of North Carolina Press, 2000.

Van Heijenoort, Jean. *With Trotsky in Exile.* Cambridge, Mass.: Harvard University Press, 1978.

Villard, Oswald Garrison. *Fighting Years: Memoirs of a Liberal Editor.* New York: Harcourt Brace, 1939.

Vrooman, David M. *Daniel Willard and the Progressive Management on the Baltimore and Ohio Railroad.* Columbus: Ohio State University, 1991.

Warren, Frank. A. *An Alternative Vision: The Socialist Party in the 1930s.* Bloomington: University of Indiana Press, 1974.

Weinstein, James. *The Decline of Socialism in America, 1912–25.* New York: Monthly Review, 1967.

Young, Arthur Nichols. *The Single Tax Movement in the United States.* Princeton, N.J.: Princeton University Press, 1916.

Zieger, Robert H. *Republicans and Labor, 1919–1929.* Lexington: University of Kentucky Press, 1969.

ARTICLES

Bohn, Frank, "The Socialist Party and the California Labor Party." *International Socialist Review* 11 (June 1911): 762–7.

Burner, David. "The Election of 1924," in Arthur Schlesinger Jr. (ed.), *History of American Presidential Elections, 1797–1968*, 3: 2459–90. New York: Chelsea House, 1971.

Coffey, William. "Matthew S. Holt." *West Virginia History* 39 (January 1978): 200–9.

Debs, Eugene V. "A Plea for Solidarity." *International Socialist Review* 14 (March 1914): 534–8.

——. "Our Party – Its Past and Its Future." *Socialist World* (June 1924): 2–3.

——. "Sound Socialist Tactics." *International Socialist Review* 12 (February 1912): 481–6.

Engels, Friedrich. "Preface to the American Edition of *The Conditions of the English Working Class*," in Karl Marx and Friedrich Engels, *Collected Works*, 26: 434–42. New York: International Publishers, 1990.

Hawkins, Howie. "Independent Progressive Politics." *Z* (March 1996): 17–20.

Haywood, William D. "No Labor Party Representatives." *International Socialist Review* 13 (August 1912): 145.

——. "What Haywood Says on Political Action." *International Socialist Review* 13 (February 1913): 622.

Haywood, William D. and Bohn, Frank. "News and Views." *International Socialist Review* 12 (December 1911): 375.

Hillquit, Morris. "Moscow and London." *Socialist World* (July 1923): 6–7.

——. "The Story of the British Labor Party." *Socialist World* (September 1923): 3–4.

Hunter, Robert. "The British Labor Party: A Reply." *International Socialist Review* 9 (April 1909): 753–64.

Johnson, Daniel J. "'No Make-Believe Class Struggle': The Socialist Municipal Campaign in Los Angeles, 1911." *Labor History* 41 (February 2000): 25–45.

Jones, Peter d'A. "Introduction to the Torch Book Edition," in Robert Hunter, *Poverty*. Reprinted edition. New York: Harper and Row, 1965), pp. x–xii.

Kerr, Charles H. "Shall Bossism Prevail in the Socialist Party." *International Socialist Review* 13(July 1912): 77–8.

——. "National Convention of 1912." *International Socialist Review* 12 (June 1912): 807–31.

Miller, Sally M. "Milwaukee: Of Ethnicity and Labor," in Bruce M. Stave (ed.) *Urban Socialism*. Port Washington, New York: Kennikat Press, 1975, pp. 41–76.

Panken, Jacob. "What We Got." *Socialist World* (January 1925): 9–11.

Shachtman, Max. "A Visit to the Island of Prinkipo," *Militant* (May 10, 1930).

Shapiro, Stanley. "'Hand and Brain': The Farmer-Labor Party of 1920." *Labor History* 26 (Summer 1985): 405–22.

Snow, William R. "Why an Independent Labor Party?" *Socialist World* (January 1923): 11–12.

Troy, Leo. "Labor Representation on American Railways," *Labor History* 2 (Fall 1961): 295–322.

Walling, William English. "Laborism versus Socialism." *International Socialist Review* 9 (March 1909): 683–89.

NEWSPAPERS AND BULLETINS

Daily Worker
International Press Correspondence
Labor
Labour Leader
Minneapolis Tribune
New York Call
New York Times
Northwest Organizer
Socialist Appeal
Socialist Call
Socialist Party Monthly Bulletin
Socialist World

Index